Printed in Canada
ISBN 1885596-24-3
LC Number 2001092467

Designed by Carol Haralson

Jacket photos of Ray Ackerman by
Michael Ives; background photo on front
cover courtesy *The Daily Oklahoman*

OKLAHOMA HERITAGE ASSOCIATION

OKLAHOMA CITY

BY BOB BURKE WITH JOAN GILMORE

FOREWORD BY LEE ALLAN SMITH

SERIES EDITOR: KENNY A. FRANKS

ASSOCIATE EDITOR: GINI MOORE CAMPBELL

OLD MAN RIVER

the life of RAY ACKERMAN

OLD
MAN
RIVER

PUBLICATION MADE POSSIBLE BY

ACKERMAN MCQUEEN

ANN SIMMONS ALSPAUGH

BANK OF OKLAHOMA, N.A.

MR. AND MRS. CLAYTON I. BENNETT

G. T. BLANKENSHIP

B. C. CLARK JEWELERS

DEVON ENERGY CORPORATION

GREATER OKLAHOMA CITY CHAMBER OF COMMERCE

GRIFFIN COMMUNICATIONS

INTEGRIS HEALTH

THE KERR FOUNDATION, INC.

KFOR-TV

KERR-MCGEE CORPORATION

JOHN E. KIRKPATRICK

CLIFF AND SYBIL KNIGHT

LSB INDUSTRIES, INC.

LOVE'S TRAVEL STOPS AND COUNTRY STORES

FRANK AND NADINE MCPHERSON

HERMAN AND LADONNA MEINDERS

OGE ENERGY CORP.

OKLAHOMA CITY COUNCIL NAVY LEAGUE OF THE UNITED STATES

OKLAHOMA CITY UNIVERSITY

OKLAHOMA NATURAL GAS CO.

GEORGE AND NANCY RECORDS

REAR ADMIRAL AND MRS. GREG SLAVONIC

7-ELEVEN STORES OF OKLAHOMA

MR. AND MRS. BILL SWISHER

RAY SAYS, "LIFE WITHOUT HER THESE PAST FIFTY-THREE YEARS,
AND IN MY REMAINING TIME ON EARTH,
I CAN'T EVEN IMAGINE."
—THE AUTHORS

CONTENTS

The World's Longest Sculpture
The Oklahoma River
Inland Water Port
Don't Trash Oklahoma
Advertising Oklahoma
New Flag for Oklahoma City
Tie State Flag to State Song

Clockwise from top: Ray as rodeo man (with Ray Anthony and Stanley Draper, Jr., left and middle); family man with second grandchild, Alexander Fuller, 1988; Navy fighter pilot; ad man receiving the industry's Silver Medal Award from Laura Snyder, Oklahoma City Ad Club president, in 1982; civic leader as president of Kirkpatrick Center in 1990 thanking General Tom Stafford, USAF (Ret.), for his many contributions to the Air Space Museum; and father of the bride with his fourth daughter Amy Lou, at her marriage to Dr. Jeff Shaver in 1988.

Oklahoma City has been deeply enriched by the contributions of Ray Ackerman, Chairman Emeritus of Ackerman McQueen Advertising Agency. Since he arrived in Oklahoma from Pennsylvania in 1947, Ray's life has been unselfishly given to one project after another, and one organization after another.

From leading the United Way to chairing the National Finals Rodeo to overseeing a citywide pride campaign, Ray has left an indelible mark.

No one is prouder of Oklahoma City's leap to great city status than Ray, especially of the Bricktown Canal and the development of the North Canadian River. He has been appropriately nicknamed "Old Man River."

Ray is blessed with boundless enthusiasm, unlimited energy, tenacity, extraordinary loyalty, and a wonderful and loving family.

As a family man, ad man, Navy man, civic leader, and great promoter of Oklahoma City, and a dear friend, Ray Ackerman is incredibly gifted. Oklahoma City is fortunate he chose to make the Sooner State his adopted home more than a half century ago.

LEE ALLAN SMITH

After 35 years of service in the Navy Reserve (top) . . . piped ashore in 1977 (right).

Writing Ray Ackerman's life story was closely akin to following the year-to-year progress of Oklahoma City in the last half of the 20th century. Both stories are inextricably intertwined.

We are indebted to Lou Ackerman and the six incredible Ackerman children for opening their scrapbooks and their hearts to our questions.

We thank Eric Dabney and Stephanie Graves Ayala for editorial and logistics support; Scott Dowell, Rodger Harris, and Delbert Amen at the Oklahoma Historical Society; David Page, Al McLaughlin, and Mick Hinton for research assistance; Debbie Neill and Shelley Dabney for transcription of interviews; Julie Huff for hundreds of hours of putting together Ray's recollections; Jon Minson for graphic assistance; and Michael Ives and Chris Carter for their splendid photography.

Paul Strasbaugh, Charles H. Van Rysselberge, Stanley C. Draper, Jr., Mex and Rodman Frates, Stokes Baggett, Chuck Piper, Warren K. "Doc" Jordan, and John E. Kirkpatrick graciously granted interviews.

As usual, Carol Haralson outdid herself in design of the book and dust jacket. We were blessed with superb editors, Dr. Kenny Franks and Gini Moore Campbell.

Without the commitment of the Oklahoma Heritage Association to preserve Oklahoma's wonderful story, this book would not have been published. Thanks to OHA President Dr. Paul Lambert, Chairman Pat Henry, and Chairman Emeritus Lee Allan Smith, who eloquently penned the foreword to this saga of a great man who fell in love with a great city.

BOB BURKE AND JOAN GILMORE

PENNSYLVANIA ROOTS

"HIS LEG WILL HAVE TO BE AMPUTATED," the doctor whispered. The grim news hit the parents of 11-year-old Ray Ackerman like a freight train. Through a dim fog created by heavy medication, young Ray saw his mother bury her head in his father's shoulder and sob. Even though his parents and the doctor talked just outside his hearing, he knew something was terribly wrong. Only when his mother took his hand and placed it to her face did his fear subside.

The physician explained that amputation of his left leg at the hip was necessary because for weeks his body failed to effectively deal with streptococcus infection. The infection had begun when Ray used a dirty handkerchief to stop the bleeding and protect his pants. He had fallen on the way home from school and scraped his leg a few weeks before Christmas in 1933.

After months of operations and efforts to drain the infection through application of heat, the physician was left with but one option—amputation.

Ray's parents and two friends spent the night before the scheduled amputation in his room, praying not for the Lord to save his leg, but rather to let him survive this drastic operation. Nurses prepared him the following morning for surgery, a gurney was moved alongside his bed, and his doctor gently peeled back his eyelids for a look. He whispered, "Please don't get your hopes up, but I'm going to wait 24 hours because I think I see a little improvement."

The Ackermans' pleas for divine intervention were answered. Although Ray had shrunk "to the size of a pencil," he began feeling better and the doctor left instructions that when he asked for something to eat, get whatever it was. He asked for watermelon, impossible to get in Pittsburgh, Pennsylvania, in the winter. The next request was for onion sandwiches. After devouring four in a row, Ray's hunger was gone, as was his love for onions for many years.

He mended quickly. The left leg was saved but three operations left 11 scars at the ankle, knee, and upper leg. After five months in bed, he limped badly and had to learn to walk again. Every evening his father walked at his side for as far as he could go, gently tapping his leg with every step saying, "You're limping, you're limping, you're limping!" If it had not been for his father, Ray says, he would have limped for the rest of his life.

Overcoming his brush with amputation, Ray later became a Navy fighter pilot, an admiral, and the chief promoter of Oklahoma's capital city.

Raymond Basil "Ray" Ackerman was born at 234 Berringer Place in Ben Avon, now known as Avonworth, a suburb of Pittsburgh, Pennsylvania, on August 7, 1922. His father, Charles Raymond Ackerman, "Ray, Sr.," an accountant with the National Tube Division of United States Steel, was born on April 19, 1898, in Benwood, West Virginia, the eighth and last child of Karl and Regina Helfrick Ackerman.

Karl and Regina migrated to America in 1871 from their homes in Bavaria, Germany, rather than face conscription into the Prussian Army. Shortly after arriving in the United States, they were married and settled in northwestern West Virginia. Karl's four brothers who came with him to America headed West and were never heard from again.

Ray's mother, Teresa Jane Grasinger Ackerman, was a homemaker. She was born in Monongahela City, Pennsylvania, on

November 28, 1900, to Joe and Catherine Bernadette Higbee Grasinger. Catherine's grandfather was a Union officer in the Civil War.

Ray Sr. and Teresa Ackerman were married on October 28, 1919, in St. Patrick's Church in Youngstown, Ohio. The ceremony was performed by Ray Sr.'s brother, Reverend Maurice Ackerman, a Capuchin priest.[1]

The Ackermans, devout Catholics, welcomed their first child, Mary Frances, "M'Fran," in 1920; then came Ray. His other sister, Kit, followed two years later, and his only brother, Karl, three years after that.

The Ackermans were an average middle-income family. The children were raised in a cozy house with good clothing, plenty of food, and a lot of family fun. Like most of their neighbors, they had no car. The children played cards and other games with their father and listened to radio shows on weekends. Before dinner and homework on school days, they listened to "Little Orphan Annie" and "Jack Armstrong, All American Boy."

Ray was born August 7, 1922, a dead-center Leo. He was the second of four children of Charles Raymond and Teresa Jane Ackerman.

Ray's parents. Charles Raymond Ackerman, right, was a strong father figure for young Ray. Once when Ray scratched the fender of a parked car with a nail, Mr. Ackerman talked the owner out of pressing charges in juvenile court, restricted Ray from any recreation for a month, and taught him to respect the property of others. Teresa Grasinger Ackerman, left, sometimes on doctor's orders, hung wet sheets in the doorways of bedrooms where sick children lay recovering from childhood diseases such as scarlet fever, chicken pox, whooping cough, measles, and mumps, believing the sheets prevented the spread of germs. Pennsylvania law was strict on quarantining children with communicable diseases. With four children in the Ackerman household, yellow quarantine signs with bold black lettering announcing "MUMPS," or other diseases, were a frequent sight in the front window of the house.

Then came the Great Depression, as hard on the Ackerman family as it was on most Americans. It had begun with the stock market crash in 1929 and worsened as factories and banks closed. Ray Sr.'s salary was slashed 45 percent on three consecutive two-week pay periods in 1930.

Raising a family with no dollars to spare brought Ray's parents into an ever closer harmony. At his father's insistence, the family did not usually buy anything on credit. However, the need to clothe four small   children caused Ray's mother to urge her husband to seek credit at Gimbel's Department Store. The elder Ackerman convinced the store credit manager to open a line of credit, promising a partial payment on the account would be made each month. Ray's father never missed a payment, but it took him 10 years to pay the account in full.

Uncle Henry, known as Uncle Hen, a bachelor streetcar conductor in Cleveland, Ohio, made up for having no children of his own at Christmas by giving his nieces and nephews gifts that Ray still remembers as magical—including a Lionel freight train one holiday. Uncle Henry tragically died from phlebitis resulting from a severe ankle injury suffered in an auto accident in his Chevy Club Coupe while returning to Pittsburgh with Ray, his brother, younger sister, and father who suffered only scratches. The car was so badly damaged that it brought only $7 for scrap. Uncle Henry's 1903 Hampton watch has been passed down to Ray's grandson, Henry Maximillian Shaver, while the Lionel freight train has been given to the only grandson with the Ackerman name, Raymond Bryan Ackerman.

The four Ackerman children. Left to right, Ray, Mary Frances, Karl, and Kit. Mary Frances was two years older than Ray. Kit was born when Ray was two and Karl came along three years later, in 1927. The first adult conversation Ray remembered was when his father burst into his room and announced that Karl had been born. Even then a visionary, Ray responded, "Yeah, but what about Charles Lindberg crossing the Atlantic Ocean!"

The Ackermans, like most middle class, Depression-era families, depended upon a wood-burning stove for heat, hot water, and cooking. Once again, the opposition to credit almost thwarted the modern convenience of a gas stove. Teresa Ackerman saw an advertisement promoting a stove installed with no down payment and small monthly payments. She took a chance and ordered the range without consulting her husband. Ray, Sr. was angry but only for about 24 hours. In his heart he knew his wife had done the right thing. Teamwork, it's called.

The Ackermans always found the best-shaped, fullest Christmas tree in town, put a lighted red wreath in every front window, and generally celebrated Christmas in grand style. Fruit and candy in their stockings and things to wear were the gifts from Santa Claus. The fancy gifts came from Teresa Ackerman's mother, "Goggy," who was a family nurse for a rich oilman in Texas, and from Uncle Hen, an older brother of his father, who Ray thought was a millionaire but who was actually a streetcar conductor in Cleveland.

One Christmas Ray talked his younger sister into letting him push out the eyes of her new doll thinking they would make a couple of good marbles. The "sale" backfired when Kit saw the holes where the eyes had been, burst into tears, and Ray got a thrashing from his dad. At that point, M'Fran remembered, "I knew he'd make a great salesman."[2]

On summer Sundays, Ray's father took the family to swim in the Ohio River, about a mile from the house. Ray was not allowed to go near the river alone but he sneaked off and played around the bank of that big river when he thought he could get away with it. When Ray was six years old, Mr. Ackerman announced that swimming was over because the Ohio River was too filthy.

All three of Pittsburgh's Rivers had become dumping grounds for sewage, chemicals, oil, and all kinds of trash. It was not uncommon for the rivers to catch fire. In 1934, city fathers formulated a plan to clean up the rivers but it was more than 40 years before they reopened to fishing, swimming, and water-skiing.

Ray walked to and from Assumption Parochial Elementary School, over a mile away. A boy in his class and his older brother often picked on him on his way home, knocking him down, calling him names, pulling out his shirt tail, always trying to get him to fight. Because he was scared of them, Ray ran when he could. One day, the older boy challenged Ray to fight his brother at the YMCA. The whole class knew about the dare, so Ray had to agree.

After an instructor briefed the boys on the Marquess of Queensberry rules, "they went at it." To his amazement, Ray was a better boxer than his opponent, and was quicker. He punched his opponent clear across the mat against the wall. And, forgetting the rules, Ray was holding his opponent's head against the wall with one glove and "about to drive it through the wall with the other" when the fight was stopped. The boys never bothered Ray again. Ray learned a few things that day—he was slow to anger, he could handle himself when he needed to, "bullies are sissies in disguise," and his dad was a good boxing coach.

In the second grade, Ray learned a lesson from his mother that stayed with him his entire life; one can always do something better than he or she just did. Ray brought home his report card one day with his grades in numbers, the method chosen by the nuns at his school. In five subjects, Ray had 100s. But in geography he had a 98. Ray flipped the report card at his mother and, looking a little smug, asked her to please sign it. She turned to him and said, "What's the problem you're having with geography?"

The Ackermans had milk delivered to their door as often as they wanted. The drink of choice was buttermilk because at 15 cents, it was a penny per gallon cheaper than sweet milk. Ray remembered the only reason they ever had sweet milk was because his sister, Kit, could not stand buttermilk. Ray still loves buttermilk![3]

Ray, Sr. and Teresa Ackerman expected a lot of their children at home and at school. Weekend chores were added to daily tasks of making beds and washing dishes. One of Ray's tasks was to polish his shoes and those of his siblings every Saturday. He be-

Ray, left, and his little sister, Kit, in 1928. The Ackerman children were assigned chores by their parents. No one over the age of four was left out.

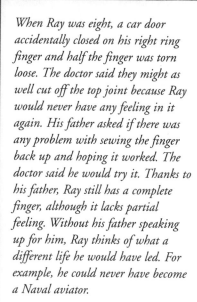

When Ray was eight, a car door accidentally closed on his right ring finger and half the finger was torn loose. The doctor said they might as well cut off the top joint because Ray would never have any feeling in it again. His father asked if there was any problem with sewing the finger back up and hoping it worked. The doctor said he would try it. Thanks to his father, Ray still has a complete finger, although it lacks partial feeling. Without his father speaking up for him, Ray thinks of what a different life he would have led. For example, he could never have become a Naval aviator.

came pretty proud of his ability to put a good shine on a pair of shoes and, to this day, he still shines his own shoes. Another big weekend chore in the summertime was weeding the family rock garden. Ray hated weeding, and still does.

Ray also helped his dad make beverages, root beer for the kids and home brew for the adults. His parents also made elderberry blossom wine with blossoms picked by Ray who was assigned to squeeze the juice out of sugar sacks in which the blossoms fermented.

Ray was in the third grade when he became an altar boy and learned the Mass in Latin. Taller than the other altar boys, Ray became the Cross bearer for processions when he was in the seventh grade. Midnight Mass lasted three hours one year and, at the age of 12, Ray felt pretty big sitting in the Sacristy with two six-year-old candle bearers asleep on his lap.

In the third grade, Ray was introduced to the world of multi-flavored ice cream. Up to that time, ice cream cones in drugstores came in vanilla, strawberry, and chocolate. However, a Swiss company, Isaly's, established a chain of ice cream stores in Pittsburgh and other cities with 35 flavors and an extra-large scoop for a nickel. Every Pittsburgh area elementary and secondary school student was given a ticket good for one free ice cream cone at a new Isaly's store. Instead of going home after school at the regular time of 3:30 P.M., Ray stood in line to get his free cone and arrived home at 7:00 P.M. The local police department had been swamped with calls about tardy children. Astute police officers finally caught on and assured parents their children would be home soon.

Well into adulthood, M'Fran and Ray reminded each other of the "caramel trick" and laughed hysterically without ever telling the younger children what they were talking about. The trick involved a box of caramels that arrived from a relative more than a month before Christmas. The children drooled over the candy but their mother instructed them to leave it alone until

Christmas Day. M'Fran noticed that the caramels were packed in the box on their sides. She and Ray conspired to take 20 percent of the caramels out of the box and repack the remaining candies flat, making the box look untouched. What a feast they had, and what fun they had for about 40 years before they finally caved in and explained the trick to their brother and sister!

About once a year his dad took Ray on a train to visit his grandparents who lived on the Ohio River in Wheeling, West Virginia. Old pictures showed a grassy lawn from their wooden house's porch to the river where Ray's dad and his brothers had fished when they were small boys. But in later years, a railroad track was laid between the house and the river and trains in the middle of the night just about bounced everyone out of bed. Toilet facilities were outside about 30 feet from the back door of the kitchen. Grandpa would send Ray to the icehouse with a quarter and a wooden bucket to get it filled with beer. Once when the Ohio River flooded, grandpa and grandma had to sit on their roof to keep out of the water, but their children could not convince them to move. They cleaned out three floors of mud and stayed put!

On one visit to Wheeling Ray's dad and uncles took him to a German beer garden. The older brothers bought Ray, age eight, his first glass of beer. When his dad protested that he was too young, they said, "It won't hurt him, let the kid drink his beer."

Ray's grandma served unsalted "sweet" butter which Ray still loves to this day. She always wrapped a pound of it in layers and layers of brown paper for him to take home on the train.

In April of 1932, when Ray was completing the fourth grade, the family moved to 530 Tingley Avenue in the Borough of Bellevue, about 7 miles from downtown Pittsburgh. The beautiful little house about 25 feet above street level had a big back yard, partially wooded, adjacent to a heavily-wooded area. They had an open-fire pit and frequently put on wiener and marshmallow roasts, with all the neighbor kids invited.[4]

When Ray was 10 years old, he received a spring-loaded Daisy B-B Gun, the Buzz Barton model. Walking through the woods one day, he heard a bird chirp overhead. He brought the gun straight up, fired, and a sparrow dropped dead at his feet. Ray never had any desire to be a hunter after that.

Mrs. Ackerman's only brother, Uncle Sam, went into business in Texas selling the first gas refrigerators made by Servel. He gave one to the Ackermans. It was hotel size, half as big as their kitchen. They provided some storage for friends and were the envy of the neighborhood, with no more pans to catch the ice melt, and no more cards in the window indicating to the ice man the number of pounds needed that day.

Two days a week during summer vacation from grade school, Ray's clever mother got him off her hands from 10:00 A.M. until 8:00 P.M. for just 25 cents. For 15 cents, he bought two streetcar tokens, which took him to and from the Pittsburgh Pirates baseball park, Forbes Field. It was an hour and a half trip each way with one transfer. That left a dime for a hot dog and an ice cream bar, each costing a nickel. As a member of the Knot Hole Gang, admission to Forbes Field was free two days a week. He saw great players such as Lloyd and Paul Waner, Jay Hanna "Dizzy" Dean, John Leonard "Pepper" Martin, and Carl Hubbell, all from Oklahoma, and Bill Terry, Pie Traynor, Gabby Hartnett, and the Gashouse Gang from St. Louis.[5]

On March 17, 1936, when Ray was in the eighth grade, Pittsburgh had its worst flood ever, referred to as the famous St. Patrick's Day Flood. The watermark on buildings in the heart of the Golden Triangle downtown was about 12 feet above the street.

A Boy Scout at the time, Ray had to circulate flyers at night in an assigned area to all the occupants, advising them to boil their water. There were no lights except candles and it was pretty scary. Ray admits he was not sure who was more scared, him standing on the porch with his flyers, knocking on the door, or all the residents around a single candle coming to the door to see what the racket was. The river must have been more than a mile wide when the scoutmaster borrowed a huge rowboat for Scouts to deliver food and medical supplies across the Ohio River to stranded residents of McKees Rocks.

With everyone out trying to buy candles, Ray's mother had the bright idea of buying vigil candles at the Catholic bookstore. On the way home in a neighbor's car, the Ackermans sat on a hill on the north side of Pittsburgh to watch the floodwaters. It seemed as though a major structure, a house or barn, went floating by every few minutes, many with people and/or pets on the roof.

Each Fourth of July, Ray's neighborhood sounded like war had broken out. There were no legal bans on shooting firecrackers anywhere. Cherry bombs and miniature TNT barrels, capable of blowing a five-gallon can inside out, pierced the early morning hours, signaling the celebration of independence.

The most exciting activities Ray recalled from Boy Scout camp at Laurel Mountain, Pennsylvania, were how to catch and carry a rattlesnake, how to weave a 6- to 8-foot black snake through a volleyball net, and how much fun it was to play "Capture the Flag," particularly after dark. Camp cost $5.00 a week and one week was all his family could afford. Because Ray was growing so fast, he towered over his fellow Scouts and his Scoutmaster. It made him feel strange and he dropped out of Scouting after reaching Star Scout rank. He always regretted not going on to earn his Life and Eagle ranks.

Assumption Church always had a summer carnival to make money, giving Ray a chance to learn about gambling and to develop his entrepreneurial spirit. A couple of neighborhood buddies and Ray built several gambling games and held carnivals in their backyards, winning all the pennies from other kids. One summer it rained on the carnival and they moved it into the cellar. Ray's mother intervened and shut down the carnival for good when she saw all the pennies stacked in front of him. The cellar full of smoke from "Indian stogies," a long skinny cigar-like bean from the catalpa trees which Ray and his friends smoked, did not help either.

When Ray graduated from the eighth grade in June, 1936, he won the American Legion Medal for Scholarship and Leadership for boys. A girl named Catherine Lewis won the same medal for the girls. In a chance meeting 50 years later, she told Ray's friend, former Oklahoma Attorney General G.T. Blankenship, she thought winning the award was a sign she and Ray would get married some day.[6]

In the summer of 1936, a man named Earnest Wahl knocked on the Ackermans' door on a Sunday and introduced himself as a second cousin to Ray's dad from Germany. He spoke with a very heavy German accent. After a brief conversation, Wahl was accepted as a cousin and invited for dinner. Ray was not the least bit interested in the conversation and the only thing he remembered about Wahl was that he had vanilla ice cream for dessert and stirred a spoonful in his coffee, a first for Ray's eyes.

Ray remembered when the family purchased a new telephone and a new service agreement from the phone company. Basic monthly charge for the phone included 40 phone calls. His father had a log mounted beside the telephone and when anyone made a call, the date and time, to whom it was made and for what purpose had to be posted on the log. After 40 calls, something as serious as the house being on fire was the only reason good enough to justify using the phone as additional calls cost a nickel each.

Goggy, Ray's grandmother on his mother's side, came to live with the Ackermans when Ray was 12 years old. A fourth for Bridge was needed and Ray was "it." By the time he went into the Navy, Ray had become a good Bridge player and generally won a little money every time he played.

When Ray was 13, he attended his first boy-girl party. Even though heavily chaperoned, the teenagers managed to get in a few games of spin-the-bottle and Ray learned that kissing girls was a lot of fun. In those days, every Sunday sermon was fire and brimstone and Ray believed that if he did not quit going to those parties, he was going to die one day and go straight to hell. With that on his mind, plus a lot of prodding from his eighth grade teacher, Sister Rose Gertrude, he accepted a high school scholarship to Duquesne, a Catholic prep school.

Young Ray Ackerman fully intended to become a priest.

BIG ACK

TOWERING TO SIX FEET THREE INCHES as he
started high school, Ray quickly became known as "BIG ACK."
Duquesne Prep had been a very prestigious high school at one
time, located on what was called "The Bluff" in downtown Pittsburgh. Ray spent his freshman year there but a university had
been spawned and the Prep School was pushed off The Bluff.
His sophomore year was spent in a building built in 1867, as
Ray recalled, "really the pits." Most of his classmates were pretty
rough Polish kids from an orphanage. Because of the dirty building and Ray noticing how cute girls looked with their skirts
swinging back and forth, his thoughts of being a priest weak-
ened. Instead, Ray began thinking about transferring to a public
high school for his last two years.

Sports was another reason Ray wanted to switch schools.
Duquesne Prep School did not have any organized athletic
teams. There were no locker or shower facilities in the old gymnasium. The school did have a gym class and Ray and his friends
had to tie the legs of their boxer shorts in knots to protect their
manhood. With his parents' permission, Ray transferred to Bellevue Public High School after his sophomore year.

Ray's family moved to a fabulous, much bigger house at 224
North Balph in Bellevue where an attractive girl named Jean

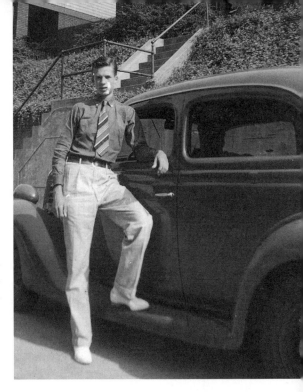

"All legs" Ray Ackerman was busy in high school. After basketball or tennis practice, he delivered 60 newspapers, ran home for dinner, and returned to school for school play practice. It was good training for his simultaneous career of 50 years in advertising and 35 years in the Navy Reserve while he and his wife were raising a large family and he was getting his college degree at night in the earlier years.

Breen lived next door. Ray remembered Goggy one day asking his sisters what those little things on the Breens' clothesline were and when his sisters said, "panties," Goggy almost fainted.

Ray landed a paper route delivering the *Pittsburgh Sun Telegraph* to 80 subscribers. There were two editions of the evening paper for home delivery, but the station manager, "a smart old geezer," kept all of his subscribers getting the early edition so he could go home early. Ray wanted to try out for the basketball team but the only way he could make practice immediately after school was if all his customers took the late edition instead of the early.

He quietly persuaded 60 of 80 customers to switch to the late edition. Ray paid a neighbor 75 cents a week to deliver the 20 early edition customers, leaving him $4.25 a week for spending money. Ray was no longer a favorite of the station manager after dumping 60 transfers to the late edition on his desk. It lengthened the manager's working day by about two hours.

The newspaper rewarded carriers who signed up a certain number of new subscribers by a deadline. A typical reward was a free ticket to a Pittsburgh-Notre Dame football game. Ray knew a lot of the non-subscribers on his route; some attended his church. He could always get 10 or 12 to sign up for home delivery and win his ticket to a football game. They all knew they could quit the paper a few weeks after the game and most of them did. About the third time Ray pulled off his subscription scam, he was challenged by the station manager's supervisor for cutting the deal.

Realizing that someday he might be caught, Ray had a rehearsed reply. He said, "It's my job to get non-subscribers to try the paper; it's the paper's job to be good enough to keep them." Although his manager never questioned him after that, the scam worked only a couple more times before Ray quit delivering papers. Actually, he never felt bad about what might be called a minor deception because several subscribers continued to take the paper. The paper carrier business was tough in those Depression days. Some people took only the 6 dailies at 3 cents each because they could not afford the 10-cent Sunday paper and many times some families hid from him on Saturday when Ray came around to collect his 18 cents.[1]

Although he fell in love with a girl the first week in the public high school, Ray was too shy to ask for a date. His sisters moved him in that direction by having a "real nice girl with a great personality," actually the homeliest girl in their sorority, ask him to one of those girl-invite-boy dances. Being new at it, Ray was not a very graceful dancer even after expert instruction from his "ballerina-graceful" sisters. He remembers pushing his heavy-set first date around the dance floor and sweating profusely. The smell of her gardenia corsage was overwhelming. In fact, Ray hated the smell of gardenias for about 25 years thereafter.

Finally Ray worked up the nerve to date a very pretty girl. After getting in trouble with his parents, still waiting up when he got home at 3:00 A.M. after a date, Ray said, "I really didn't want to start dating, but all of you just kept pushing and pushing and pushing me and now that I am, I really like it!"

In high school, only 50 cents was needed for a Friday night date, a dime for gas for the rare student who could borrow his father's car and 40 cents for two burgers and two Cokes at the local jukebox and dance joint. The boys were skilled in ending a dance far away from the jukebox, as they had no extra nickel to play the next song.

The family had a huge, six-person sled, perfect for the up-and-down roller coaster-like hill in front of the house. One night, with both hills rock-solid with ice, Ray was lying on the sled steering with five friends on top of him. The sled began drifting toward the curb because the runners were not cutting the ice. Ray yelled for everyone to jump because there was a parked car where the sled would start up the second hill. Everyone got off in time but Ray and the sled went under the car, stopped by his buttocks against the bumper. He was in bed for a week. The Navy never spotted any damage but some years later, civilian doctors spotted the after effects of the collision with the bumper.

Though he started competitive sports late, Ray made the tennis team and the reserve basketball team in his junior year at Bellevue High School. He landed a spot on the first-string varsity basketball team his senior year. The squad won its division and went on to the Western Pennsylvania Interscholastic Athletic League playoffs. All starters were over six feet tall but only 17 years old. Bellevue High was eliminated in the playoffs by a team of 23-year-olds from Rankin High School. Ray remembered, "Those guys had whiskers about a quarter inch long and had worked in the coal mines for five years before coming back to complete high school; they literally scared our team to death."

After Ray's junior year, the man who coached both basketball and football spent many summer evenings on the Ackerman front porch trying to talk Ray's parents into letting him play football his senior year. His parents refused because Ray still had the 11 scars on his left leg, still blood red and possibly susceptible to breaking open. Ray and his parents had some terrible fights at home over that issue.

Karl, five years younger than Ray, was not overly interested in polishing his own shoes when his dad told him to. Ray was on Karl's back all the time about his muddy shoes. One Sunday, Karl's shoes were shining brightly and Ray complimented him. His sisters laughed hysterically before blurting out that Karl was wearing a pair of Ray's shoes.[2] He did learn to shine his shoes, graduated from Notre Dame in political science, and spent 30 years with the country's State Department. He married Majorie Thornton, a Parisian model and the daughter of a TWA executive, in Paris.

Once he started dating girls in high school, Ray, along with a dozen other guys, fell in love with the class beauty, a young lady named Nancy Duff. It was really hard to get a date with her and it seemed she had to be asked weeks and maybe months in advance. In October of his senior year, she unexpectedly asked Ray to a girl-asks-boy dance at Christmas time. He was so elated that his "feet did not touch the ground for days." Then, remembering that "all is fair in love and war," Ray conceived a diabolical plan to get rid of his competition.

Ray called a meeting of all the girl's suitors and suggested they stop the ridiculous competition. Ray suggested that whomever the girl invited to the dance, for which Ray already had a secret invitation, would be the winner and the other suitors would go away. All but one agreed. However, Ray considered one competitor better than 10. The romance ended the following June on the night of the Joe Louis-Billy Conn prize fight, which was scheduled for the same night as a big school dance.

All the guys could hardly wait to get to the site of the dance so they could go in the back room and listen to the fight on the radio because Billy Conn was "a Pittsburgh boy," who they all thought could beat Louis. On the way to the dance, Ray was telling the driver of their car to hurry so they could hear the fight, and his date said, "What fight?" Ray decided at that moment he could not live with a woman who did not know what was going on in the world of sports, so they parted company.

They did have one more date. It was in the fall of 1944 when Ray was home on leave from the Navy and his brother was captain of the Bellevue High School football team. His old sweetheart, Nancy, was married to a Navy officer by that time, but he was at sea. His brother's football game was being played on Friday afternoon, and Ray asked his mother if she thought it was alright for him to invite Nancy to go to the game. His mother approved, so they went. Ray told Nancy how he got rid of the competition back in 1939. She was so mad she did not speak to him again until the 50th anniversary reunion of their graduation class in 1990.

YOU'RE IN
THE ARMY NOW

WHEN RAY WAS IN HIGH SCHOOL, the Army had a program called Citizens Military Training Corps (CMTC). It was a month-long summer military training camp. If a student attended four summers and passed all the requirements, he received a second lieutenant reserve commission, the same as for four years of Reserve Officers Training Corps (ROTC) in college.

During his senior year, a brochure about the program was circulated in Ray's high school. He remembered the words, "Swimming, boating and recreation at beautiful Fort George G. Meade, Maryland." It sounded good so Ray and a buddy, Paul Himmelman, signed up. They were told to report to the train station in downtown Pittsburgh at "1800, 5 July 1940, with a change of socks, underwear, handkerchief and toilet articles, all of which would fit in a shoe box." But there was an optional list of suit, shirt, tie, good shoes, and a musical instrument. Ray and his friend brought everything on the list, including his friend's French horn. The other 2,998 guys who showed up for the same train had only shoeboxes.

The train coaches, the oldest on the Pennsylvania line, had

...ay in his Army uniform at
...itizens Military Training Corps
...amp, Fort George G. Meade,
...Maryland, in July, 1940.

broken-out windows which allowed soot to blow in. Ray caught a cold. At noon the next day, in 110-degree heat at Fort Meade, 3,000 boys disembarked and were ordered to double-time across a field, which was about 500 yards down to an opening in a fence. It was quite exhausting with two heavy bags and a French horn.

Ray and his buddy were assigned to a bunk house to drop their gear before heading several places to get uniforms, shots, and quick physicals. The guy next to Ray was not able to complete the urine test, so Ray jokingly said he would give him some of his. He took it. Ray admitted it was one of the most foolish things he had ever done. The recruit could have been "at death's door" or had a communicable disease that would have gone undetected.

No sooner had the exhausted Army recruits lay down on their bunks than a sergeant yelled, "Fall in on the street." He then announced kitchen police (KP) for the next morning, to report to the galley at 4:00 A.M. With a name like Ackerman, Ray was first on the list. Breakfast ran from about 5:00 A.M. to 7:00 A.M. Afterwards Ray started washing greasy pans and was still at it at 9:00 A.M. when his friend Paul came in and said he was going home. It seems he had a hernia.

Ray was so homesick, he could have cried. Seventeen years old, out on a little hill listening to someone's radio playing, "I'll Never Smile Again," by Frank Sinatra, he never felt so lonely. He got over it as he busied himself playing on a championship softball team and getting his Marksman and Sharpshooter medals with the old 1903 Springfield rifle. Water was hosed into a dusty low spot on the base to make mud and the rookies learned to slither through it on their elbows with their rifles held high. The maneuver could have had something to do with Ray picking the Navy when the big war started.[1]

Ray made it into Washington, D.C., a couple of times on liberty. He had only a few dollars, so he slept on park benches. When he left Fort Meade on August 3, 1940, he had completed the first phase of Basic Instruction in the Army Infantry.

When Ray returned from basic training, his dad asked him again what he was going to do with his life. It was unspoken, but Ray knew there was no money to send him to college. Ray finally said he was going to be an accountant like his father. He signed up for night school in Accounting and Commercial Law at the Robert Morris School of Business, then got a job ushering in the Stanley Theater in downtown Pittsburgh where the weekly fare was a movie and a stage show. Once Mickey Rooney was the stage show attraction, and he and his manager went up to the "peanut gallery" where Ray was stationed. A couple of fans saw the movie star and yelled, "There's Mickey Rooney!" Ray was knocked off his feet and rolled down the steps all the way to the front of the balcony. Frank Sinatra was another budding star Ray saw there.

In September of 1940, Ray went to work as a messenger boy for Mellon National Bank. He had to wear a suit, tie, and hat to work even though his job was as an errand boy, doing such work as returning insufficient checks in the downtown area for a starting pay of $70 a month. If he had to return an insufficient check more than a mile, he was given two streetcar tokens, one for each way. Ray recalled he "ran like hell and saved the tokens for going to and from work."

He was promoted to the Proof Department at the bank and learned to operate a large black machine that endorsed checks, sorted them into 24 different pockets, and added the checks individually by pocket. One objective each day was to get as many checks through the machine as possible before 10:00 A.M., when the checks were sent to the Citywide Clearing House. The banks had informal competition and Ray was the citywide champ for getting the most checks through the machine in a morning. When war was obvious and the bank started bringing retired ladies back to work because the younger employees were probably going to war, Ray was their teacher on the big machine.

In the late fall of 1941, Bing Crosby's "White Christmas" was introduced. It was selling out of retail stores as fast as they were getting it in. Ray told his sisters he would find the record. He walked all over the Golden Triangle in downtown Pittsburgh one Saturday trying to find the record, then crossed the Allegheny River on the Sixth Street Bridge to the north side and finally found a copy after five hours of searching.[2]

Ray's gross monthly pay at Mellon National Bank rose from $70 to $125 over the two years he worked there but most of the increases were called cost-of-living bonuses rather than raises for merit. The theory was the country was having inflation because of the war and once the war was over, the bank could stop the bonuses and take the employees back to minimal salaries.

There were good things about working at the bank. Ray believed that management promoted romance, hoping to see their young people get married and get so deep in debt they could not quit the bank. In addition, there were many bank holidays. One November, employees worked 16 days and had 14 days off; five Saturdays, five Sundays, Election Day, Armistice Day, and two days for Thanksgiving. To help retail sales with a longer Christmas buying season, President Franklin D. Roosevelt encouraged states to move Thanksgiving to the next to last Thursday rather than the last Thursday in November. Some states did, some states did not. Pennsylvania could not make up its mind, so the Keystone State ended up with two Thanksgivings.

You had to live in Pittsburgh to know how dirty it was before it cleaned itself up. Many times, Pittsburgh was as dark at noon as it was at midnight; street and store window lights had to be turned on. Under the leadership of Paul Mellon, a plan was formulated in 1934 between private business, city, county, state and the federal government. The plan gave major industry 25 years to convert from the dirty, soft coal to anthracite coal, electricity or gas. Twenty-five years later, in 1959, an amazing transformation was complete and the Golden Triangle became as beautiful and sparkling at night as the core of any city. Pittsburgh was the first of the large, older cities east of the Mississippi River to embark on such an ambitious plan.

While working at Mellon National Bank and going to night school, Ray played semi-pro basketball for three different teams, Mellon National Bank; Gulf Oil Company; and The Aces, a local YMCA team. Most weeks he played five games. When the season started, he weighed 188 pounds; when it was over, he weighed 168. Wet laundry was hung in the cellar in the winter in those days but the Ackermans never had room for anything except Ray's basketball uniforms. Notre Dame scouts showed an interest in him for a basketball scholarship but the war put an end to that.

The bank had a Christmas party every year for employees. Bank officers sat at a head table about 10 feet above the employees, wearing their white starched collars and dark blue suits and looking very severe. Knowing a war was coming on, there was a devil-may-care attitude among the young guys and one of the messenger boys with too much to drink took a nearly empty shrimp bowl with water and ice in it, climbed up to the head table, walked over to the bank's cashier, and dumped it over his head. It was the last employee Christmas party Mellon National Bank ever had.

On Sunday, December 7, 1941, Ray had just begun his homework when the news of Pearl Harbor came over the radio. He closed the books and never opened them again, though he did manage to finish a third semester in January.

ANCHORS AWEIGH

WORLD WAR II WAS RAGING IN 1942. Nightly radio reports of heavy fighting in Europe and the slaughter of American troops in the Pacific convinced most everyone that the war would last at least 10 years. So when an influential neighbor, Judge Harry Montgomery, called and said he had an appointment for Ray to the United States Naval Academy at Annapolis, Maryland, Ray leaped at the chance. Montgomery had been unsuccessful in landing an appointment for Ray when he graduated from high school two years earlier.[1]

The only condition of the new opportunity was that Ray must pass six written examinations. Because he was always a quick learner, but not too good at retaining information he did not use, Ray found a tutor. He passed the tests with flying colors, except for Physics, which he failed by one-tenth of a point.

Ironically, Ray found out later that because of making good grades in high school, he needed to take only the English and Math tests, and not Physics or the other tests to gain admittance to the Naval Academy.

The near-miss appointment to the Naval Academy worked out well for Ray. Had he attended the Academy, he would have been commissioned as an Ensign in the regular Navy (USN) in

June, 1945, 22 months after he was commissioned an Ensign in the United States Naval Reserve (USNR).

Ray chose to enlist as a Naval Aviation Cadet (NAVCAD). Wartime scholastic requirements had been dropped to passing an intelligence test, rather than requiring four years of college, later reduced to two years. His second and third choices were the Army Air Corps and paratrooper training.

Ray's first obstacle was to pass the Naval Aviation physical, considered the most demanding in the military. Navy Air doctors could see the 11 scars on his leg and literally made him "jump through hoops" to prove he was fit for flying in the Navy. Doctors wanted a second opinion on Ray's leg condition and a questionable ear, a result of infections from childhood. Physicians were not certain that a hole required to drain infection from his ear had healed. The request for a second opinion delayed by 30 days any progress on his Navy application as the examining physicians came to Pittsburgh from Philadelphia only once a month.

When Ray appeared for the second opinion, he was covered with poison ivy. He could hardly stand to walk from the bus to the recruiting office because of his pants rubbing his red-whelped legs. Ray remembered, "It was so bad my hands had to be tied at night because one night I dreamed I was peeling tomatoes and awakened to find I had scratched my sores so badly my legs were bleeding." The doctor took one look at Ray and said, "Put your clothes on and go home. We'll see you next month." Another 30-day delay.

A month later, Ray passed both the physical and written exams. On August 22, 1942, two weeks after his 20th birthday, Ray was sworn in as a Naval Aviation Cadet, and was complimented for enlisting when told it would be at least a year before he would be drafted.

While waiting for orders for active duty, he continued to work at Mellon National Bank, completed a course in Celestial

Navigation at Buhl Planetarium and one in both sound and blinker Morse code. Both courses were completed in night school. When Ray learned that carrots improved an aviator's eyesight, he began eating them at least twice daily, prompting his sisters to "believe he was turning orange."

On Labor Day, in front of City Hall in Bellevue, a large sculpture was unveiled depicting World War II veterans and listing all the local men and women who were serving their country in the military. All six feet three inches of Ray, in the first row, towered over the crowd. As the sheet covering the sculpture was removed, Ray was shocked to see his name first on the alphabetical list. The Navy had certainly moved fast. He could see people looking at him, wondering why he was still at home. When the draft speeded up and all his friends were gone by November, Ray began to go into hiding. For example, he would wait until after dark to go the movies and then would sit in the back where no one could see him. Finally his orders came to report to Flight Preparatory School at the University of Pennsylvania in Philadelphia on January 3, 1943.

On New Year's Eve, just three days before Ray was scheduled to leave for active duty, he and a friend attended a party. They decided to see what it was like to drink alcohol. After a glass of rum, Ray was green with nausea and asked a friend to take him home. He nearly threw up when he saw an outdoor advertising sign selling rum eggnogs. With a terrible hangover the following evening, Ray was the family's guest of honor at New Year's Day dinner. When his mother announced that Ray, Sr. had a special treat for the occasion, "eggnog," Ray threw his chair back from the table and barely made it up the stairs to the bathroom.[2]

Ray reported for active duty and searched in vain for the Navy office in the building to which he was ordered to report. About to panic, he saw a Navy lieutenant and asked, "Pardon me, sir, but could you tell me where the Navy office is?" The reply was, "Hell son, I just put this uniform on for the first time this morning and I'm looking for the office too." The lieutenant was Dallas Ward, later a football coach at Colorado, who had been commissioned as a physical education instructor.

Ray was assigned to a room with seven other cadets in an 1889-era dormitory in a courtyard called the quadrangle. It reminded him of Duquesne Prep School, with the water tank on the wall above the toilet for gravity flushing and droplights with green shades. Once suitcases were dumped on the bed, cadets were told to report to the swimming pool. Ray thought he was a swimmer because he had spent much of his teenage years swimming from one side of the Bellevue pool to the other, as he recalled, "to check out the girls."

The first test of Navy training was the classification of a cadet as a "swimmer" or "sub-swimmer." The stakes were high. Sub-swimmers were demoted to Seaman Recruit and sent to boot camp at Bainbridge, Maryland. Swimmers were allowed to keep their NAVCAD designation and continue training in Philadelphia.

Ray and many other recruits failed the first test of staying afloat in deep water for five minutes without touching the sides. They were given one week to become swimmers, defined as "staying in deep water for one hour without touching the sides." Fortunately, the swimming instructor was Jack Medica, a Princeton University graduate and winner of three gold medals in swimming at the 1932 Olympics. Medica was a tough trainer. When a cadet tired and touched the sides of the pool, Medica dragged him from the water and made him do pushups until he was exhausted. Then Medica rolled him back into the pool. Somehow, after the week's training, Ray was officially classified a "swimmer," but tests continued through the first four of seven required levels of competence, D-C-B and A, which he passed successfully. AA, AAA, and AAAA tests were to be taken at the next duty station.

Because of the quick start up of the Navy Flight Preparatory

School at the University of Pennsylvania, the recruits had no uniforms. Finally, someone came up with a box of Watch Caps, an official uniform item but which was a simple blue knit stocking cap. When the producers of a radio show, Spotlight Band, visited the school to film military personnel marching for newsreels, an enterprising public affairs officer begged 200 striped khaki uniforms from the local Coca-Cola bottler and removed the Coke logo. With black ties begged from a clothing store, the watch caps, and their Coca-Cola uniforms, the unit marched smartly in formation.

Taking the Morse Code course in Pittsburgh put Ray ahead of his fellow recruits, allowing him more time to become proficient in the study of aircraft engines, aerology, and the most difficult course, dead reckoning navigation.

Even though Ray and his fellow cadets were trying to becoming aviators, they still had to learn to march. Once when Ray was leading and calling cadence, he called, "Platoon right, march" and then, "Platoon, by the right flank, march," when only about half the troops had made the turn. Ray recalled, "Suddenly it looked like 42nd and Broadway in New York at midnight on New Year's Eve, with the cadets running into each other." The instructor told Ray he would never be a platoon leader, which was all right with him because he never wanted to be one.[3]

With free food and lodging and a $120 monthly salary, Ray considered himself living rich in the college dormitory. He was able to spend two weekend liberties in New York City gawking at the big buildings, drinking beer, and trying to meet girls. He remembered sleeping one night in the vestibule of his date's apartment.

Naval Aviation cadets were glamour boys to the girls, so it was not surprising to see an invitation on the bulletin board to sign up if one wanted to go to a Sunday afternoon dance in Upper Darby, the most affluent part of Philadelphia. Ray went one Sunday, got off the train and was walking up the hill with his buddies to a big house, only to find out that it was the servants' quarters and the main house was the size of a castle on an adjacent hill.

On Saturday mornings, the last thing on the rigorous physical education routine for 200 cadets was pushups. Lieutenant Dallas Ward's instructions were simple, "Do as many as you can and then roll over." Those who rolled over before Ward blew his whistle had to run another mile before being turned loose on liberty. Ray strained mightily each week and could see there was only a handful of men still doing pushups when he had to turn over. When he was leaving the school, Ray asked Ward when he decided to blow the whistle. His answer was, "As soon as you rolled over on your back."

In March, 1943, the Navy decided it needed some Air Navigators in a hurry. A quick commission was offered to selected cadets who could complete an 18-week navigation course and an aerology course beginning in April in Hollywood, Florida, and they were guaranteed orders back to flight training in a year. More than half of the 200 cadets signed up to compete for the school's quota of 20. Because of his proficiency in code, enabling him to concentrate on dead reckoning navigation, Ray had no trouble winning one of the slots. Getting commissioned a year earlier was the big opportunity, all but eliminating the possibility of being cut from the program and being sent to Bainbridge as a seaman apprentice.

Ray was given five days leave before reporting to Florida. Not wanting to go home without a uniform, and embarrassed to return in civvies after being listed on the monument at City Hall, he outfitted himself in Navy Blues from the John Wanamaker Department Store in Philadelphia.

Leaving Pennsylvania by train on a cold, dreary April morning, Ray arrived in Hollywood, Florida, late the following afternoon. Never having been south of Washington, D.C., and never having seen the ocean, Ray was awestruck by the warmth and beauty of Florida in April. He rode a Navy bus from the airport on a tree-lined highway to the Hollywood Beach Hotel.

A Navy lieutenant with a thick southern accent told the arriving cadets that he expected all of them to graduate and be commissioned. As a result, he was going to treat them as officers and gentlemen, "starting now," and he did.

Ray was assigned with seven other cadets to a three-room suite on the eighth floor of the hotel that had been a noted resort for the rich and famous in the Roaring Twenties. Before the Navy took it over in 1942, the suite was bringing $80 a day, an unheard of hotel rate at the time.

The Navigation School moved at an easy-going pace with some classes even held on the beach. Ray noticed the ocean side of the façade of the hotel had a slight color change at the fifth floor and was told a tidal wave from a hurricane in the late 1920s reached that high on the building.

Ray remembered, "Nothing is sacred in a fraternity of guys like those in Naval Aviation." The cadets got pretty tan on the beach but the 11 scars on Ray's leg from the childhood operation stayed white. One cadet asked about them and Ray told the story, prompting the friend to say, "You should have let them cut your leg off and you would have had the distinction of being the only one-legged Naval aviator."[4]

The most difficult task Ray encountered in physical education was how to get into a lifeboat from the stern. There was only one procedure that would not tip the boat over. Instructors included Dixie Howell, the halfback end of the famous All-American passing attack at the University of Alabama, Howell to Hutson, and Curly Stebbins, a star halfback at the University of Pittsburgh.

Classroom instruction was easy for Ray. More than half the students came from schools such as the University of Pennsylvania where the primary studies were dead reckoning navigation and Morse Code. The remaining cadets came from pre-flight schools with a modest amount of instruction in celestial navigation. Ray was the only student who already knew something about both areas of navigation study, so it was not a surprise when he finished tied for first place in the class of 200. He also had plenty of extra time to become a proficient aerologist, the second field of study.

White and khaki uniforms were issued immediately upon arrival at navigation school. Of course the cadets thought they were "hot stuff." Decked out in white uniforms with black shoulder boards each highlighted with a gold star, Ray and his fellow cadets were often mistaken by Army "dogfaces" as admirals or generals and saluted. Nonchalantly, the Navy cadets returned every salute.

Ray and his suitemates became good friends. The eight cadets were all about 20 years old except for one "old man" of 25. They ignored the weekly admonition of the Catholic chaplain who pointed in the direction of Miami Beach and said, "Stay out of that cesspool of Hell." The older cadet was the only man in the suite experienced with girls. His roommates could hardly wait to get with him after he went on a date to learn what happened. He told Ray to date the rich girls in south Florida, saying, "It's just as easy to fall in love with a rich girl as a poor one and there's no point in taking chances."

Navigation training missions were flown in the SNB aircraft out of Opa Locka Naval Air Station in Miami. However, because Opa Locka's primary mission was the training of fighter pilots, the missions flown by Ray and his fellow navigation cadets took second place to the fighters. It was a common occurrence for SNB's to wait a long time at the end of the runway for takeoff.

Because the Navy was short of first line fighter aircraft, the best fighter plane, the F4F Wildcat, was assigned to the fleet and the fighter cadets had to fly the underpowered F2A Brewster Buffalo. The F2A was the Navy's first monoplane fighter and entered the service in the late 1930s. By the time of America's entry into World War II it was obsolete and after the Battle of Midway was withdrawn from front line service and assigned to training squadrons.[5]

Ray noticed that the fence at the end of the Opa Locka runway was often a freshly-painted green. He was told that it was patched in the evenings so the pilots trying to take off the next morning would not see the holes made by those who did not get airborne and crashed through the fence the day before.

Looking back, Ray said, "What a loss of fine young men simply because the United States was not prepared for war in 1941." Ray later heard that more pilots were killed in all the services in World War II during training than in combat, though Ray never verified the story.

The last of the swimming tests for naval aviation, AA, AAA, and AAAA, had to be passed before Ray could be commissioned. At Hollywood Navigation School, the tests involved swimming in the ocean back and forth between two anchored rowboats and breaking holds while rescuing "drowning" shipmates. Ray recalled, "Whatever advantage was gained by the buoyancy of saltwater was more than offset by waves slapping you in the face. Swimming a mile with your clothes on was no mean feat, moving fast from one boat to the other with the tide, and a murderous uphill battle against it." Ray had a lot of endurance but was one of the slowest swimmers in his class.

Ray had the choice of being commissioned in the Marines or Navy. He chose the Navy and received his Ensign bar on August 18, 1943. Being at the top of his class in navigation school gave him the opportunity to sign up for duty as a high altitude bombardier, or airbomber, as the Navy called the specialty. The following day, he reported for duty involving flying under instruction in aerial bombing as a technical observer at the Naval Air Station in Jacksonville, Florida. Within three weeks, the school was transferred to the Banana River Naval Air Station, later renamed Cape Kennedy.[6]

Most of the flight training at Corpus Christi was accomplished in four-plane flights. Ray, who went by the nickname "The Axe," and three other pilots in his flight became good friends and frequented the best, and worst, nightspots on many a night.

Because of the unexpected way Ray was commissioned as a navigator after originally enlisting to become a naval aviator, an important part of Ray's training was lost in the transition; like learning Navy protocol and rules and regulations. Not knowing any better, he wrote a nasty letter to the Supply Officer in Hollywood, Florida, when his luggage did not arrive in a timely fashion. The officer wrote a blistering letter back, notifying Ray that a copy of the letter was sent to the Bureau of Personnel for inclusion in his jacket.

The cadets trained with the famous Norden bombsight, invented for the Navy 20 years before, a fact lost in history because the bombsight was primarily an Army Air Corps asset in World War II. Once, from 16,000 feet in the Navy SNB, Ray dropped a 50-pound water-filled bomb through a 50-foot square. On the other hand, he made a mistake one day in securing his sight and dropped the same kind of bomb in a churchyard in Gainesville, Florida. As Ray remembered, "There was hell to pay when my plane returned to base."

Another famous former football player was the cadets' physical education instructor at Banana River. Forest Evashevski, the blocking back for All-American halfback Tom Harmon at the University of Michigan, always played opposite Ray, the biggest of the cadets, in pick-up basketball games. Evashevski played basketball like he did football and Ray learned the hard way the purpose of placing mattresses on the walls behind the basketball goals.

Evashevski and his wife, Ruth, hosted parties for the young bachelors. Ruth was high on marriage, saying to the Navy cadets, "Don't wait too long because if a man doesn't get married until he's over 25, he's not worth shooting."

On December 3, 1943, after successfully completing the Aerial Bombing School, Ray reported to COMAIRLANT Norfolk Naval Air Station in Virginia. He was excited about going to Europe and navigating the Navy's big Privateer bomber, the PB4Y, to the target, then jumping on the bombsight to take the pilot in for the drop. This plane was the Navy's version of the B-24 but with a radically different tail assembly utilizing a tall single tail fin and rudder. It also featured a lengthened forward fuselage, two dorsal turrets, a nose ball turret, and a two-gun "teardrop" blister on each side of the fuselage. With a cruising range of 2,800 miles at 140 mph and a top speed of 237 mph, the PB4Y-2 was ideal as a land-based maritime patrol bomber.[7]

However, while waiting for orders for Europe, Ray underwent an emergency appendectomy in the middle of the night. He was upset by having to have invasive surgery and was alarmed when he discovered that the young sailor prepping him for surgery, with straight-edged razor in hand, had been a butcher in private life. Ray was very, very still.

When Ray recovered from the appendectomy, his classmates had already been shipped out to Europe and the Pacific. It seemed no one knew what to do with Ray. His temporary additional duty (TAD) orders sent him to four different naval air stations in Virginia, to Chincoteague Navy Auxiliary Air Station for additional training as a navigator bombardier, to Celestial Navigation School in Norfolk, to the Dam Neck Aerial Gunnery School, and back to Naval Air Station Norfolk just to report in every morning to say, "I'm here."

The officer to whom Ray made his daily reports said, "I've never seen so many TAD's on TAD's. I think you could go home and nobody would find you until the war is over."

Ray played on an NAS Norfolk basketball team. The surgeon who took out his appendix told him not to play for 30 days. After exactly 30 days, he played a full game, shook all night, and thought he was going to die. His incision stretched so wide he believes it might be the "biggest appendix scar in the history of medicine."

One of the greatest shocks of young Ray's life came when a Navy lieutenant with a sidearm approached him in quarters and demanded he accompany him to Navy Security. Ray could not imagine what the problem was. He was very apprehensive. Tension mounted when Navy security officers placed him in a chair in the middle of an interrogation room. Ray recalled, "The officers were walking around me in circles, just like the interrogation of criminals I had seen in the movies."

An officer blurted out, "What do you know about Earnest Wahl?" Ray had not thought of the visitor to his parents' home since 1936, but, after a few moments of silence, replied, "He puts vanilla ice cream in his coffee." Frankly, that was all that Ray knew about Wahl. Realizing that Ray was not part of any Nazi spy conspiracy, the officers began to laugh and gave him a ride back to his quarters.

It turned out that Wahl was a Nazi spy for the Luftwaffe who toured the United States studying airports and the aviation industry. He apparently had picked Pittsburgh because of its modern airport. Ray's grandfather and his four brothers migrated to the United States in 1871 from Bavaria. It was amazing to Ray that even though his grandfather had been gone from Germany for 63 years, the Germans had known exactly how to find his youngest son and family in Pittsburgh.[8]

Ray's next duty station, on another TAD, was Quonset Point, Rhode Island, for Searchlight Training in Anti-Sub Warfare in PBY Catalinas. An amphibious patrol bomber, the PBY Catalina had a range of 2,545 miles and was used for scouting and anti-submarine patrols. The Black Cat Catalinas operated at night, when German submarines would surface to recharge their batteries. Should an enemy submarine be detected by the Catalina's radar, the PBY would swoop into the attack by fixing the powerful Leigh searchlight on the surfaced U-Boat and then drop bombs or depth charges.[9]

It was cold work flying over the Atlantic coast off Rhode Island during the winter. The searchlight operator sat forward of the pilot in a glass-enclosed nose turret that could be opened on top to allow the searchlight operator to stand up. Dressed in a leather, fleece-lined flight suit, Ray sat in the nose of a PBY, nearly freezing to death every night, learning to operate a huge Leigh light while listening to the radar operator as the aircraft tracked a submarine. A mile from the target, Ray would turn on the light and move it in a prescribed sweeping pattern until the pilot could see the submarine and fly over it to drop depth charges.

After learning what he called "a ridiculously easy procedure," Ray was assigned to the Naval Air Station at Boca Chica, Florida,

Ray liked his assignment at Corpus Christi, Texas. The weather was outstanding and honing one's skills as a pilot was exciting.

the third island north of Key West. Ray was the instructor in searchlight training of third pilot PB4Y navigators going to Europe. On nights off, he worked a couple of times as a dancer in floorshows at the biggest nightclub in Key West—a great way, as Ray remembered, "to learn how to lift those cute little dancers and spend a wonderful evening afterwards on a date."

The Bachelor Officers Quarters were not air conditioned. While Ray lay soaked in sweat one night, he received a phone call from his parents with news that his sister Kit had eloped with Bill Winkler. Ray replied, "Wonderful, that's great news." As a sure sign that Ray's father was beginning to transfer part of the family leadership to his Navy officer son, the elder Ackerman said, "Well, if Ray thinks it's OK, it must be OK." Ray had met Winkler a couple of times and really liked him, although at their first meeting Ray had to lean over and say to him, "Your fly is unzipped."

One Saturday afternoon, Ray was looking for a Catholic church in Key West so he could go to Confession. He was directed to an ancient gray stone structure, which looked perfectly Catholic to him, although he had never seen in those days the hymns to be sung on Sunday posted in the sacristy of a Catholic church as they were in this church. He discovered several weeks later that it was actually an Episcopalian church. When Ray explained his experience to a Catholic priest, the priest "blew his stack," and said, "As soon as you say 'Bless me father,' to start, he knows you are Catholic but likes to listen to all your sins so he never tells anyone of their mistake."

Ray finally entered Primary Flight Training at Ottumwa, Iowa, on November 2, 1944, still not concerned about missing the war. Frankly, one of his big concerns was hair loss. He was just 22, but his hair was falling out. He had purchased a home treatment kit with twelve bottles each of four different fluids that had to be applied to the scalp daily.

Wanting desperately to win his Wings of Gold, Ray was determined to refrain from drinking beer or any alcoholic beverage, study hard, and have very few dates, so he did not see any problem with having "gooey" hair.

Flight training in Iowa came during one of the state's coldest winters on record. Ray and other cadets learned to fly in a Stearman N2S, an open-cockpit aircraft that cruised at 106 mph. It was the same plane that Robert Ragozzino flew around the world in 2000. Ray's instructor taught by yelling and screaming at his students. Ray often was so angry in the back seat of the plane that tears of rage filled his eyes. However, the loud lieutenant allowed Ray to solo on his sixth flight, two short of the prescribed regimen, indicating that Ray was doing pretty good. Ray always found it humorous that he had a license to fly before he had a driver's license.

Flight school consisted of a half-day's instruction in ground school and a half-day of flying. Because of all his previous schooling, Ray passed final exams early in all the subjects except Aircraft Engines so he had a light load for half a day. He was promoted to Lieutenant Junior Grade (LTJG) on December 1, 1944.

The Stearmans were not equipped with radios and the cadets took off from octagonal-shaped mats, rather than runways, to allow multiple aircraft to take off or land at the same time. Once, as planes were being recalled with beacon lights during a snowstorm, Ray was breaking his glide to land when he glanced down and saw a horrified face in a cockpit between him and the mat. He pulled up just in time to avoid a collision.

The Navy provided facemasks to protect student pilots from the bitter Iowa cold. However, the facemasks were not adequate, prompting ladies from the local American Red Cross chapter to knit big woolen head socks for the young pilots. There was a slot for their goggles after they pulled the sock and helmet over their heads. It was not uncommon for pilots to return from flights with a beard of icicles hanging from the wool. It was so cold that winter in Iowa that a wet towel would freeze on the short walk from the gymnasium to the barracks.[10]

The training planes were restricted from being flown if the temperature was below ten degrees. Nevertheless, the public address system in the ready room often blared, "Pilots, man your planes, pilots man your planes. The temperature is zero but it will be ten by the time you're ready to take off." No one complained about flying in the cold. The alternative was spending the morning watching what Ray described as "terribly explicit and sickening" venereal disease warning films.

Weekends in Iowa were wonderful. In Des Moines, 90 miles away, local girls, and 5,000 students at a Womens Air Corps (WAC) training school, provided an incredible supply of potential dates. Babe's Night Club was the place to go. Babe's was voted by those who responded to a *Time* Magazine survey as the number one place for servicemen to go on liberty during the war.

A *Time* article described the typical scene at Babe's on a Saturday afternoon when a Navy man would walk up to a pretty girl and say, "Are you the kind of a girl that hopes to get married and have a house with a white picket fence, rose bushes, and babies?" If the girl answered yes, the Navy man said, "You're not what I'm looking for."

Through handling advertising for the National Rifle Association, Ray got to know the Des Moines police chief 45 years after he went through flight training in Iowa. The police chief told Ray that Babe was still alive and had a written a book. Later, a copy of the book arrived in Oklahoma City in the mail inscribed with, "The girls are still asking about you," signed "Babe."

On four different weekends while stationed at Ottumwa, Ray managed to get to Chicago on the 80-mile-per-hour Burlington train. On his first weekend in the Windy City, he met a girl named Wanda Cochran, who was an usher in the Erlanger Theater, the first stop for the road show of "Oklahoma!" Wanda had ambitions beyond being an usher and when Ray arrived the second weekend, she was singing in the chorus. By weekend number three, she was understudying the lead and, the following weekend, she was playing the lead, because the girl who was playing Laurie in the stage play had eloped.

Basketball occupied much of Ray's time after dark, following long hours of flight training in the severe winter weather. The Ottumwa Naval Air Station team actually defeated the Harlem Globetrotters one night during an exhibition game. Ray remembered, "It was one of those nights when all we had to do was put the ball in the air, and it went in!"

Before completing Primary Flight Training, Ray made a 100-mile cross-country flight in a Stearman with a canopy. Like most of his fellow aviators, Ray could not resist "flat-hatting" over wide open Iowa farms and chasing the cows and horses.

He received orders to report to the Naval Air Station at Corpus Christi, Texas. He and a friend from California, Lieutenant

Roy Falconer, dubbed "The Falcon," drove from Iowa to Texas in Falconer's convertible in March, 1945, passing through Oklahoma.

It was Ray's first time to be in the state he would someday learn to deeply love. He and his friend stopped at a gasoline station in Ardmore. As they were pulling away from the pump, the attendant said, "Ya'll come back." Not knowing what that salutation meant, Ray and his companion stopped, backed up, and asked, "What for?" It was Ray's introduction to the friendliness of the people in Oklahoma.

Ray and Falconer stopped in Dallas, Texas, en route to Corpus Christi. They checked into a hotel and looked for a bar. They discovered Texas was "dry." So much for all the wild saloons they had seen in Texas movies. Ray had saved back a bottle of Johnny Walker Black Label, purchased with extra liquor ration cards received in Iowa. When he set the bottle on the table at Pappy's Showland, a popular Dallas nightclub, the place went silent. Ray remembered, "Several girls actually walked by and dropped a note on the table with their address, telephone number, and what time they'd be home."[11]

Ray had no problem passing all flight requirements. For 24 hours, however, he was in trouble because of an incident over the Gulf of Mexico. The instructor said he would fly the plane for a while then let Ray take over, to practice instruments under the hood. While the instructor was still flying, the sun was beaming in through the canopy and Ray fell asleep. The instructor did a couple of snap rolls which awakened Ray in a hurry.

The training at Corpus Christi was in four-plane flights. Getting familiar with flying at night, "boring holes," they called it, got pretty old. But, liberty at Matamoras, Mexico, made up for the boring flying. Ray and his buddies were forewarned about the Matamoras prostitutes who literally lined the streets trying to pull guys into their hovels. Falconer, a little older than the rest of the flight, warned Ray, "You can dance with the B girls, even buy them a drink, but don't kiss one."

Ray's two closest friends were The Falcon and The Mace, who had rowed stroke for the Naval Academy crew and had arms and shoulders "like blacksmiths." One night when there was no water coming out of either faucet in the men's room at Zacchi's, a Corpus Christi drive-in, the Mace grabbed the sink and tore it off the wall. Water spouted everywhere as Ray and his buddies made a rapid exit. The Mace also enjoyed punching holes in walls in quarters. One night he hit a stud instead of sheet rock and was grounded with a swollen hand for a week.

Ray was given the opportunity to select between multi-engine or fighter planes for his future in the Navy. He eagerly selected the fighters.

Ray worked hard to be one of the Navy's best pilots. He knew it would not be long before he would use his newly learned skills in the war against the Japanese. However, that never happened. President Harry S. Truman made the decision to drop the atomic bomb on two Japanese cities in August, 1945. The devastation caused by the bombing of Hiroshima and Nagasaki forced the Japanese to surrender within days. World War II was over.

Ray was glad the killing had stopped and that his own life would not be in danger. However, there was an element of disappointment that he and his buddies did not get into the fight. He was highly trained as a pilot, navigator, and bombardier, three disciplines he did not get to use in combat.

One weekend, a hurricane was coming and everyone was confined to base except Ray and some friends who got out before the gate was closed. They rented a hotel suite in Galveston and threw a giant party while the hurricane blew around them. Ray said, "There's nothing quite like a party when no one can leave!"

Before leaving Corpus Christi in October, after completing Intermediate and Pre-Operational Training, Ray's special friend, Jimmy Hafford, got married and his mates threw him and his bride, Betty, a party in the Nueces Hotel. The party planners thought one bottle of champagne per guest was about right so three cases were laid in a bathtub with a 100-pound cake of ice. However, more than a full case remained after the party.[12]

On November 7, 1945, Ray reported to the Naval Air Station in Jacksonville, Florida, for Operational Flight Training in the FG-1D Corsair. Armed with six .50-caliber machine guns and a maximum speed of 440 mph, the Corsair and the F6F Hellcat were the two outstanding carrier-based fighters of World War II. The Corsair was the first American fighter with a top speed in excess of 400 mph.[13]

On the way from Texas to Florida, in two convertibles, Ray and five friends used champagne left over from the Hafford wedding reception to mix half and half with ale, to make a drink called Black Velvet, made famous by the movie *The Great John L. Sullivan.* Ray recalled, "We stored the leftover champagne in the trunk and brought it into whatever nightclub we stopped at, ordering the ale to mix. After we got kicked out of a club in New Orleans for shooting the champagne corks across the dance floor, we quit that practice."

The first time Ray took off in the 2,000-plus horsepower Corsair, "It was an awesome experience when I started down the runway. I thought my body was going out the back of the cockpit. I think I was at 3,000 feet before I even remembered to retract the landing gear." One of the main drawbacks of the Corsair was its elongated nose, which limited visibility during takeoffs and landings. Ray trained in the Corsair during late 1945 and early 1946 at NAS Jacksonville and NAS Miami.

Ray returned home for Christmas in 1945, as did his brother, a student at Notre Dame, his older sister who was traveling as the advance publicist for the Ice Capades, and his younger sister who had married and lived in Cleveland. His parents had moved from Bellevue to Franklin, Pennsylvania, where Ray, Sr. was the financial officer of a new plastics manufacturing company.

Ray was the last of the four Ackerman children to get home,

arriving late on Christmas Eve. A heavy snow started and they all walked to Midnight Mass where blue Christmas lights reflected on new snow like a Currier & Ives Christmas card with a "Silent Night" theme. It made such an impression on Ray that his family home is always decorated on the outside with blue lights.

It was a perfect Christmas. The family was actually snowed in and enjoyed an extra day together. Christmas, 1945, was the last time all six members of the Ackerman family were together for Christmas. It also was the last time that all four children were together for the Yuletide until 1980, 35 years later.[14]

FACING: Ray's flight training in Corpus Christi was much more intense than the early training in Iowa. He flew the 550-horsepower SNJ, which the Army Air Corps called the AT-6 Texan, out of Cabiness and Kingsville fields, learning about instrument flying, how to fly in formation, air-to-air gunnery, and night familiarization. The SNJ was the most widely used trainer ever, with more than 17,000 aircraft built. Nearly every pilot in World War II flew either the SNJ or the AT-6. Ray also flew the SBD Douglas Dive Bomber, the Dauntless, out of Beeville, Texas. It was a plane that made a major difference in the Battle of Midway. The pilot flew from the front cockpit, while an observer/rear gunner flew in the back. With a 1,200 horsepower engine and a maximum speed of 230 mph, it was a transition to the Corsair.

ON LAND AND SEA

RAY'S TIME FLYING CORSAIRS IN FLORIDA culminated with Field Carrier Landing Practice (FCLP) at Cecil Field in Jacksonville, followed by carrier qualifications out of Saufley Field in Pensacola. Making field carrier landings was not as easy as it looked. When Ray and fellow cadets observed other pilots attempting landings on a place marked on the runway about the size of a carrier deck, and were waved off because their landing gears were still up, Ray thought to himself, "How could anyone be so dumb?"

However, after he was waved off on his first two attempts because his landing gear was not deployed, Ray realized the extra things a pilot had to do when landing on the narrow deck of a carrier—flying slower, putting the tail hook down, following the directions of the Landing Signal Officer (LSO), and landing on an exact spot. The saying, "On any given day, anyone can make a stupid mistake, so don't get cocky!" made a lot of sense to Ray.

Ray qualified on the USS *Ranger*, a carrier that was famous for having the narrowest deck in the Navy, only 60 feet wide. Launched in 1933, the *Ranger* was one of the oldest aircraft carriers in the Navy. After serving with the Atlantic Fleet, participating in the American invasion of North Africa, and service with the British Home Fleet, the *Ranger* was relegated to aircraft carrier training operations in late 1944. Designed just as the United States Navy was beginning to develop its aircraft carrier tactics, the *Ranger* had four smoke stacks on the port side of her flight deck. To provide a clear path for a wave-off, the smoke stacks were lowered to a horizontal position for landings.[1]

Landing his Corsair on the narrow deck was a challenge. It was difficult to see through the windshield of the plane because of several cross bars. In fact, the plane's cockpit was called "the birdcage." Flying at the necessary low speed to come in for a landing made it difficult to see the LSO because of the Corsair's long nose. To land, Ray had to lean partially out of the cockpit, position the LSO right against the engine, alternately open and close the cowl flaps to keep the engine cool, get the signal to cut the engine while in a turn, and then level out to land in the middle of the narrow deck. Ray surprised even himself by landing eight times in a row without a wave-off, sufficient for certification.

Ironically, Aviation Boatswains Mate Third Class George Nigh, later Governor of Oklahoma, was a plane handler on the USS *Ranger* on the same day that Ray qualified, May 1, 1946. After reading Nigh's biography, *Good Guys Wear White Hats,* Ray said, "Maybe the kid from Pittsburg County, Oklahoma, was disengaging the hook after the kid from Pittsburgh, Pennsylvania, made his landings."[2]

Before going to Norfolk, Virginia, to join a fighter squadron, Ray had a few days leave and went to New York City to see the Yankees play the Boston Red Sox. In the heat of a pennant race, Yankee Stadium was sold out. Boston was on a 15-game winning streak and in first place. The Yankees, expected to win the pennant, were not far behind in second place. It was Ladies' Day and the offer of free nylon stockings drew a giant crowd to the ballpark.

Ray walked around the stadium twice, looking for a scalper with a ticket. About to give up, Ray noticed the Marine captain in charge of the color guard wore his green uniform, similar to the Naval Aviator greens Ray wore. The captain allowed Ray to march into Yankee Stadium with the color guard, one of the few times anyone successfully crashed the gate at the famous ballpark. Ray had to sit on a concrete step on the aisle but saw a great game. The Yankees won 3-2 and both Ted Williams and Joe DiMaggio hit home runs.

In June, 1946, Ray reported for duty as a member of Squadron VF-4, called the Red Rippers, at Norfolk, Virginia, Naval Air Station. The squadron was assigned to the USS *Tarawa,* an Essex Class carrier, the last class that was not too large to go through the Panama Canal. Even at that, the side elevator on the *Tarawa* had to be removed so the carrier could squeeze through the canal.

The *Tarawa* (CV-40) had been commissioned into service on December 8, 1945, and conducted its shakedown cruise in the vicinity of Guantanamo Bay, Cuba, from February until April of 1946. After returning to Norfolk, the carrier, with Ray aboard, sailed for San Diego, California, on June 28, 1946.[3] The ship's skipper was Captain A.T. Malstrom who had a reputation for commanding the cleanest ship in the Navy. The crew was always chipping and painting, starting at the bow. As soon as they finished at the stern, they went to the bow and started over.

It took Ray weeks to become accustomed to the 90-feet wide landing deck of the *Tarawa.* He kept crowding the LSO as he had to on the *Ranger* and the LSO kept diving into his safety net after frantically giving Ray a wave-off.

The USS *Tarawa* sailed from Norfolk, through the Panama Canal, and on to San Diego, California, arriving July 15, 1946. When the carrier dropped anchor, Ray and the other pilots flew their planes ashore and headed for the Officers Club. The married officers had their wives drive cross-country to meet them.

As the newest man in the squadron, Ray was ordered by the commanding officer to "Go get some dates for the single guys."

He remembered, "I went sailing through swinging barroom-type doors just as three girls walked in the front door of the club. When they answered yes to my question if they wanted to go to a party, I had them back into the room before the door even stopped swinging!"

The captain took one look at him and said, "From now on, you are the Welfare and Recreation Officer." Ray remembered, "The young ladies I recruited were typical of many widows in the area who had lost their husbands fighting the Japanese. Most of them were looking for husbands."[4]

From San Diego, the *Tarawa* sailed to Pearl Harbor, Hawaii, where it was equipped with brand new fighter planes, F4U-4's. Ray and the other pilots began practicing strafing and dive bombing. The target, called a sled, was dragged by the carrier. After one of the pilots was killed when his tail separated from the fuselage as he pulled out of a dive, all Navy Corsairs were grounded for several weeks while Navy and Grumman engineers analyzed the problem. Additional rivets was the answer. Another Air Group pilot was killed enroute to Saipan when the ring attaching his SB2C Helldiver to the catapult broke.

Half the time on this tour of duty, Ray's Air Group operated off the carrier and the other half off the airstrip on Saipan. Between September 28 and October 3, the *Tarawa* was in port at Yokosuka, Japan, and then from October 7 to 11, it was at Sasebo, Japan. However, it was ordered off the shore of northern China to help stabilize the situation during the Nationalist-Communist Chinese warfare and arrived off Tsingtao, China, on October 15.

While off the shore of China, Ray and other crew members were allowed liberty ashore and time to travel on a day's round trip to Peking, China. One night in Tsingtao, Ray had a date with a white Russian girl named Helen Hloboshema, "white" referring to the fact that she was not a communist. She took him to dinner at her home in the nearby hills where he learned a new

card game from her rather sizeable family who won all his money amid great laughter. He had to walk back to the dock with no flashlight in total darkness. He recalled, "I had improvised and made a weapon out of my belt and buckle, expecting thieves and murderers to drop out of the trees at anytime." He was not attacked but arrived back at the dock minutes after the last boat had left for the carrier.

After a less than adequate night's sleep on a bench, Ray awoke at 6:30 A.M., wondering how he could get to his ship for 8:00 A.M. muster. There was a Chinese junk not far off and Ray signaled wildly, pointing to the carrier. Ray overcame a definite language barrier and convinced the owner of the junk to carry him out to his ship. After negotiating a course to the opposite side of the carrier, far from the view of the Officer of the Day, Ray climbed aboard when a sailor threw him a knotted rope. He arrived just in time for the 8:00 o'clock muster. About the time

Ray was considering how lucky and smart he was to get back to the ship, reality set in. The junk was probably a regular taxi service every morning a Navy ship was in port.

The electricity on Saipan frequently failed, meaning no refrigeration for beer. On such days, Ray's squadron flew a "beer flight." An airplane, loaded with beer, was flown long enough at high altitude to chill the beer in time for Happy Hour.

Ray, like most military men stuck on an island, grew a mustache and beard. That is until one morning when one of the long, straight mustache hairs appeared to be mixed with his powdered eggs.

Ray was the Squadron Transportation Officer and had a jeep at his disposal. So when a young dancer he dated in Key West showed up in a USO show, he was able to have a date every night as her troop moved from base to base on Saipan.

After a few days of operations on the carrier, Ray landed back on Saipan and learned his USO girlfriend was in that area of the Pacific for only one more night, on the nearby island of Tinian. Ray talked his commanding officer into allowing him and two friends to fly to Tinian and spend the night. Tinian was so close to Saipan that Ray and his friends did not have to raise the gear of their aircraft. Looking at his manual, he discovered that the Tinian field was closed that day. However, Ray landed with his friends anyway, intent upon having his last date for several months. As the three were tying their planes down, a jeep driven by a lieutenant with a full commander passenger drove up. Ray explained why they were there. It was the wrong answer. The commander said, "There are several thousand men on this island, only eight girls on this USO tour, and you three guys show up to take three of the girls away and make the odds even worse."[5]

Ray suddenly recognized the officer as the former commanding officer of Cudahy Field in Corpus Christi, close to where Ray was stationed at Cabiness Field. Ray remembered the commander's proficiency as a party giver, and his reputation for saying, "Lock all the doors and windows, don't let anyone in or out, we're gonna' have a party." Warming up at the recollection, the commander invited Ray and his friends to spend the night in his quarters. He and the major in charge of the small Army unit on the island, whose turn it was to host the USO, soon figured out that because Ray knew the USO girls, their odds of getting dates were pretty good. Sure enough, Ray was able to line up the girls for himself, his two friends, and the commander and major. That left three girls for the remaining several thousand troops.

Ray, number 7 on the back row, was part of the basketball team on the USS Tarawa *that won the Pacific all-Navy basketball tournament in February, 1947. The Air Group team beat the ship's team soundly every time they played so the ship's captain combined the two teams for the Pacific tournament. The hangar deck on the carrier was ideal for basketball and the forward elevator, when lowered, was an excellent volleyball court. Navy commanders encouraged their men to play sports, both on the ship and when in port.*

The Tinian party lasted all night. Ray and his friends woke up after 8:00 A.M., the time they were scheduled to be back in Saipan. His new found friend, the commander, said, "Don't worry. I'll send your CO a message and everything will be OK. Let's go have some fun."

However, while watching the daily destruction of ammunition and bombs on Tinian, an important post-war activity, Ray noticed a lone Corsair circling. It was his skipper, trying to find "his boys" and "rescue" them. It turned out that the message he received said "I'm detaining," not "I'm entertaining."

Ray and his two friends were ordered to appear before the Air Group Board within minutes of their arrival back on Saipan. Four of the five officers on the board could hardly contain their laughter about the situation. However, their skipper was stern and threatening and confined the three to quarters for several days, except for the time they were required to work as grease monkeys on the squadron's ground transportation.

The punishment meted out by the skipper may have been agitated by the fact that Ray fulfilled his promise to bring the skipper back a gift from his night on Tinian. At the end of the tongue-lashing, Ray laid a hand grenade down in front of the skipper. The gift had no particular significance until New Year's Eve when someone stole the grenade and blew the Air Group Commander's quarters off the island. Ray and his friends were out of favor again.

In March, 1947, Ray received his orders discharging him from active duty. His Air Group had just completed war games in the Pacific, simulating attacks on ships, striking Johnston Island, even attempting a sneak attack on Pearl Harbor, and was then shore-based on Maui.

Ray was ordered to catch the USS *Bairoka,* a jeep carrier, for transportation from Pearl Harbor back to the mainland. Jeep carriers were the common name for merchant ships that had been converted to small aircraft carriers during World War II. Many served in an anti-submarine role for convoys during the fighting, but were converted to transport aircraft to the larger fleet carriers as replacements in the latter stages of the war.[6]

The squadron's only transport, a Beechcraft, was down for maintenance and Ray had no way to get to Pearl Harbor to catch his ride home. He asked his skipper, Commander John Lacoture, how to get down to Pearl. His answer was, "That's your problem."

Taking matters into his own hands, he "borrowed" a Corsair and flew to Ford Island at Pearl Harbor, tied down the plane, boarded the *Bairoka,* and sailed for home. The incident resulted in a letter of reprimand in Ray's jacket from the skipper of Fighting Squadron Four for "stealing" an airplane. It was the next to last paper in Ray's jacket at the Navy Bureau of Personnel to end his active duty career in the Navy, preceding his Honorable Discharge. It was a "bookend" with the other letter of reprimand received from the Supply Officer at Navigation School, the second paper in Ray's active duty jacket following the paper commissioning him as an Ensign.

Ray arrived in San Diego, California, was detached from active duty on March 22, 1947, and began 60 days of terminal leave. When he was turning in his Navy gear, including his Colt .45, the sailor checking in the equipment said, "Keep the pistol. Everyone else does." Ray has his pistol to this day.[7]

GO WEST YOUNG MAN

RAY IMMEDIATELY went to see his older sister, M'Fran, in Hollywood. She was the advance publicist for the Ice Capades, which had been strictly a man's business until Anita Colby, a former movie star, became the first traveling female in such a job. M'Fran was the second. She was in Hollywood because the traveling season of the Ice Capades was over and the skaters were there to create and practice routines for the new year. The owners rented one of the old mansions and built a temporary arena for practice. It was M'Fran's job to prepare photographs and publicity material for the next season.

M'Fran wanted to do something nice for Ray so she took him to Clark Gable's tailor and had a grey flannel double-breasted suit made for him. She also arranged for a photographer to take some really glamour-type pictures in both uniform and flight gear for the family album.

The idea for a life in advertising had popped into Ray's mind one night in Saipan during a conversation with his Navy buddy, Gus St. Clair. To help him with his intended career, M'Fran introduced Ray to people she knew in the advertising business in Los Angeles. Their advice was to work for a newspaper in a medium-sized city.

While still in California, Ray visited the parents of his Navy friend Jimmy Hafford, who unexpectedly died of pneumonia while still on active duty. Hafford's father owned the Pastime Bar in Benecia, California, a small town near San Francisco. When Ray arrived at the bar about 3:00 P.M. one afternoon, he was told that Hafford was out visiting competitors but would be back shortly. Ray sat down and had a beer, noticing that the bartenders stared at him, then checked snapshots tucked in a mirror. The photographs were of Jimmy and Ray together. Once Ray was recognized, he never bought another beer.

It may have been the wildest three days of Ray's life. While a houseguest of his late friend's parents, Ray was offered an interesting proposition. If he would marry Jimmy's widow, Betty, and take care of her and the baby, the bar would be signed over to Ray and he would inherit the entire Hafford estate. Ray remembered, "Betty was a cute little girl and being out of work and shortly having to find a job I was mildly tempted for about 60 seconds, but with such an offer of desperation, it was not easy to say no and leave town."[1]

Ray headed east. He stopped in Los Alamos, New Mexico, to visit a former Navy WAVE who taught him in a Link trainer in Florida. They had been exchanging letters for months. In fact, Ray thought they were in love. He realized it one day when a letter from the WAVE asked if he was serious, and if he was not, she was going to marry someone else. Ray, believing he could not live without her, wrote passionate letters and promised, "I'll be back!" The girl said she would not marry another anxious suitor before Ray came home.

Anxious for Ray to stay in New Mexico, his girlfriend landed him a job interview at a radio station in Los Alamos. Fortunately, Ray did not get the job, and after a few days, and the realization he and the lady were not cut out for each other, headed eastward to Oklahoma. It was snowing heavily when his bus pulled out of the Los Alamos station. Looking at her teary face through the snow, Ray fell in love all over again.

Ray arrived in Oklahoma City on a crisp April day in 1947. He was impressed by the clean air and the two tall buildings in

Oklahoma's capital city silhouetted against a deep blue sky. Oklahoma City was a natural stop on Ray's trek eastward because his mother's only brother, Uncle Sam, and his wife, Esther, and their five children lived there.

Uncle Sam Grasinger, always fond of his nephew, was intrigued by Ray's announcement that he wanted to go into advertising and that he had been advised to work for a newspaper in a medium-sized city. Sam had worked with an advertising agency executive, George Knox, at Tinker Field in Oklahoma City during the war and used his contact with Knox to get Ray an interview with O.C. Brown, advertising director of *The Daily Oklahoman* and *Oklahoma City Times,* owned by the Oklahoma Publishing Company (OPUBCO).

The next thing Ray knew, he was being interviewed by Brown. Even though he was still in uniform and had not made up his mind where to settle, Ray knew his Uncle Sam had gone to a lot of trouble to set up the interview at the newspaper so he completed a job application for an advertising sales position.

After staying with Uncle Sam and Aunt Esther for a few days, Ray traveled to South Bend, Indiana, to visit his brother who was a student at the University of Notre Dame. Ray also stopped by Louisville, Kentucky, to see the Kentucky Derby. He picked a horse, Jet Pilot, to win the race. With 20-to-1 odds, Ray would have won nearly $4,000 with the $200 bet he planned. However, he suddenly became frugal and decided to save his money. He had stayed on active duty longer than he needed to because the year-long cruise was so enjoyable, making it easy to save a little for the future.

Ray went home to Franklin, Pennsylvania, halfway between Pittsburgh and Lake Erie. It had been said that Franklin had more millionaires, 13, than New York City in the 1890s. Franklin was near Oil City, the site of the first oil discovery right after the Civil War, and it was home to the country's first oil barons. Ray visited a number of college campuses in western

Pennsylvania, still uncertain whether to go to school, get a job, or do both at once.

One day, while agonizing over his choices, Ray received a wire from O.C. Brown in Oklahoma City. The wire simply stated, "If you want the job you applied for, be here at 8:00 A.M. on Monday morning, June 12."[2]

Ray weighed his options—go to college near his home, or make a new life in Oklahoma City. He wanted to fly in the Naval Reserve and could do that at the Naval Air Station, Dallas. And, he could get a degree at night at Oklahoma City University. Lastly, Oklahoma City was warmer and cleaner than Pittsburgh, which he still called home, even though his parents had moved.

After soul searching, Ray wired his acceptance and faced a new hurdle. He needed a new car to get to Oklahoma, a near impossible task since America's appetite for automobiles immediately after World War II had resulted in a shortage of new cars for sale. In fact, Ray's father had been unable to reserve a new car for his son before he got home from active duty. The pent-up desire for new cars created a bad situation. Dealers often expected "under the table" money from anyone wanting a new car.

Luck was with Ray. The local Chevrolet dealer called to report that his girlfriend had a 1941 Coupe that she might sell for the right price. Ray offered the lady her asking price of $1,100 for the shiny Chevy with only 8,700 miles logged in the six and a half years she had owned the car. The lady cried as Ray drove off in the car that had a 1943 newspaper in the back seat and a trunk that smelled as if it had never been opened.

Ray prepared to pack all his worldly possessions for the trip west to Oklahoma. However, his closet was bare. His mother said his younger brother had grown up to within two inches of Ray's height and used the suits, sport coats, and pants Ray left behind to enter the Navy. Ray asked about one lone pair of shoes that remained in the closet. His mother replied, "Your brother went through that size before he wore them out."

Ray bought a few items of clothing and loaded them into his new car along with his tailor-made gray flannel suit and his electric train, then headed west toward his new job. He detoured briefly, to New Mexico, to see if there was any future with the girl in Los Alamos. But again, after a few days, he decided to forget girls and get to Oklahoma City to bear down on work and school. [3]

AD SALESMAN
AND STUDENT

RAY SPENT HIS FIRST NIGHT IN OKLAHOMA City at the Biltmore Hotel. He reported for work the following morning and was assigned to travel with one of the more experienced advertising salesmen. After a few weeks of training Ray was given several small downtown Oklahoma City accounts, mostly chain stores that regularly advertised in both the morning and evening papers. One of the first accounts Ray was assigned to was B.C. Clark Jewelers, an account that later played a major part in Ray's advertising success.

Most young men such as Ray lived in rooming houses or private households that took in boarders. Ray lucked out and moved into a room in the home of the widow of a Judge Miley at 733 Northeast 19th Street. His quarters were tiny, but comfortable. Mrs. Miley said she expected Ray to be an ideal boarder like one of her previous tenants, newspaper reporter A.S. "Mike" Monroney, who later served as Congressman and United States Senator from Oklahoma.[1]

On his first Saturday in Oklahoma, Ray traveled on a business trip with his Uncle Sam and his cousin, Sam, Jr., to Fort Smith, Arkansas. As they approached the Arkansas border, out of nowhere there was a traffic jam trying to get across the river into Fort Smith. Uncle Sam explained that Oklahoma was dry and the people were going to Arkansas to buy whiskey for the weekend. Ray had not realized Oklahoma was dry.

Coming back from Fort Smith on Sunday afternoon, there was a jam of people in Arkansas trying to cross the river into Oklahoma. Ray asked his uncle about the people crossing into Oklahoma and was told Arkansas was completely dry on Sundays; not even beer was sold. As a result, Arkansas citizens were going into Oklahoma to drink beer. Ray began to wonder if he had made a bad move in coming to this "crazy part of the country."

In addition to work, Ray got busy immediately with school, signing up for a summer course in Psychology at the OCU night school. With a profession of advertising, Ray looked at a college degree as being more of an insurance policy for promotion rather than being directly helpful to his career. He thought studying Psychology would help him get through fast and in good style by practicing it on his teachers. Also, he reported for duty as an active reservist at NAS Dallas and was assigned to Fighting Squadron VF-56A, effective June 30, 1947.

OPUBCO paid Ray $45 per week. At first, Ray believed he could easily get by on the salary but soon realized how many living expenses he had not had to pay while in the Navy. The $50 in his pocket when he arrived in Oklahoma City and his first two paychecks were gone in those two weeks. He realized his spendthrift days were over.

FACING: Ray met Lucille Frances Flanagan in the record department at Harbour Longmire in 1947. Lou had graduated from Oklahoma City's Classen High School in 1945 and was a student at Rosary College in Chicago, Illinois. From the beginning of their relationship, Ray described Lou as "a cute little maid with a million-dollar smile and a two-million dollar laugh."

Ray worked out of the OPUBCO branch office in a building on the southeast corner of Main Street and Hudson Avenue in downtown Oklahoma City. On one fateful day, he walked a half block down the street to visit his cousin, Teresa Jane Grasinger, who worked in the record department at Harbour Longmire. While there, he was introduced to the other girl in the department, Lucille Frances "Lou" Flanagan, the Irish Catholic daughter of George Smarr Flanagan and Kathleen Bradley Flanagan of Oklahoma City.

Two days later Ray invited Lou to an Oklahoma City Indians baseball game. A few days later, Lou invited Ray to a family picnic on the Fourth of July at Broadlawn Lake in northwest Oklahoma City. Ray thought that spot had the scenery closest to Pennsylvania he had seen and vowed to build a house on the lake if he ever had the chance.

Ray grew serious about Lou. But, there was a problem. Lou wore the fraternity ring of one Wally Borden, her boyfriend in Chicago. Ray made the elimination of Borden his priority mission. He wanted Lou to stay in Oklahoma City and not return to Rosary College in Chicago nor enroll in the Kansas City Art Institute she was considering.

Borden's ring on Lou's hand irritated Ray. Finally, Ray said, "If I ever move into first place ahead of Wally, just don't wear the ring and I'll know." The next week, when Ray picked up Lou for a date, he noticed the ring was gone. He began singing and whistling as they drove down the street. Lou asked, "What's the matter with you?" Ray pointed at Lou's hand and replied, "No ring!" She burst his bubble when she said, "Oh my gosh, I forgot to put it back on after I finished washing the dishes."[2]

Ray desperately tried to impress Lou to keep her in Oklahoma City. He thought maybe an airplane ride would do the trick and scraped together a few dollars to rent an old Stearman from Keith Kahle Aviation at Will Rogers Airport. It was the only plane Kahle owned that Ray had flown before and it was the only one he could afford to rent for 30 minutes. Ray placed Lou in the rear cockpit and explained certain safety procedures including how to bail out. Then he explained all the acrobatic maneuvers he planned to do, starting with a loop.

Ray remembered the Stearman from primary flight training as having a ceiling of about 8,500 feet, but the old Kahle clunker would not climb higher than 3,200 feet. That meant that Ray had to dive a little lower than Civil Aviation Administration rules for the minimum altitude for acrobatics. The Stearman always coughed a little bit when the engine went through the horizon on the way up, but this one coughed and then quit completely. Ray frantically kicked everything in the cockpit to restart the engine but finally picked the riverbed of the South Canadian River to land. When he was about 20 feet from landing, he got the engine started and immediately flew back to the airport. Lou, who enjoyed immensely the short flight, did not know the engine had conked out. When they landed, she said, "I thought you were going to do a lot of tricks for 30 minutes." He never took her up again.

CARPETBAGGER
WITHOUT PORTFOLIO

RAY HAD ANOTHER PROBLEM in winning Lou's hand. Her mother, Kathleen, insisted on calling Ray a "carpetbagger." She often challenged Lou, "What do you know about that carpetbagger from Pennsylvania who arrived in town without portfolio?"

The label resulted in quite a few conversations between Lou and her mother. During one discussion, Lou showed her mother one of the glamour photographs of Ray that Mary Frances, his sister, had purchased for him in California. On the picture, drawing from Ray's and Lou's favorite song, "Peg O' My Heart," Ray had written, "It's your Irish heart I'm after. Love, Ray." Mrs. Flanagan, still convinced that Ray was up to no good, scoffed at the photograph and said, "I'll bet there's a girl in every port with one of those."

Wally Borden came to Oklahoma City to pursue his courtship with Lou who agreed to see him one evening. It was a lonely, agonizing night for Ray. When Lou called and said Wally had gone back to Chicago, Ray knew he was winning the battle for Lou's hand.

On Lou's birthday, September 3, 1947, Ray took her to St. Francis of Assisi Catholic Church on Northwest 18th Street, lit a couple of candles, and asked her to marry him, after ascertaining she, like he, wanted a large family. Ray asked, "How many children would you like to have?" When Lou answered, "Six," the same number Ray was thinking, he knew he had found the girl for him.[1]

Lou accepted an engagement ring and a wedding date of June 14, 1948, was set. However, one final obstacle remained. Ray had to ask her dad for Lou's hand. Lou's sister, Kay, and her husband, Al, and Mrs. Flanagan, who had begun to like Ray, planned an evening for the big question. They advised Ray that the best time to ask George such a delicate question was at dusk when he was putting his two cars in the garage.

When Mr. Flanagan got behind the wheel of one of the cars, Ray walked up to the window and blurted out, "George, I would like your permission to marry Lou." Mr. Flanagan said, "Good grief!" started the car, and just drove it into the garage.

Moments later, even though it seemed like an eternity to Ray, Mr. Flanagan walked out of the garage to get the other car and asked, "How much money are you making?" Ray had been given a raise to $50.00 a week but lied and said, "$55.00 a week." Lou's father started the engine, looked out the window and said, "I think it'll be OK."

There was one final approval process before the wedding, the formidable family, which happened to be gathering for their annual Christmas party in 1947 at Lou's parents' house. The Flanagans, the Flynns, the Bradleys, the Rolekes, the Browns, and a wide variety of uncles, aunts, cousins, and babies, immediately stopped talking when Ray appeared at the door that evening. He was really uncomfortable until Lou's brother, George, took him to the kitchen for some spirits.

OPUBCO was owned by E.K. Gaylord, the most powerful and influential force in Oklahoma City. Ray had worked for Gaylord only a few months when he was pressed into service on the advertising department's solicitation team for the United Way, called the "Big One" in those days. As the junior salesman, Ray was assigned to solicit contributions, normally from $10.00 to $25.00, from dance halls, pool parlors, bowling alleys, and gambling joints. He surprised his team leader when he returned from his eight calls, going way over his $200 quota. Leaving one bar, a poker player who was doing well that day, asked Ray what he was doing. When Ray said he was raising money for the United Way, the man gave Ray five crisp $100.00 bills. It was Ray's first successful fund-raising effort. In 2001, he was a volunteer for the United Way of Metropolitan Oklahoma City, for the 55th consecutive year.

In November, 1947, Ray's parents moved to Oklahoma City. For years, Ray, Sr. had been told he should move to a drier climate for a throat problem. Because Ray was the first of the Ackerman children to settle in a drier climate, the move was made. Ray's father became an accountant at the Big Red Warehouse, later Evans Home Furnishings. He later was chief financial officer for Paddock Pools. Ray's mother worked in the lingerie department at Halliburton's Department Store. She later worked as buyer in the lingerie department at Kerr's Department Store. Once the Flanagans met Ray's parents, any lingering doubts they had about the carpetbagger from Pennsylvania were gone.

Ray looked for restaurants with an atmosphere to take Lou for dinner. He remembered that you could shave by the bright light in a booth or at a table in all restaurants except for Dolores' Restaurant on Northeast 23rd Street, near the State Capitol, where he and Lou dined by candlelight. Nearby was Mike n' Nell's, a place to take his lady for dancing. The establishment had strange rules, however. There was an open courtyard and a building on one side that was used for dancing. If one wanted beer, he had to walk across the courtyard to another building, buy it, and bring it back to the table. Other favorite dating places for Ray and Lou were the Blossom Heath Ballroom on

Northwest 39th Street and Willow Springs, an abandoned sand-pit filled with water from springs, an ideal swimming hole.

Lou took some night classes with Ray at OCU and they often had a date for a beer after school. Ray never knew Lou did not like beer until after they were married.

About a month before their scheduled wedding, Ray rented an apartment at 2309 North Florida Street, across Northwest 23rd Street from OCU. He and Lou shopped newspaper classifieds and bought a second-hand bed and two unfinished chests of drawers. At night, Ray stained and varnished the chests of drawers, readying the house for his new bride.

The wedding took place at St. Francis of Assisi Catholic Church in Oklahoma City on June 14, 1948, at 9:00 A.M. Ray was 25, Lou was 20. Ruth Evashevski's remark that men are no darned good if they are past 25 when they get married had nothing to do with setting the date of the wedding. Nevertheless, Ray was glad the wedding was 54 days before he turned 26.

Lou was a beautiful bride in her long, white gown. Ray, according to his mother, was "very handsome" in a new navy blue suit, new black shoes, and a conservative tie over a white shirt. She said she could have cried with joy, and then when Ray knelt down, she just cried. Out of all that elegance leaped bright white leather soles on Ray's big new shoes, almost enough to put her in shock. From that day forward, Ray had the soles of new shoes stained black before he wore them.

After a reception at the home of Lou's parents, Ray and his new bride took a taxi to a service station at Northwest 7th Street and Broadway, where his brother, Karl, had hidden Ray's car, to avoid the traditional tying of tin cans to the bumper. Ray's Uncle Sam stopped the taxi just long enough to toss a deck of cards in the window, saying, "Just in case you get bored."

Ray and Lou spent the first night of their honeymoon at the El Sombrero Hotel on Harry Hines Boulevard in Dallas, Texas. After a night in Houston, Texas, they settled in the Edgewater

The "carpetbagger" from Pennsylvania, Ray passed muster and won the hearts of Lou's extended family at a giant Christmas gathering in December, 1947. It was the last hurdle Ray had to overcome to win the support of the Flanagans for his marriage to their daughter.

Ray and Lou at Turner Falls in the spring of 1948.

Ray and Lou on their honeymoon, in a self-taken photo.

Left to right, George Flanagan, Kathleen Flanagan, Lou, Ray, Teresa Ackerman, and Charles Raymond Ackerman, at the June 14, 1948, wedding of Lou and Ray at St. Francis of Assisi Catholic Church in Oklahoma City.

Ray carries Lou across the threshold of her parents' home at 2215 Northwest 18th Street in Oklahoma City for the reception that followed their wedding.

Gulf Hotel, halfway between Gulfport and Biloxi, Mississippi, where they spent most of their honeymoon.

The first morning, Ray forgot to close the louvers on the bottom of their old-fashioned door—until he glanced over and saw the upside-down face of a maid in a kerchief staring at them.

When the newlyweds went out to the pool for a swim, their first, Ray dove in and came up in the middle, just as a girl surfaced at the same spot. She was an old girlfriend and Ray quickly told her he was not available.

On their way back to Oklahoma City, they visited some of Lou's family in Vicksburg, Mississippi, and stayed one night in New Orleans where they dined at Antoine's. A half century later, they visited the famous restaurant and found everything the same, except the prices. The final part of the honeymoon was spent in Dallas with Ray performing his monthly Naval Reserve drill.

Ray was very happy. In a year, he had found a beautiful and loving bride and a wonderful place, Oklahoma, to call his home forever.[3]

THE CRADLE WILL ROCK

THE NEXT three and a half years were a whirlwind for Ray. While holding down a fulltime job as a display advertising salesman for OPUBCO, he earned a degree in business at OCU. He went to school continuously, averaging 30 credit hours a year, and graduated in January, 1951, Magna Cum Laude, with 32 A's and 4 B's. One weekend a month, he flew out of NAS Dallas and each summer took two weeks active duty, flying out of a Navy field, usually at a coastal city.

In September, 1948, during his squadron's two weeks active duty, the pilots landed aboard the aircraft carrier, USS *Lexington,* off Pensacola, Florida. It was the first time "weekend warriors," as they were called, had ever gone back aboard a carrier after leaving active duty. The pilots proved themselves admirably, with only two of them sent back to shore without qualifying.

Nine months and eleven days after their marriage, Lou gave birth on March 25, 1949, to their first baby, a darling daughter they named Patricia Ann. Thirteen months later, on April 18, 1950, a second little girl, Ann Carol, was born. Family entertainment was no problem for the young Ackermans. Ray's brother in law, Bill Veeck, owned the Oklahoma City Indians, so all the family had passes to home games. After school, Ray would meet his father in about the fourth inning at the old Texas League

The young Ackerman family's 1949 Christmas card proudly displayed their new arrival, Patsy. Lou was pregnant with their second child at the time.

ballpark at Northwest 4th Street and Pennsylvania Avenue. One night when Ray looked particularly tired after a long day of work and school, his father said, "Maybe we should have let you play football in high school so you could have gotten a scholarship to Notre Dame like your brother and then you wouldn't have to work so hard." Ray remembered the moment, "I darn near cried."[1]

In 1949, Ray, Lou, and Patsy moved into a tiny rent house with a meticulously groomed lawn and garden at 3240 Northwest 15th Street. However, in the fall of 1950, the owners realized they loved their smaller home more than the new one they bought, and

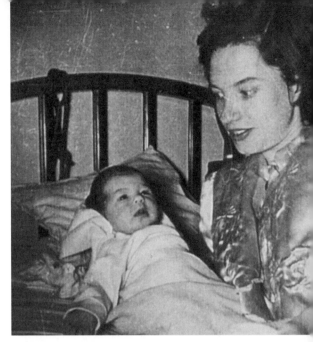

Lou, beaming with joy after the birth of her first child, Patricia Ann, in March, 1949. Patricia Ann soon became "Patsy."

Patsy left, with her little sister, Ann Carol "Annie." The Ackerman family doubled within 13 months with the birth of the two girls.

announced their intention to move back into the house Ray and Lou had fallen in love with. Lou had some indication that the owners missed the home because the lady often stopped, hopped out of her car to pull a few sprigs of crabgrass, then drove away.

Ray was promoted to full Lieutenant in the Navy on November 30, 1950, as the conflict in Korea worsened. Worried that his squadron might be called to active duty, Ray was concerned about Lou being left with the job of moving from one rental property to another. So they jointly made the big financial step to buy a new home. Ray remembered, "We got up one Saturday morning and went out and bought a house being built." They were in such a hurry to purchase a home, they hardlly realized the house at 4300 Northwest 22nd Street had only two bedrooms, not nearly enough space for a family with two children and headed for an even half-dozen offspring.

The new house was scheduled to be completed in January, 1951, but the couple that owned the rent house would not wait, forcing the Ackermans to move into a duplex at 2715 Northwest 20th Street in November. It was a miserable holiday season, with another move to the new house in January hanging over the family. To make matters worse, Kentucky beat Oklahoma 13-7 in the Sugar Bowl on New Year's Day and Patsy and Annie came down with 104-degree fevers.

Lou and Ray were excited about living in their own home. While it was being constructed, they visited neighbors. Two couples, Caye and Stokes Baggett and Brazil and Chuck Piper, became their lifelong friends. Lou and Ray moved in on February 2, 1951, immediately after his graduation from OCU. Neighborhood bridge parties with the Baggetts, Pipers, and three other couples began. Also, alternating among homes for cocktails, the group would then go out for dinner together. When it came time for cocktails at the Ackerman house, Ray decided to do something different than the normal bourbon-and-branch water drinks other couples served. Using two Waring blenders, Ray

The growing Ackerman family on a Sunday outing at Will Rogers Park in northwest Oklahoma City in 1951. Left to right, Annie, Lou, Patsy, and Ray.

mixed up margaritas with plenty of limes, rum, and grenadine syrup. The guests began ordering seconds faster than Ray could make them. Most of the neighbors did not make it to Vic n' Honey's Restaurant that night for dinner.

That spring, Ray had to put in a lawn, front and back. A friend obtained permission for him to transplant Bermuda sod from a farm at the southwest corner of Northwest 10th Street and Meridian Avenue. The grass was coarse, but nice and healthy. The neighbor across the street, Lee Stocker, who was planting a very fine-bladed grass, wandered over one day, looked at Ray's grass

In December, 1950, Ray, second from right, was selected as Oklahoma's student representative to the National Association of Manufacturers (NAM) meeting in New York City. Already considering himself a conservative Republican, Ray pledged to return to Oklahoma to make speeches on subjects such as the importance of passing a right to work law. He wrote a paper summarizing his experiences at the New York conference and strongly urged management to pay more attention to white-collar workers before they began organizing and creating more union problems. The local NAM executives were aghast at the thought and never asked Ray to make any speeches.

and said, "I think you're transplanting crab grass!" Ray did not get much sleep for three nights until he was assured that his grass was just "rough, old, mature Bermuda."

For a $100.00 stock purchase, Ray and Lou joined the Sportsman's Club on Northwest 39th Street at Portland Avenue. The club had a great swimming pool where they took the children almost every Sunday. On Saturday nights, Ray and Lou dined and danced at the club.

One hot, summer Saturday night, after the club closed at midnight, Ray and Chuck Piper looked at the cool and inviting Sportsman's Club pool on their way to get their cars. The men looked at each other, and without words, went into action. Ray remembered, "Before you could bat an eyelash, Piper and I were over the fence, out of our clothes, and had a wonderful moonlight skinnydip. I have often wondered how that could have read in *The Sunday Oklahoman*, "Ad and Oil Execs Jailed for Indecent Exposure.'"

Ray enjoyed selling advertising for OPUBCO. Because his accounts were small businesses, he actually became their advertising manager. He conceived marketing ideas and wrote and laid out the ads. Because he had more free time in the evenings after college graduation, Ray set up a side business, providing additional services to some of his accounts such as B.C. Clark Jewelers, Connolly's Menswear, and Park's Menswear. He charged them each $50.00 a month for spending extra time creating and producing the advertisements that appeared in *The Daily Oklahoman* and *The Oklahoma City Times.*

Ray was a dedicated salesman. For three of the four Christmases he worked at OPUBCO, he won a cash prize for selling the most Christmas greeting ads.

His only complaint about his job was that OPUBCO rules mandated he wear a hat, coat, and tie even on Oklahoma's horribly hot and humid summer days.

His boss, O.C. Brown, grew weary of hearing Ray ask if the

In 1950, Ray's sister, Mary Frances, married baseball legend Bill Veeck, a member of the National Baseball Hall of Fame. Veeck was part-owner of the Oklahoma City Indians from 1949 to 1951 and was general manager and part-owner at different times between 1948 and 1961 of the major league Cleveland Indians, St. Louis Browns, and Chicago White Sox. Mary Frances co-hosted radio and tv shows with Bill in every city. Best known for publicity stunts, such as hiring a midget to bat for the Browns in 1952, Veeck was a sound baseball executive. He died of lung cancer in 1986. One of his sons, Mike, followed in his footsteps and owns an interest in several minor league teams.

rules could be changed to allow him to carry his coat over his arm and go hatless as he made his business calls. One morning when Ray arrived for work, Brown informed him he had an appointment with E.K. Gaylord at 9:00 A.M.

Gaylord, in his 70s at the time, invited Ray into his spacious and impressive office, offering Ray a heavy chair which he placed beside his desk. The publishing baron recapped the gist of Ray's complaints about the OPUBCO dress code and, while feeling the material of the jacket he was wearing, offered a solution. Gaylord said, "Mr. Ackerman, have you tried these seersucker suits? They are really lightweight and I think you would feel a lot cooler in these than what you have been wearing." End of meeting, and the end of Ray's complaining about what he had to wear on the job.[2]

One of Ray's accounts was the Broadway Pawn Shop owned by two brothers, Benny and Irwin Fagin. When Ray called on the Fagins at their shop at Broadway and Grand, now Sheridan Avenue, he sometimes wore his Hollywood tailor-made, grey flannel suit given to him by his sister. The Fagins, having an eye

Lou and Ray, 1951. Even with two quick children, full-time college, and an ever-increasing desire to succeed as an ad man, Ray's hair was still thick, thanks possibly to the hair tonics he had faithfully applied in 1944.

for quality, and wondering how a low-paid advertising salesman could afford such a suit, made a bold move one afternoon to learn the maker of the suit. Irwin Fagan jumped over the counter, snatched Ray's coat open, saw the label and screamed, "Russo!" as he recognized the name of the famous tailor. Ray never told the Fagins how he got the suit.

One Christmas season Ray visited Broadway Pawn carrying presents he had received from other accounts. Benny Fagin asked about the presents. Ray hesitated, not wanting Fagin to think he was looking for a present from him but finally told him they were gifts from other accounts. Fagin said, "Ray, I want you to pick out a couple of shirts and couple of ties," pointing to his stock of new goods he carried in addition to his pawned items. Ray protested and protested but, not wanting to hurt Fagin's feelings, went over and picked out two shirts and two ties. Fagin immediately went to the cash register, rang the items up, and said, "That will be $35.00 please."

Ray started to protest but swallowed hard and paid for the goods. He had learned a lesson in selling from a master. To make matters worse, a sleeve fell off one of the shirts the first time it was washed.

The $40.00 a month Ray received for flying in the Navy Reserve was important to the family budget. The money allowed luxuries such as attending the annual Oklahoma-Texas football game at the Cotton Bowl in Dallas. Ray and Lou could leave the girls at home with grandparents and spend an entire weekend in Dallas in a new motel for $50.00. His Navy drills always fell on the OU-Texas weekend. Ray always found a way to get to the football game.

Ray did get a little disturbed when the telephone bill arrived one month, noticing an unexpected long distance call from Golden, Colorado. He asked Lou about it and was informed that an old schoolmate had called her collect. Ray told Lou not to accept any more collect calls.

A few days later, Ray came home and Lou proudly said she

Photographs of Patsy and Ann appeared on the 1952 family Christmas card. In the upper right hand corner of the card was an angel, joyful announcement that a third Ackerman baby was due in May, 1953. However, complications with her pregnancy after the trip to see the St. Louis Browns caused Lou to be bedridden for weeks. On April 23, she gave birth to a little girl named Beth. However, the infant had an enlarging heart that doctors were unable to help. She died six weeks after birth.

had turned down a collect call from a Jimmy Black in Norman, a long distance call in those days. Ray flew in Dallas with Black who said he thought his could get Ray and Lou 50-yard-line tickets for the upcoming OU-Texas football game. Ray had told Black to call him collect if he lined up the tickets. Ray quickly called Black back, saved the tickets, and eased up on the collect-call rule with Lou.[3]

Ray was still worried about losing his hair. His brother in law, George Flanagan, was losing hair at an even faster pace and bought every product on the market that touted its ability to stop hair loss. One of the more novel approaches was the theory that if you could separate the two layers of skin on the top of one's head with a toilet plunger, health and vitality would return to the hair. George tried the suction on Ray's head a couple of times but the march to baldness continued.

By late 1951, Ray wondered how far he could advance at OPUBCO. His boss, advertising manager O.C. Brown, had given Ray and Lou a carving set as a wedding present with a note saying, "For the day you earn enough to buy a roast." Ray told Brown that three years after his marriage he still was not making enough to buy a roast and asked what the future held for him at OPUBCO. When Ray received the same "Be patient, we have great plans for you" answer, he began looking around for another job. Within weeks, Ray had two options. The company that handled advertising on the inside and outside of city buses offered Ray $500.00 a month. The George Knox Advertising Agency offered him $400.00 per month. Another advantage of the higher paying job was that Ray would be home every day by 5:00 P.M.

Ray told Lou that if he took the advertising agency job, she might not see much of him. Wisely, Lou suggested that Ray take the job that appealed to him the most. Because the bus advertising job was a dead end, and knowing that he might be able to build a real future working in an ad agency, he took the job with Knox.

When Ray told O.C. Brown that he had taken another job, Brown said, "Sorry to hear that because we had great plans for you." When Ray asked why he was never told about the great plans, Brown replied, "We were afraid you might start letting up." When Ray said that if he were given a glimpse of his future and did let up, that would prove they were grooming the wrong man. Brown had no answer for that comment.[4]

BUILDING
AN AD BUSINESS

RAY REPORTED FOR WORK at George Knox Associates on the 11th floor of the Colcord Building on February 12, 1952. The agency consisted of George Knox and three staff members. On the day of his arrival, Ray was informed that Knox was leaving for three weeks, that he needed to find new space because the agency office lease expired in three months, a new color postcard needed to be produced promptly for the Hotel Black, and City National Bank needed a new television commercial.

Knox Advertising billed about $250,000 a year, one third of it from the Progress Brewing Company; another third from Hales-Mullally, an appliance distributor; and the balance from a number of small accounts. Mullally was the grandfather of television actress Megan Mullally.

George Knox had been the advertising manager for Hales-Mullally in the 1930s before launching his own agency in 1939 with Hales-Mullally as his first account. The second account was Hank Moran Insurance. Knox had coined a line and logo, "Hank Moran the Insurance Man."

When Knox began to spend more and more time in Colorado, Ray was left to run the small agency. His experience at

OPUBCO had well equipped him to handle large accounts such as Hales-Mullally that primarily ran newspaper ads for local appliance retailers throughout the state. Using free-lance photographers, artists, and radio and television talent, he was able to satisfy the needs of other clients.

Ray's squadron at Dallas had been flying Corsairs since he joined it in 1947 but the pilots eagerly anticipated transitioning to jets. Although this did not happen until the spring of 1955, in August, 1952, Navy Dallas received a few FH-1's from Grumman and all the pilots had their first jet flights. The FH-1 was a tiny airplane that only carried enough gas for a 60 to 90 minute flight. It had three gasoline tanks with no automatic transfer from one to the other, causing the pilot to constantly remember to think about switching tanks every 30 minutes.

Ray made his first flight in an FH-1 before the Supply Officer at Dallas had received any anti-blackout gear, neither the old harness nor the more modern flight suit, both of which inflated bladders in the stomach and thighs to prevent the pilot's blood from leaving the head and upper body. In his first loop in the FH-1, without the anti-blackout gear, Ray totally blacked out as he soared straight up, with just enough consciousness to slowly pull the stick back and finish what he remembered as "maybe the biggest loop on record."[1]

During the long Labor Day weekend of 1952, Ray and Lou traveled by train to St. Louis to visit with Bill and M'Fran Veeck. The baseball club owner had purchased the St. Louis Browns and had renovated a portion of the old offices in Sportsman's Park as living quarters for his family. Games were played at night and players came by Veeck's apartment after games for beer. Others regularly came by the apartment for breakfast before batting practice. It was exciting for Ray and Lou to meet such famous stars as Leroy Robert "Satchel" Paige.

On January 1, 1953, the agency changed its name to Knox-Ackerman. It was a change in name only because Ray, even though he was running the place, was still an employee of Knox.

The agency "partnership" came just in time for a 1953 Progress Beer crisis. Progress sponsored live wrestling on television weekly for several years, using flip-card cartoon commercials. However, the sale of beer was declining in taverns and skyrocketing in supermarkets so live wrestling was no longer a good advertising vehicle for Progress.

To replace it, Ray purchased a 30-minute syndicated weekly television show called *My Favorite Story,* starring Adolf Menjou. With a small budget, and just four weeks to prepare, Ray set out to produce a new series of Progress Beer commercials.

He hired a local handsome, articulate television announcer, John Harrison, and cameraman Doc Smith to produce three one-minute spots. After the spots ran the first time one Friday night, Ray received a frantic call from Harrison who requested the commercials not be used anymore. Harrison's father, Walter Harrison, the former editor of *The Daily Oklahoman,* was running for mayor of Oklahoma City and thought his son selling beer on television might hurt his chances of election.

Ray did not have a contract with Harrison and had no choice but to comply with his request. Because television stations had a policy of not allowing live commercials for alcoholic beverage products, Ray faced the challenge of producing new spots within six days. He said to himself, "I like beer, I certainly know the product well, I have a reasonably good speaking voice and appearance—why not use myself as talent?" He did.

The commercials were terrible. Ray remembered, "Doc Smith, the photographer, tried me without beer, with a few beers in me, and with a lot of beers in me. But the results were always the same—bad." Ray warned Progress Beer management that the commercials were bad and that he would have new ones produced the following week. However, Progress received a couple of favorable phone calls from people who liked the commercials because, as one caller said, "The announcer is obviously not a professional, he seems like a good ol' country boy who is believable about your product."

Ray, right, was elected president of the Oklahoma City Advertising Club in 1954. Here club members, left to right, Clayton Anderson, Walt Sanders, Bert Horner, Leon Srago, and Ray, head for Dallas for the Advertising Federation of America national convention.

For 13 weeks the commercials ran, and Ray was the butt of jokes of advertising people in the area. One of Ray's Navy flying buddies from Shawnee, Oklahoma, telephoned after seeing the commercial and said, "You look like a Chicago gangster with pneumonia." People began recognizing Ray. A state trooper stared at him one day at the midway station on the Turner Turnpike and, after introducing himself, said, "Aren't you the guy who drinks Progress Beer on television?" Ray was relieved the trooper was not eyeing him as the recipient of a traffic ticket.

In all the commercials, Ray "chug-a-lugged" an entire glass of Progress Beer at the end, a violation of Federal Communications Commission (FCC) rules. The television stations received many calls from viewers opposed to drinking but allowed the commercials to run, only warning the agency about future commercials.

Even in church, a little boy pointed to Ray and said loudly, "Mommy, there's the man who drinks beer on television." The comment was ill-timed. Lou was wearing a new type of skirt, made by Page Boy for expectant mothers. The skirt had a huge hole for a pregnant stomach to protrude through and with a ribbon to tie around the body above the hole. The little boy hollered just as Lou and Ray stood for the reading of the Gospel, the ribbon-tie came loose, and Lou's skirt fell to the floor. All the parishioners turned to see who the boy was talking about.[2]

Ray in his new office in the Classen Terrace Building at 1411 Classen Boulevard in Oklahoma City. Knox-Ackerman moved into the new quarters March 3, 1955. Courtesy Ray Jacoby.

At the Naval Air Station in Dallas, Texas, Ray, second from right, won the annual .38-caliber pistol shooting competition in 1955.

George Knox spent most of his time in Colorado running a luxury soap business so Ray suggested that he buy the agency. A deal was completed to turn over ownership to Ray for $38,500, to be paid over five years. Ray thought, "If the whole thing turns to worms, I would call Knox and say, 'Hey! I'm giving this thing back to you.'"

The opening balance sheet for Ray's agency was frightening. The agency's only assets were an $1,800 cash loan Knox left to help Ray get started, $27,000 good will, a $9,000 covenant not to compete, and $2,500 worth of office furniture and equipment. Ray realized that he could not make any mistakes or he would be out of business quickly.

The first political account the agency handled after Ray assumed full ownership was for William "Bill" Logan of Lawton, Oklahoma, who was running for governor. Ray had been advised to insist on advance payment from political clients and was handed $10,000 cash outside a smoked-filled "Logan for Governor" rally at the Huckins Hotel in downtown Oklahoma City. Ray had never seen that much cash. He started to put the money in the City National Bank night depository, then worried that he could not trust the person opening the depository the following morning. Instead, Ray stuffed the cash under his mattress and slept on it.

The Corsairs flown by Ray's squadron at Dallas were also flown by Marine squadrons on different weekends. When Ray reported to the air station for his two weeks active duty in 1953, he learned that, because of a mix-up, the Corsairs had been flown to California by the Marines for their two-weeks training. Ray was informed that if he wanted to go on active duty at Pensacola, Florida, he would have to check out in the F6F Hellcat.

Normally, to check out in a new high-performance fighter plane, one had to spend a few days in ground school, make several flights accompanied by an instructor in another plane, and

Lou and Ray appeared in a Progress Beer commercial produced by Knox-Ackerman in 1955.

pass both a flying and classroom test. There was no time for all that, so Ray was given a handbook on the aircraft, told to study it, and be ready for an 8:00 A.M. take-off the next morning. Ray remembered, "It was one of those 'read the book, kick the tires, and have someone show you how to start it' kind of moments." The Hellcat was a great airplane and Ray enjoyed the opportunity to fly it.[3]

In 1954, Norman Pearson and Howard Furlow hired Ray to come up with a name for compost being produced from city garbage at the dump in Norman and to produce a brochure and bag to hold the product. Ray was mesmerized by the idea of solving two of the world's biggest problems; converting garbage into a usable product and increasing food production by using compost to improve the soil. Ray came up with the name "Naturizer" and wrote some memorable advertising lines such as "Smells sweet as the woods after rain."

Ray was so intrigued by the compost idea that he bought a five percent interest in the company for $1,250, his and Lou's total savings at the time. Ray fully expected to get rich quick off of compost.

The aircraft industry was in the doldrums with many companies looking for diversification. Westinghouse and Lockheed joined Naturizer and built a garbage conversion plant in the San Fernando Valley in California. With big corporate names behind the idea, the stock escalated wildly. Ray estimated his $1,250 investment was at one time worth $250,000.

When the aviation industry rebounded after the Soviet Union launched the Sputnik in 1957, Lockheed lost interest in compost. However, the State Farm Insurance Company bought out Lockheed's interest in the product, and with Westinghouse and Naturizer, formed the International Disposal Corporation (IDC), headquartered in Shawnee, Oklahoma. The compost product was manufactured at the Naturizer plant in Norman, Oklahoma, but the name of the product was changed to CURA.

One of the big attractions to cities and towns about making compost from garbage was the claim that a number of small plants could be built within city limits, adjacent to country clubs, housing, and hospitals, because there would be no odor, no pollution from incineration, and no long, costly hauls to landfills.

As a test of the theory, IDC built a plant beside a country club in St. Petersburg, Florida. An electric fence, intended to destroy any small odor that leaked out of the plant, was constructed around the property. Ray never forgot a photograph that appeared in the St. Petersburg newspaper that showed city council members with their noses to the air to see if the plant worked. When the council voted 4-3 that they could smell a mild odor, it was the end of the company and of Ray's involvement with the process to solve two of the world's biggest problems.[4]

In 1954, the Progress Brewing Company offered Ray the lucrative job of sales manager, with a contract to become president of the brewery within one year, because the two men who ran the company, Mark Dykema and Elmer Streich, wanted to retire. To be the head of a brewing company at age 33 was a big temptation for Ray.

When Knox was advised that Ray might give the advertising agency back to him, he offered to cut the original sales price by $17,000, if Ray could come up with immediate cash for the balance due. Ray's banker at City National Bank suggested a counter-offer of $2,500 less or he would not make the loan. When Knox agreed, Ray borrowed the money by pledging his meager assets plus a guarantee of the note by his father in law, George Flanagan. Lou also had to co-sign the loan the very afternoon the money had to be wired to Colorado. Ray was perturbed at the banker who insisted she drive downtown in a raging rainstorm five months pregnant and with two little girls because the bank would not wait 24 hours. Ray never forgot the sight of Lou and the girls walking into the bank soaking wet.

"With his heart in his mouth," Ray told the owners of Progress Brewing Company his decision to stay at Knox-Ackerman and breathed a sigh of relief when they kept their account with the agency.

Not every story of Ray's early advertising career had a successful ending. Once Ray tried to win the Townley Dairy account. The major milk and dairy product producer was looking for a new agency so Ray scheduled a Saturday morning appointment with the owner, Sam Townley, who went by the initials S.E.

Connolly's Menswear was one of Ray's accounts and owner Joe Connolly kept Ray dressed "better than local bank presidents." He gave Ray a new Oxxford suit each Christmas and sold other clothing to Ray at a 40 percent discount. Connolly also convinced Ray to wear a narrow-brimmed hat, the fashion rage back East.

When Townley opened the door as Ray knocked, the milk company owner's eyes shot right to Ray's hat and back to his eyes. Townley said, "You're from Boston, ain't you?" Ray knew he was a dead duck because his competition to get the account was Hugh Wallace, who owned the Galloway-Wallace agency, and who "snapped galluses with Mr. Townley in the kitchen and got the business."

Ray's appearance was not the only reason he did not land the Townley account. He sent a telegram to Townley, pointing out that agency personnel had 32 children who all drank Townley's milk. Unfortunately, the telegram was phoned to the Townley home at 2:00 A.M. and woke up the entire family. Defeated by his own mistakes, Ray scratched Townley from his prospect list.

On another occasion, Ray made a presentation to the owners of KOCO Television who had Federal Communications Commission approval to move its transmitter location from Enid to Oklahoma City as the city's ABC affiliate. Their formidable challenge was to compete successfully with already established KWTV (CBS) and WKY (NBC) Television. During the presentation, one of the station's owners fell asleep. Ray had worked hard on the presentation and woke the man up with sharp words, telling him to pay attention. When the meeting was over, all parties concerned ended up yelling at each other in the parking lot. However, Ray was notified the following day he had won the account.

Ray had to be creative just to survive in the small advertising agency, such as when the owner of Kilpatrick Lumber Company discovered the price of every louver shutter in a Knox-Ackerman produced brochure was $3.00 too high. Even though the mistake was made by the lumber company, its owner thought otherwise, under the old cliché, "the customer is always right," and insisted Ray pay for reprinting the brochure. Ray simply did not have the $400.00, so he came up with an ingenious plan.

Ray proposed an insert for the brochure that announced a $3.00 discount for each shutter purchased by a certain date and owner John Kilpatrick approved. The gimmick worked for everyone. It cost Ray only $20.00 to print the insert and shutter sales at the lumber company hit an all-time high.

Ray went to the books to study English heraldry to help meet the desire of Oklahoma City businessmen Frank Hightower, Joe Connolly, and Warren Ramsey who wanted their new jewelry and gift store, Hightower's, to look as if it had been there for a hundred years the day it opened. Ray designed ancient-looking large copper shields heavily patinaed, depicting the owners' names—for Ramsey there was a ram on one side standing upright on one hind leg holding a telescope to his eye; for Hightower, a tall medieval-style tower on the other side; and for Connolly, a knight's helmet and visor across the top to depict valor, which the word Connolly means in Irish.

On September 3, 1954, Ray was promoted to Lieutenant Commander in the Navy. Also in 1954, he became president of the Oklahoma City Advertising Club.

The Ad Club was responsible for the speaker for an annual

meeting in conjunction with the Oklahoma City Chamber of Commerce. Ray felt lucky to have scheduled the president of Coca-Cola to speak at the joint meeting. However, the day before the meeting, the Coca-Cola executive was hospitalized and could not make the speech. Frantic, Ray picked up the evening newspaper and discovered J.C. Penney was in Oklahoma City for a meeting. He called the Skirvin Hotel, got right through to Penney, and told him of his problem. Much to Ray's surprise, the world-renowned retailer accepted the invitation to speak. Ray recalled, "Talk about coming out smelling like a rose!"

In May, 1955, Ray's squadron transitioned from flying the Corsair to the Grumman Cougar, the F9F-6, a jet fighter. Orders were cut for five days of special active duty for ground school and flying to complete the transition to jets. It was quite a learning process. Divisions of four prop planes would rendezvous at 3,000 feet over a television tower as the leader could always see the other three planes climbing into formation. The orbits of the tower were so large in the high-speed jets that the pilots had to learn a whole new technique.

The first time the pilots tried air-to-air gunnery over the Gulf of Mexico off Corpus Christi, one of the pilots got lost. The runs were made from a position called the perch, which was above and forward of the target. In an s-turn shallow dive, the pilots zeroed in on the target. The pilot who got lost came in too steep, pulled out too late, and could not see nor catch up with the rest of the flight.

The F9F-6 was underpowered at low altitude, resulting in a close call for Ray when he took off from Lambert Field in St. Louis, Missouri, one day when the temperature was over 100 degrees. Evidence of the inability of the airplane to lift off quickly was the couple of small tree branches that were caught in the wheel-well doors of Ray's aircraft that day.

The F9F-6's were replaced with the better performing F9F-7 in 1956 and the squadron flew them successfully until 1960 when a transition was made to the North American Fury—first the FJ3M, and then the FJ-4B.

Ray was scared to death about the pitfalls of being a one-man shop. In his short life, he had already had the experience of almost dying while being bed-ridden for five months with an infection and of being in an automobile accident that killed the driver, Uncle Hen. Any similar bad luck would put him out of business and cause his family to suffer. Ray looked for a way to make employees as dedicated to the business as he was and to therefore share in the company's potential growth.

SHARED OWNERSHIP

RAY BELIEVED that the only way to attract and keep quality people was to share ownership with his employees. However, his first experiment with that theory was a disaster. By 1956, with the agency expanded by three more men, Bill Shrouf, Ken Juergens, and Harvard Page; and two women, Edith Bardsley and Beverly Theus, Ray turned the personal automobiles of the three account men into company cars and issued stock for their value. He also raised their pay, with the money earmarked to buy agency stock.

Within a few months, five days before Ray was leaving for two weeks of active duty in the Navy, the three men resigned to start their own advertising agency. Ray was busy trying to keep his clients from leaving with them and managed to keep all but one. He would have saved that client, Cullimore's Furniture Store, if he had been able to talk to owner James Cullimore earlier. Cullimore told Ray, "I really don't like what they did to you but I had to keep my advertising going." The crisis caused Ray to miss his scheduled summer Navy duty, the only time he missed the annual training in his 35-year Navy career.

Ray again owned 100 percent of the agency but looked for new people to share ownership responsibilities and potential gain beyond a salary. This time, the shared ownership theory worked perfectly. Ray hired Al Fiegel, an Oklahoma State University graduate and a creative talent with experience in radio and television in Lubbock, Texas, as well as at KTOK Radio and KTVQ Television in Oklahoma City. Fiegel was made agency vice president and creative director and was assigned a stock option. The agency was never again owned by one person and in 2001 was owned by 12 employee-stockholders.[1]

Fiegel and Ray made a good team for a number of years. Ray was "Mr. Outside," as the agency's account executive to clients. Feigel was "Mr. Inside," responsible for creating ads that sold products and services for the clients.

Without a doubt, Fiegel's major creative achievement was the B.C. Clark "Jewelry Is the Gift to Give" jingle, introduced on Thanksgiving Day, 1956. The jingle was written by Fiegel, produced in Dallas at a total cost of only $300, and became one of Oklahoma's most memorable tunes, helping transform a relatively small store into a major player in the state's jewelry business. In 2001, Oklahoma City's Emmy Award-winning actress Megan Mullally, appearing on NBC's The Tonight Show, wowed host Jay Leno by singing the B.C. Clark jingle.

Eddie Miller, a University of Oklahoma journalism graduate and former newspaper editor, became vice president of public relations for the firm, which continued to be called Knox-Ackerman, even though George Knox had been out of the firm for some time. Miller had great credentials, including being the son of R.G. Miller, longtime writer for *The Daily Oklahoman.* However, Ray and Miller's idea of working after hours were not the same and Miller soon left the agency. Ray remembered, "I got so paranoid about hearing Miller push back his chair and turn out his light at exactly 5:00 P.M. each night, I just couldn't stand it."

Nita Krautlarger was the bookkeeper and office manager and Jan Gordon was the copywriter-film editor. Jack Moses was the agency art director, production manager, and an important member of the agency for 18 years.

Ray always served the special needs of his clients. The Nichols Seed and Feed Company met once a week at Ray's office to plan future advertising. The feed company owners wanted to open their store on West California Street at 6:00 A.M. for the farmers and insisted on the weekly ad meeting occurring before that early hour of the morning. Ray obtained a key from the landlord of his building and arrived at 3:30 A.M. to have coffee ready for the Nichols weekly session at 4:00 A.M.

Though never in his business experience did Ray refuse an appointment with a salesman, he did use his experience with Nichols to ward off salesmen who were trying to land an appointment with him for no particular good reason. He would suggest they meet at 6:30 A.M. after a Nichols meeting. Ray recalled, "It was amazing to see how many salesmen changed their minds about wanting a meeting."

A "Nichols red-plaid" sport coat was the trademark of employees of Nichols. Bill Hill the tailor made one for Ray for $35.00, a coat Ray proudly wore to the Nichols annual sales dinner scheduled each New Year's Eve. Earl Nichols admitted to Ray that he scheduled the event on New Year's Eve to keep his staff from partying as long as possible. The Reverend R.T. Williams, known as the "singing pastor" of the Nazarene Church, was the principal entertainment at the Nichols New Year's Eve dinner.[2]

Ray's clients often presented interesting new challenges. When Hales-Mullally saw its middleman role as an appliance distributor fading, the firm fostered a young inventor, Robert Anderson, who developed the Mark IV air conditioner for automobiles. Knox-Ackerman was employed to design the first brochure for aftermarket auto air conditioning. Unfortunately, for Hales-Mullally and Knox-Ackerman, Anderson left the company and took his invention to Dallas.

Hales-Mullally also contracted with Ray's agency to design brochures for Sola Cell, a small device that dangled inside an automobile radiator, claiming to stop rust from forming. Knox-

Ackerman worked with the Nash Motor Company and the Lincoln-Mercury division of Ford Motor Company to produce boxes and brochures for the Sola Cell. Ray believed he was on his way to big business, as he traveled to Detroit and worked with big auto companies. However, Sola Cell lost out to additives.

Ray always actively practiced his Catholic faith. He will never forget one Christmas Eve when he went to St. Patrick's Church on North Portland Avenue in Oklahoma City. It was 5:30 P.M. and Ray asked the priest, who was leaving for dinner, to stay a moment longer to hear his confession. After confession, Ray was alone in the church whose parishioners had elegantly decorated for Christmas with tall evergreen trees in an enclosed but not covered courtyard. Ray remembered, "As I was saying prayers, I saw snow falling on those green branches. It was so quiet and peaceful, you literally could have heard a pin drop. I have never had, before or since, such a beautiful moment with God."

When Patsy and Annie were six and five years old, Ray took them to the State Fair of Oklahoma. Being normal kids, they were interested in midway games where contestants tried to win dolls and toys. Being a good father, Ray got two rolls of 20 nickels and began the pursuit of a large, beautiful Panda doll for each of his young daughters.

The idea of the game was to land a nickel in a very shallow ashtray on the head of a doll. Nickel after nickel skipped off the ashtray and fell to the ground. But on the 18th nickel, Ray won a doll for Patsy by bouncing the nickel off the Panda's forehead into the ashtray, despite the huckster's warning he was leaning too far over the rail. The pressure was on for Ray to win a doll for Annie. Using the same forehead-bouncing technique, Ray won a doll for Annie on the 19th nickel of her roll.[3]

On Christmas Eve afternoon of 1955, Ray stopped at Chuck Piper's house on his way home from the office. Chuck had just started assembling a small race car for his son in the garage and asked Ray to help. Following the instructions, and with a little

Raymond Karl Ackerman was born October 5, 1954.

Schnapps under their belts, the job was apparently finished. Ray remembered, "We had that sucker put together in three hours, except for the steering column. It just would not go in!" To their dismay, Chuck and Ray discovered they should have put the steering column in at the beginning of the assembly, so they were forced to take the racer apart and start all over, a process that took another two hours.

Several Christmases later, son Ray K. was old enough for a little racing car and, remembering his experience at Piper's, Ray ordered one from Sears to be delivered to his neighbor's house fully-assembled. Lou called the office one day and said the racer had been delivered. Ray commented, "Great!" Lou continued, "In a flat box."

Ray called Faye Hixon, manager of the Sears store at Northwest 23rd Street and Pennsylvania Avenue told him of the problem. Hixon said he would get on it, called Ray back, and said, "The racers are all gone except the floor model." Ray said, "I'll take it!" That night, it began to snow heavily as the family was on their way to church to see their two little girls in a Christmas play. Ray sneaked out of church, had to park four blocks from Sears because of the heavy Christmas traffic, and ended up pushing the racer four blocks through the snow to get it to the car.

In 1956, publisher E.K. Gaylord asked to speak to the Oklahoma City Ad Club to urge the creation of a public service campaign. Gaylord told advertising executives that the population of the greater Oklahoma City area was about 550,000 and needed to grow to 600,000 by 1960. Norman Hall, another local advertising agency owner, and Ray co-chaired a committee to create a plan. Their photograph appeared in the newspaper together with an article that suggested they were considering a campaign slogan, "I'm an Okie and Proud of It."[4]

Three of Ray's clients, still smarting from the terrible publicity given the word Okie in John Steinbeck's *The Grapes of Wrath*, threatened to pull their business if the word Okie was used in any fashion. The idea was dead for the moment although Republican Oklahoma Governor Dewey Bartlett used Okie pins to promote the state effectively a decade later.

Mark Ackerman was born June 15, 1960.

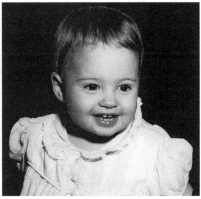

Susan Marie "Susie" Ackerman was born April 29, 1957.

Ray was especially proud of his light blue 1956 Plymouth DeSoto. He drove it to Naval Air Station Dallas in 1957 to commence his two-week active duty. At about 10:00 P.M. the first evening, he and two friends started out in the DeSoto for a Chinese restaurant in North Dallas. Traveling on a very narrow road that had been newly blacktopped with no center line, edge markings, or shoulders, they went up over a little hill. The road curved sharply to the right but Ray drove straight ahead, thundering over some exposed railroad tracks and coming to a halt with the king pins on both front wheels broken and each at a right angle to the rest of the car.

With his two friends pushing and pulling and Ray trying to get a little traction with the rear wheels, they tried mightily to get the car off the train tracks. Several men passing by stopped to help. One of them leaned in the window as Ray was still trying to get traction and said, "You better hurry, there is a train due by here any minute."

A good-sized crowd had stopped to help and one of Ray's friends and passenger, John Ashby, suggested he and Ray should go back to a motel they passed on the other side of the hill to call a friend of his at the police station for help. They left their other buddy to supervise the ever-increasing crowd trying to get the car off the tracks.

At the motel, they convinced the owner to let them use the phone, then began jogging back up the hill. Suddenly they heard a train whistle. The headlight of the train disappeared behind the little hill, and, as Ray recalled, "Thank God, it emerged on the other side without hitting anything."

The car was off the tracks. As Ray and John arrived, so did a police car. All the help was gone and their friend was asleep in the car. One of the police officers said, "Hi, John, looks like you need some help." The officer asked for Ray's permission to haul the car to a local Dodge dealer for repair, suggesting that the Dodge dealer had a better reputation than the DeSoto dealer for good work. Naturally, Ray agreed. Then the officer took the three men in his car to the Air Station.

Charley Franklin was the third man in the car. Ray and Ashby took him by the dispensary to get some glass pulled out of his head from breaking the windshield.

The next morning, the squadron was flying to Port Isabel at South Padre Island for five days of aerial gunnery practice over the Gulf of Mexico. Before they departed, Ray called his insurance agent, Hank Moran, in Oklahoma City, still a client of the advertising agency, and told him the problem and that his car had to be repaired and back in service by Friday, when the wives were coming down to join the guys for the weekend. Hank said he would see what he could do. Luckily, he got the job done and Lou never knew about the accident until Ray told her about it six months later.[5]

Ray cornered John Ashby about his close relationship with the police department. Ashby said that on the previous Christmas Eve, he had left a party in downtown Dallas at dark and was heading home on the Central Expressway when he heard a siren and saw the lights of a police car behind him. Having had a little Christmas cheer, he decided to outrun the police car, got well ahead of it, ducked off at an exit, went about a block, turned off the engine, and laid down on the floor of the car. Two minutes later, two officers shined their flashlight in his face. He had forgotten to turn off his headlights. He spent all night, Christmas Eve, in jail, absent from his home where his four small boys prepared to celebrate Christmas. Ashby told Ray, "On such an occasion, one gets very well acquainted with the policemen on duty."

On another occasion, Ray, Lou, and Naturizer executives Norman Pierson and Howard Furlow with their wives, left the Ackerman home during a snowstorm to have dinner at Vic 'n Honey's Restaurant on North Council Road in Oklahoma City. As the blizzard worsened, Ray made a wrong turn and slipped off a narrow road into a bar ditch. As the snowfall diminished, they could see the lights of Vic 'n Honey's. The men considered traipsing across the field to the party but the ladies, in their open-toed shoes, vetoed the idea. Residents of a nearby house allowed Ray and his friends to sit in their living room all night, waiting on a wrecker. However, it was a black hearse, rather than a tow truck that came to pick up the stranded couples the following morning. The appearance of the hearse created quite a commotion and speculation along Northwest 22nd Street.

On April 29, 1957, Susan Marie Ackerman was born in Oklahoma City. About halfway through Lou's pregnancy, she and Ray recognized they needed more room than their 900-square-foot house offered.

Remembering Broadlawn Lake where Lou took him to a picnic on the Fourth of July, 1947, and his pledge to try to build a home there someday if he could buy a piece of property, Ray checked all possibilities. However, no one would sell any lake frontage. Ray contracted with Jack Johnston, the famous builder and developer of Oklahoma City's Quail Creek Addition, to build a house north of Northwest 63rd Street and east of May Avenue, overlooking a small lake.

On the day before the slab was to be poured, Ray received word that a man named Bill Falter was willing to sell a piece of property adjacent to his home on Broadlawn Lake. The land was 225 feet deep with 75 feet of lake frontage. Ray called Falter, raced over to see him, and bought the lot for $6,000.

Ray called Johnston and asked, "Is there any chance you might let me out of the contract on the house you're starting tomorrow?" Johnston replied, "Let me see the piece of property on the lake you're talking about and if I think it is something special, I might let you out."[6]

Johnston looked over the lake property and thought it was something special. He permitted Ray to cancel the building contract. It turned out to be a good deal for him also. While looking at Ray's lot, Johnston discovered the water-filled abandoned sand pit south of Broadlawn Lake on Northwest 50th Street, across the street from the first Putnam City High School. He later developed the property with lakeside apartments.

A Navy flying buddy of Ray's from Shawnee, architect Chapin Howard, and Lou designed the house. Howard acted as builder, which saved Ray money. Howard knew how much money Ray and Lou had to spend and said he was going to design the house to spend all the money on sufficient room for a big family, and that the Ackermans could "worry about the amenities when they had the money."

The new house was 3,500 square feet, four times as large as the house on Northwest 22nd Street, and designed specifically for raising a big family and having fun on the lake.

It was easy for Ray to get a permanent loan from Jefferson Standard Life Insurance Company. However, he went to his client, City National Bank and Trust Company of Oklahoma City, for construction financing. Bank vice president Spence Miller scheduled a time to meet Ray at the property to look it over before approving the construction loan. When Miller arrived, much to Ray's surprise, bank owner and chairman of the board Dan Hogan got out of the back seat. Hogan was more than 90 years old but obviously still working.

Hogan nodded to Ray, looked south for about five seconds, looked west for five seconds, looked north for five seconds, and then looked east for about ten seconds. He turned to Ray and said, "Bad drainage," nodded to Miller, got in the car, and they drove off. Ray and Lou had to turn to their architect's bank in Shawnee for construction financing. Hogan was right about the drainage, as Ray would discover later.

In anticipation of moving into a big house, Ray and Lou ordered a new master bedroom suite, complete with a king size bed. Ray could not wait for the move to get into his new bed so he measured their tiny bedroom on Northwest 22nd Street and figured he could set up the king size bed if he moved Susie's crib into the dining room already used as a bedroom with Ray K. Lou agreed with the understanding that Ray would install a folding door on the dining room before moving Susie. Ray bought the folding door but procrastinated on installation.

Arriving home at 8:00 P.M. on a Sunday from his Navy weekend in Dallas, Lou reported that the new bed had been delivered, was set up, that Susie's crib was in the dining room, and if Ray was going to keep his word, the folding door had to be put up before he went to bed. Ray took the door out of the box, only to find it was four inches too narrow. He found four one-by-four boards in the garage, screwed two on each side of the door frame, painted them, installed the door, painted it, and went to bed at 3:00 A.M.[7]

Moving from a 900-square-foot house to a 3,500-square-foot house, Ray and Lou knew they were going to need lots of furniture and had set aside $5,000 to begin furnishing the new house. Ray began to get concerned as the house was being built because his architect-builder kept coming up with items like "a new sliding door just on the market that is a lot better than the one planned on and costs only $500 more." It was typical of several dozen such changes.

One night, at Ray's insistence, he and Howard used an old adding machine to total up the invoices, only to discover that the Ackermans had not only blown the $5,000 furniture stash, but were a few thousand dollars in the hole. The next day, all the workers were sent home and Howard and Ray hung the kitchen cabinets, bought cheap cloth to hang over the windows, and had $2.00 a yard carpet, with pad, installed. The carpet actually lasted five years.

Lou and Ray were happy as could be when they moved in on February 3, 1958. The three oldest children were eight, seven, and three. Susie was not quite a year old and Mark and Amy were still in the planning stage. Over the next 25 years the Ackermans would live in the house on Broadlawn Lake, coming close to fulfilling their desire to raise their family in just one home. They transferred from St. Patrick's Catholic Church to a brand new church, St. Charles Borromeo, at Northwest 50th Street and Grove. Only the school had been built and its gymnasium was a temporary church. The pastor, the Reverend Charles Beckman, used the small house on the property as a rectory.

In December, 1957, Father Beckman was trying to raise money for his new parish and was selling Christmas trees. Ray bought one, stepped inside the rectory to pay for it, and fell through the rotten wooden floor. A new rectory was the second building for the parish. Strapped for funds to furnish the new school, Father Beckman hauled off a pile of old desks discarded by the Oklahoma City School District. Ray and a couple dozen other men spent many a long summer night in 1958, sanding, staining, and mounting the old desks on rails.

In August, 1956, Ray changed the name of his advertising agency to Ackerman Associates, Inc. The new agency also became a member of the American Association of Advertising Agencies (Four A).

Upon the admission of Ackerman Associates, Inc., to membership in the American Association of Advertising Agencies (Four As), Ray was welcomed by representatives of the three other Four A member agencies in Oklahoma City. Left to right, Lowe Runkle, Lowe Runkle Co.; Ray; Hugh Wallace, Galloway-Wallace Advertising Agency; and Warren Humphrey, Erwin, Wasey & Co, which later became Humphrey/Williamson and Gibson.

The agency's membership in Four A put it in the Southwest Council of the organization. Because the council was so small, as early as 1960 Ray was the incoming chairman, which meant he was in charge of the annual meeting. He convinced the Southeast Council to combine its annual meeting with the Southwest Council and meet in New Orleans, which was more or less on the border between the two councils. Ray had never been in charge of a big meeting but was determined to make it memorable.

Don Halsey, President of Fitzgerald, the only Four A agency in New Orleans, agreed to handle all local arrangements with the about-to-open Royal Orleans Hotel as the headquarters hotel. Ray put together the program, inviting big names from all over the country, with little regard for expenses.

Halsey persuaded Ray and Lou to come to New Orleans to celebrate Mardi Gras the weekend before the Four A meeting started on Ash Wednesday. Ray remembered, "What a blast it was, culminating on Fat Tuesday. Halsey had matching clown costumes delivered to our room, told us to go to a certain corner to see the parade, to watch for him on a pogo stick following the parade, and to get in the crowd following him to a tour of the grand old homes and enjoy free lavish spreads of food and drink. We got back to the hotel at 9:00 P.M., totally exhausted."

The Four A members voted the New Orleans convention the best advertising convention they had ever attended. Four A president Fred Gamble of New York, in a backroom luncheon at Arnand's, said it was bigger than the Four A Central Region meeting in Chicago and as good as the national meeting at the Greenbrier.

Gamble did not know, nor did Ray at the time, that Ray had spent not only the registration fees, intended to cover the entire cost of the convention, but also had blown the organization's $10,000 treasury. On top of that, each member had to be assessed $100.00.[8]

After those financial disclosures, the Four A office in New York controlled the next annual meeting in Dallas. It consisted of one day, no wives, no overnight, and no parties. However, for years, even with the treasury depletion and the assessment, members told Ray the New Orleans convention was still the best Four A meeting ever.

In the 1950s, Ray became active in programs of the Oklahoma City Chamber of Commerce. His first big assignment was as publicity chairman for a Chamber-sponsored air show in 1954 that Ray named the Air Fair. The Navy's new jet-powered Crusader fighter plane was the big attraction. He also served as chairman of the Education Committee and each year had his photograph taken with the winning teacher from each school district in the state. He always received clippings from teachers who returned home and saw the stories in their hometown newspapers.

In January, 1960, Chamber president, Edward L. Gaylord, son of OPUBCO publisher E.K. Gaylord, appointed Ray as chairman of the chamber's public relations division. A few years later, Ray was elected to the Chamber's Board of Directors, a position he held continuously into 2001.

A NEAR MISS

IN EARLY 1960, Ray was promoted to Executive Officer of VF 704 in Dallas and on June 15th, his second son, Mark, was born. Twenty six days later, on July 11, Ray's squadron was on its way to Oceana, Virginia, for two weeks of active duty, making the long trip in two plane sections of FJ-4B fighter aircraft. The plane was called the Fury and it was the Navy's version of the Air Force's F-86 Saberjet.

The FJ-4B was the most powerful and the heaviest of the Fury line and was introduced in December of 1956. Its maximum speed was 680 mph and it was utilized as a carrier-based fighter-interceptor. In its close-support role it could carry six Sidewinder or five Bullpup missiles, bombs, or rockets, or four external fuel tanks, in addition to four 20-mm cannon.[1]

While climbing through 37,000 feet over Marshall, Texas, on the way to his assigned altitude of 41,500 feet, Ray looked around and did not see his wingman, not unusual in the loose formation flown on a long trip. He thought the wingman was probably behind him and either above or below. Ray was just keying his microphone to ask where the wingman was, when a garbled transmission came through. Ray thought the wingman said he was going to make a dummy gunnery run. However, he was not sure, so he asked for a repeat. No sooner did Ray get the words out of his mouth than the wingman flew into him, cutting off the tail of Ray's plane three inches behind the cockpit and severing his own left wing. The fact that Ray had not acknowledged the gunnery run was not a factor in the mid-air collision as he would have continued in his climbing attitude in any event.

The impact was not as severe a shock as one might think because the wingman had pulled out of his dive a little late and got sucked into Ray's plane by a Venturi-effect.

Ray's plane immediately inverted. He did not realize he had lost his tail so he tried to turn right side up several times, but the plane just flipped over. Of course he realized he had lost his engine and was falling toward earth, so he prepared to eject.

Spinning wildly with irregular centrifugal force, Ray tried to get his finger on the switch to lower his seat to the floor so that he could eject with a straight backbone. Failing to do so, he had to go out with his neck bent. His parachute opened successfully, but when he went to actuate his portable oxygen, the little green ball connected to the actuating cable came off in his hand. Ray had to wrap his finger around the steel cable and pull to get the flow of oxygen.

He never did see the two halves of his airplane. But, having to eject downward, they were above him and he might have been scared to death had he seen one part falling close to his parachute. He tried to check his wristwatch to time his descent so he would know exactly at what altitude he opened the chute, but the wristwatch was gone. Ray had not paid any attention to instructions not to wear an expansion band in case of ejection, the advice being that the band would stretch to its maximum length and the watch would sail off into space, which is what he assumed had happened.

Recalling lectures on safety in parachuting, he tried to steer the parachute because, as he remembered, "It looked like I was coming down in the middle of a lake." But every time he pulled the cords on one side of the chute, the rate of descent increased substantially and scared him to death. As he got close to the ground, he remembered to cross his legs, because the book said, "you just might come down across a barbed-wire fence."[2]

It was late morning when he landed unhurt in a thicket of bushes about ten feet high. He had just finished gathering up his chute and was walking out of the brush when a preacher came over a little hill reading his Bible, with a group of people following him. They all thanked God that Ray was still alive. One of them offered him a cigarette, and although Ray did not smoke anything but cigars, that one cigarette did taste good.

Ray had been on the ground close to an hour when he felt something in his armpit. It turned out to be the watch, which had gone up his arm rather than off his hand. Ray could not imagine the amount of adrenaline it took to keep him from feeling the watch for an hour.

A funeral parlor in Marshall sent out a hearse, of all things, to transport Ray to town. When he called Lou, she said, "I thought you were flying to Virginia this morning. Where are you?" Unthinkingly, he said he was in a funeral home in Marshall, Texas, then quickly explained what had happened. Fortunately, he caught her when he did, because his employees at Ackerman Associates thought he was dead, having heard a radio announcement that reported something like, "Two Oklahoma City Navy pilots were involved in a mid-air crash over Marshall, Texas, this morning. Lieutenant Hal Joines sustained minor injuries." It was correct, but the announcement did not say Ray was unhurt and the inference was that he was dead because pilots do not generally survive mid-air collisions. Incidentally, Joines' plane flip-flopped for about five miles before he ejected safely.

By his near miss, Ray became a member of the Caterpillar Club, membership open only to those who have jumped to save their lives, not just jumped. He was flown back to Naval Air Station Dallas for a physical, which revealed no apparent injury, a safety debriefing, and the presentation of the traditional bottle of fine Scotch to the sailor who packed the parachute which carried Ray safely back to earth.

Of course, there was a celebratory party at the Officers' Club followed by a midnight breakfast at Lucas B and B in the Oak Cliff section of Dallas. Joe Roark, the man who sold Lou and Ray their first house, was speeding in his convertible on the Dallas to Waco highway when he heard about the mid-air on the radio. He made it back to Dallas for the party.

Lou flew to Dallas for a couple of days and, for the first time in the 12 years they had been married, said something about his flying. She said, "Don't you think you should quit flying?" He said, "No" and the subject never came up again in his Navy career.

Ray thought afterwards, "After not having gotten into the Battle of the Pacific during World War II, it would have been a crime for me to have been killed in a 'kamikaze' attack by one of our own planes!"[3]

Ray believed he had divine intervention through Padre Pio, an Italian priest with stigmata, frequently referred to as "The Patron Saint of Aviators," who was canonized in 2002. There were many stories about him appearing in the cockpit to pilots who were in trouble during World War II. A number of aviators gave Padre credit for helping them find their way when they were lost. Shortly after Ray married Lou, her cousin, Margaret Bradley, sent Ray a medal of Padre Pio. Ray put it on his key chain and never thought much about it.

The FJ-4B had a small compartment in the side to store street clothes and a toilet kit. Ray's key chain was in one of the pockets of the uniform. In the crash, everything in that compartment burned to ashes except the pocket carrying the key ring and the Padre Pio medal. It was just like several other pockets in size, stitching, and design, yet, the fire burned up to the seams on all sides and stopped.

Ray had the medal gilded at B.C. Clark's Jewelers and wore it on a gold chain around his neck. It had a little picture of Padre Pio in it, which Ray thought was under glass. In a hot whirlpool one day, the picture came out, leaving just a hole in the middle. It was not glass over the picture; it was plastic which had melted.

Ray could not find a nice medal of Padre Pio in the United States, but a friend discovered a jeweler in Florence, Italy, a devotee of Padre Pio, with a selection of medals and sculptures. Ray purchased an 18-carat large gold medal of the Padre which he has worn around his neck ever since.

Noting in 1981 that Padre Pio was being considered for canonization, Ray wrote to his Eminence, the Cardinal Casaroli, the Secretariat of State for the Vatican, giving a report of his experience and asking that it be included in Padre Pio's canonization file. A letter, dated July 27, 1981, was received in acknowledgement from E. Martinez of the Secretariat of State's office that Ray's story had been duly transmitted to the Sacred Congregation of Causes of Saints with a request that the matter be given appropriate consideration. The number assigned to Ray's story on this acknowledgment is 70592.[4]

As soon as possible after his brush with death, Ray joined his squadron at Oceana and got back in the air, knowing if he waited too long he might be scared to do so. A Division Leader in the squadron, he was leading four planes out for a rocket run on a target a few miles off the coast of North Carolina. Not being as familiar with the area as he should have been, he thought he spotted the target and started to get his division into formation to attack. Fortunately, his wingman called and said, "Sir, I think you are looking at the Kitty Hawk Memorial."

About a month after his safe ejection, Ray began to experience pain in his neck and left arm. He went to the famous Oklahoma City orthopedic surgeon, Henry Freede, who diagnosed Ray with a small crack in a vertebrae and a slight injury in his neck.

A Navy doctor at the Air Station in Dallas claimed that his x-rays showed no injury and that Ray must have hurt his neck in the previous 30 days. As Ray had not been involved in anything particularly physical during that 30 days, Freede knew the Navy was mistaken and told Ray how important it was for him to prove it. He said Ray needed a report of the injury in his Navy medical record just in case he needed government medical assistance later in life.

Dr. Freede called Ray one morning and asked how quickly he could get into a hospital bed in the next day or two. Freede said he was winning the argument with the Navy doctor but that it would be important for Ray to be in bed getting treatment before the Navy ordered him to its hospital in Corpus Christi, Texas. Freede said, "You might be in their hospital for weeks or months."

The Ackerman agency office was near United FoundersTower and Baptist Hospital had just opened its first small building across the Northwest Highway. Ray told Freede he could probably be in the hospital in five minutes. Two days later, the doctor called and said, "Get into the hospital." Within minutes, Ray was in bed at Baptist with his neck in a harness, attached to a rope which went though a pulley on the back of the bed. The rope was attached to several bricks, the weight intended to stretch his neck. The quick action kept Ray from having to go to Corpus Christi.

The neck-stretching went on for seven days. Ray was in absolutely no pain and, unbelievably, the hospital was so new and understaffed, he could smoke cigars in his room.

In Ray's double room there was a young man who had undergone an operation for appendicitis. A couple of days after the operation, the young man needed to go to the bathroom and rang for a nurse. After numerous rings, and no sign of a nurse, he asked Ray if he thought it was OK for him to go to the bathroom. Ray said, "Sure!"

Ray, back center, with neck brace, was still hurting from his aircraft ejection in July, 1960, when he attended an advertising party at KOCY Radio in Oklahoma City three months later. By successfully parachuting from his plane, Ray became a member of the Caterpillar Club, a unique group of pilots who jumped to save their lives.

On July 1, 1961, Ray became Commanding Officer of the Navy Fighting Squadron 704.

However, as the young man started toward the bathroom, he promptly fainted. Ray rang the call button a half-dozen times with no response. He could not get out of his bed to summon help so he threw a bedpan into the hallway. The loud clanking of the metal brought immediate help for his young friend.

About 25 years later, Ray was making a business call at the Fleming Company in Oklahoma City. A man introduced himself and said, "Mr. Ackerman, I don't believe you remember me, but I'm the guy you helped with the bedpan at Baptist Hospital."

The new hospital was so loose with rules, policies, and procedures, that on a Saturday, some of Ray's Navy friends came down the hall with a cargo parachute as sort of a canopy, hiding a picher of martinis and a box of cigars. Ray recalled, "Closing the door of course, we had a helluva' party while watching a football game on television that afternoon."

Ray served briefly on the boards of the Oklahoma City Urban League and the Red Lands Council of the Girl Scouts of America. However, because he usually worked past 8:00 P.M. at the agency and both boards met at night, he resigned the positions. He also served on the Board of Directors of the Catholic Foundation of Oklahoma and Mercy Hospital.[5] The agency had provided free advertising services for the National Cowboy Hall of Fame and Western Heritage Center, later renamed the National Cowboy and Western Heritage Musueum, in Oklahoma City since the Hall opened. The agency handled the first Western Heritage Awards dinner in the Tower Club of the Skirvin Tower Hotel and not only conceived the idea for the Western Heritage Awards, but also designed the award itself. The museum was so short of funds that Ray's secretaries and receptionist worked as waitresses for the first Western Heritage Award dinner.

In October, 1961, Ray went to B.C. Clark, Jr., with the idea that his "Jewelry Is the Gift to Give" jingle still had good lyrics but that the music should be updated. Clark agreed and a new jingle went on the air Thanksgiving morning. By noon on the day after Thanksgiving, B.C. Clark Jewelers had received so

The Good Old Summer Dime.

7-11 convenience stores in greater Oklahoma City was a major client of Ray's agency. Other significant accounts handled were Star Manufacturing Company, DEMCO, Sirloin Stockade, Hahn-Cook Funeral Home, Founders Bank, Parks Menswear, Frigette Auto Air Conditioners, Acme Tool, Standard Roofing, Southwest Factories, H and R Block, United Founders Life Insurance Company, the Oklahoma State Fair, Kerr's Department Store, Fife Manufacturing, Oklahoma City Beautiful, Oklahoma Christian College, Evans Home Furnishings, George Farha Toys, G.T. Blankenship for Attorney General, Keller-Williams Furniture, GASO Pumps, and Stripprinter.

many calls from customers who wanted the original music back that the new jingle was pulled and the old commercial substituted within hours. B.C. Clark, Jr., remembered, "The phone started ringing immediately. We got letters. People said, 'You changed the jingle and it isn't the same!'"

In 1967, when Amy Ackerman came home from the last day of school before Christmas, Ray asked her what her class did that day. Amy replied that students gave their teacher presents, exchanged Christmas cards, had ice cream and cake, and sang "Silent Night," "Jingle Bells," and "Jewelry Is the Gift to Give."

On another occasion, several Oklahoma Cityans were attending a big wedding in Canada. When someone said, "Let's sing the Oklahoma song," the group broke into "Jewelry Is the Gift to Give."

*Ray labored long
hours to build his
advertising agency
into one of the most
successful in
Oklahoma in the
1960s.*

*Clayton Anderson,
left, president of the
Oklahoma City
Advertising Club,
presents the 1964
Ad Club
Distinguished Club
Award to Ray.*

*Ray and his
"crew"
hashing out a
new project in
1962. Left to
right, Ray,
Jack Moses,
and Bob
Cooper.*

Amy Lou Ackerman was born November 15, 1961, the last of the six living Ackerman children. With each child, Lou's time of labor was shorter, prompting her physician, Dr. Gerald Rogers, to say before the birth of the last two children, "Let's induce labor. Otherwise, you'll be frying an egg some morning and look down on the floor and say 'Oops!'"

In 2001, 45 years after the B.C. Clark jingle hit the airwaves, it was still one of the most recognized slogans in the nation. Most adults who grew up in Oklahoma City could sing the words of the jingle on command.

Military cutbacks resulted in the June 30, 1962 decommissioning of Ray's fighter squadron in Dallas. Ray considered retiring in August with 20 years of service but had a stroke of good fortune in being selected as deputy to the staff commander, the senior reservist at the Dallas Naval Air Station, for one weekend each month. No longer assigned to combat fighters, Ray was relegated to fly twin-engine aircraft, the SNB and US2B, but his Navy career continued.

Gone was the requirement that Ray spend his two weeks active Navy duty in the summer. He was finally free to plan family vacations. In a new Pontiac station wagon, Ray drove the family through the West several times and once to Florida.

In the summer of 1965, the Ackermans adopted North Padre Island on the Gulf Coast as the family's regular summer vacation spot. The first year, they stayed at a condominium called The Island House, but the following year they went to the newer, bigger, nicer Gulfstream for two weeks and went back every summer thereafter until 1990.

Everyone in the family was a sun, sea, and sand worshiper to the point that, in 1971, Lou and Ray decided to retire on Padre at some time in the future. They bought a residential lot on a waterway and two adjacent commercial lots on Padre Island Boulevard, the main thoroughfare. Building, owning, and operating a radio station on the commercial property was one thought Ray had for retirement Another idea was to build and operate a health club. As time went by, Lou and Ray began to realize how much they loved Oklahoma City, how all their friends and most of their family lived in the Sooner State, how suddenly the sun was less attractive because of skin cancer, so they abandoned the idea of moving after retirement.

Children and grandchildren still visit North Padre Island about every other year with Ray and Lou joining them occasionally for a few days. Ray fondly remembered the area, "South Padre Island has developed into sort of a Coney Island or Atlantic City, while North Padre Island Gulf frontage remains pristine by comparison. People talk about Oklahoma being landlocked in the center of the country, not remembering that Oklahoma City is just a good day's drive from the saltwater off Padre Island—about 550 miles."

TOMORROW BELONGS
TO OKLAHOMA

IN 1964, the 75th anniversary of the Oklahoma Land Run of 1889, Ray published a book entitled *Tomorrow Belongs to Oklahoma!* Ackerman Agency staffers did the research and Joe Park helped Ray with the writing.

Ray's stated purpose for his book was to inspire a greater sense of pride in Oklahomans. He wanted to arouse the interest of out-of-state industrialists in Oklahoma, to cause Oklahomans to become impatient for "tomorrow," and to give them a sense of direction for speeding the day when "tomorrow" would arrive. OPUBCO publisher E. K. Gaylord wrote the foreword to the book, and referred to Ray as "one of Oklahoma City's young, eager, and progressive businessmen."[1]

In *Tomorrow Belongs to Oklahoma!,* Ray cited the 20th century prediction by pioneer investment counselor and economic forecaster, Roger Babson, that the "Magic Circle," squarely in the center of the United States, could become the world's greatest international trading center.

Babson's Magic Circle encompassed 500,000 square miles, reaching from below Oklahoma's southern boundary to include Arkansas, Missouri, Nebraska, and Kansas, before circling back past the Oklahoma Panhandle.

The Ackerman Building after its completion in 1964. It was a modern, two-story structure built near the United Founders Tower in northwest Oklahoma City. In 2000, 16 years after the agency moved out, the north and south walls were extended a few feet and a third floor was added, converting the building into a Quality Inn.

In 1963, ground was broken for a new building to house the Ackerman agency. Left to right, Ray, George Soter, and Paul Sprehe, co-owners of the building. Soter and Sprehe owned an engineering company. Holding the starting gun is Al Fiegel, Ackerman vice president whose creative genius resulted in the "Jewelry Is the Gift to Give" jingle for B.C. Clark Jewelers. A special guest at the ground-breaking was Hank Moran, the second client of the Knox Agency, the predecessor to Ackerman.

The 1963 Ackerman Agency Christmas party was held at The Levee, a popular nightspot on Northwest 39th Street in Oklahoma City. Left to right, Bill Roberts, Jack Moses, Cathy Davis, Jim Ulman, Jerry Bell, Bob Cooper, Ava Milburn, Jeri Beard, Glenna Hammack, Ray, Al Fiegel, Beverly Theus, Nadine Pease, Jim Blacketer, Pat Padgham, Ginger Pelofsky, Ruth Ann Campbell, Jack Sherry, Tom House, and Joe Park. George Knox had started an annual Christmas Media and Trades party in 1939 for people in the media and vendors that the agency bought time and materials from. The party was so popular that representatives of national media in New York, Chicago, and Dallas scheduled their quarterly or semi-annual visits to Oklahoma City to coincide with it. Ray continued the tradition until attendance at the annual function reached almost 600 because of guests bringing uninvited spouses or dates. The great expense, and the concern for guests driving home in the days before designated drivers, caused Ray to discontinue the celebration in 1970, after 31 years.

Ray bragged that Oklahoma City had become the largest city, in size, in America. He said, "This expansion began with one of the boldest planning experiments in the nation. The plan called for land growth by annexation for industrial development." In 1956, the city grew from 49 square miles to over 600 square miles by a skillfully executed annexation plan that took less than 24 hours to formulate. Ray remembered, "Like a Panzer-tank movement, the city annexed corridors between surrounding towns and cities and then fanned out and annexed around them. The result is that Oklahoma City controls its own destiny."[2]

Ray thanked Zach Taylor, the executive director of the Association of Central Oklahoma Governments, for helping to maintain a cordial relationship among all the cities in central Oklahoma.

A billboard celebrating the publication of Ray's book, Tomorrow Belongs to Oklahoma!, *in 1964. Many people at Ray's agency helped compile material for the book that painted an exciting future of economic development for Oklahoma City and the state of Oklahoma. Joe Park shared writing responsibilities with Ray..*

In March, 1964, Ray purchased the Srago Advertising Agency in Oklahoma City. Here, Ray and Leon Srago, left, sign the contract to consummate the sale. With the purchase came two prominent clients, Emmer Brothers Clothing Stores and L & S Bearing Company. Ray became good friends with Jack Golsen, president of L & S, who later became chief executive officer of LSB Industries, a holding company primarily in the chemical and air handling businesses. In 1993, Ray joined the LSB Board of Directors.

Ray wrote, "When other cities are choked by hundreds of separate surrounding communities, each with its separate laws and ordinances, with inept taxes and conflicting standards; while other cities starve for water that is cut off by boundary lines, lose airports to overcrowded developments and jobs for the lack of a place to put new industry, Oklahoma City will just be beginning its growth."

Ray also applauded the vision for Oklahoma demonstrated by the leadership of United States Senator Robert S. Kerr and long-time Oklahoma City Chamber of Commerce manager Stanley C. Draper.

In encouraging Oklahomans to work together for a greater state, Ray wrote, "The time for quiet building is over. It's time to shout 'to wave the flag, to stand and sing "Oklahoma!" ' at public gatherings. Our history, our resources, the belief of Babson, Kerr, Draper, and you and me in Oklahoma and its potential, justifies our pride and self confidence."[3]

Ray built a terrific team of talent around him at the agency. Among the key people besides Al Fiegel were Darlene Murphy,

Ralph Combs, Pat Marchiando, Dan Thompson, Pat Catlett Austin, Cathy Davis Lawhon, Sonja Sullivan Adams, Marge Luebker, Ralph Stuart, Dorothy Gutsche, Bill Davidson, Tom Webster, Rick Duiker, Don Spencer, Ray Scales, Ray Arkekta, Joyce Outhier, Sandra Brown, Dotty Cecil, Todd Van Every, Jim Stowe, Jim Ulman, Jack Sherry, Jerry Bell, Jeri Beard, Jim Blacketer, and Bill Shdeed.

In early 1963, Ray was approached by Paul Sprehe, a fellow member in the Serra Club, an organization of Catholic men to promote vocations, to consider jointly building an office building. Sprehe and his partner, George Soter, wanted to join forces with Ackerman Associates to build an office building that would house the Soter and Sprehe Engineering Company, the advertising agency, and smaller tenants, whose space could be used later for expansion of the owner firms.

Remembering the old saying, "Why pay rent when you could be making payments instead on a permanent asset," Ray leaped at the opportunity. First the group considered building on North Classen Boulevard. However, Horace Rhodes, president of the United Founders Insurance Company, and one of Ray's clients, offered a choice lot near the United Founders Tower for construction of a new facility.

Ray liked the idea but first had to break the rented space lease at 1411 North Classen with Hudgins, Thompson & Ball (HTB), an architectural firm that owned the building. Ray had two other problems when he met with HTB President Ed Hudgins. He wanted to keep HTB as a client of the agency, yet wanted to use another firm to design the new office building because "of wanting more creativity than he saw in HTB's work."

Ed Hudgins actually received the news well, sold Ray on a new young creative architect he had just hired, Tom Glover, to design the new building and allowed Ray to break his lease at the old location. HTB also remained a client of Ackerman Associates.

Soter and Sprehe Engineering and Ackerman Associates were equal partners in the construction project that also resulted in a deep friendship between the Ackermans, Soters, and Sprehes. In the spring of 1964, Soter and Sprehe moved in. Ackerman Associates moved into 75 percent of the second floor in the fall. On December, 11, 1964, Ray hosted an open house to celebrate the new offices. The special guest was Hank Moran, the second client of the agency in 1939. A feature of the event was the introduction of a new cigarette made from dried lettuce leaves. Its name is long forgotten as is the cigarette.[4]

One of the features of the new building, dubbed the Ackerman Building, was a snack bar manned by George Soter's mother-in-law, Kate Samaras. "Mama Kate" always had something different every day for a hot meal plus sandwiches and desserts. There were only five seats at the counter but often a dozen people lined up, saying Mama Kate's hot food and personality made it a better place to eat than the nearby Queen Anne Cafeteria.

By the mid 1960s, Ray was heavily involved in civic and charitable causes in Oklahoma City. In 1963, he chaired the committee to combat high school dropouts in the Oklahoma City School District. In 1964, he received the second annual Outstanding Graduate Award from the Oklahoma City University School of Business and was the recipient of the Distinguished Service Award from the Oklahoma City Advertising Club. The same year he was Campaign Chairman for the United Way of Greater Oklahoma City. Under his leadership, the fundraising goal was exceeded by nine percent, a record that stood for 13 years.

In 1964, Ray and Lou were able to buy a matching piece of lake frontage on the north side of their home from Bill Falter, as well as a 150 foot by 300 foot lot on the west side. The additional land increased the size of the Ackerman homestead to nearly 2.5 acres.

A small stone house, built like a castle, came with the new lake frontage. It was built in the 1920s to be a gatehouse for a huge castle-style house the owners planned to build. The owners divorced and their great plan produced only the gatehouse. The Ackermans used it as a guest house and a bath house. They later rented it for a few years to a divorced artist who wanted to sort of disappear, then to a single girl who wanted to do likewise.

The day the artist, Joan McCrary, was moving out, she leaned some of her paintings against her station wagon. The Ackerman's black schnauzer, Jet, according to Ray, "sashayed up to one of them, sniffed it, and lifted his left hind leg and—yes he did!" Joan commented, "That has got to be my severest critic!"

The additional lake frontage was so low it was almost like swampland, except on the west end where the stone house stood. As part of a big home improvement project, which included fencing the property on the west and north sides, building an entrance on the north, a concrete driveway, a 1,000-square-foot patio on the north side of the house, and a half basketball court, Ray decided to dredge the lake in front of the property and pile drive a steel retaining wall. The wall, among other things, would make it feasible to bring in fill dirt and raise the level of the swampland to a usable height.

The wall was scheduled for construction on the Monday after Mother's Day. To rule out the possibility that a thunderstorm could carry silt into Ray's newly-dredged frontage before the wall was in place, his brother-in-law, Bill Winkler, helped cut half-dead willow trees in the swamp area, chain-saw them into logs, and stake them into dams in the low run-off area.

Sure enough, storm clouds were gathering as they cleaned up for dinner. As they sipped their pre-dinner cocktails on Mother's Day, it rained so hard they watched out the window as a torrent of water tore out the stakes and fired the logs into the lake like torpedoes.

The project also included building a diving board, a floating raft connected to the steel wall, a badminton court, tetherball facility, and horseshoe pits, all necessary for the fabulous picnics which followed.

The west lot was bare and Ray planted a variety of saplings such as black walnut that the kids watered faithfully, partially by buckets because the water pressure from the wells was not sufficient for hoses to reach all the way to the new plantings on the west end.[5]

The Ackermans discovered that living on a lake is unique from living on a street. People used to ask Lou and Ray if they worried about the kids drowning. They did not, and all the children became excellent swimmers. One year in the Sooner State Games, the four daughters made up a relay team that came in second to one boys' team, while beating three others. Ray said, "On a lake, one doesn't have to worry where their kids are, as it is an attractive meeting place for their friends."

In the 1930s, there was an article about the lake in *Life* Magazine, showing some Broadlawn Lake homeowners planting water lilies in a secluded finger of the lake. By the mid-1960s, the lilies had spread to the point where one could almost walk across the lake on them, just north of the Ackerman's frontage. Over an entire summer, Ray almost single-handedly cleaned them out, living in the lake on Saturdays and Sundays until he thought he was developing webbed feet.

The children helped—somewhat. Ray would tell them to look for any new lilies emerging on Monday morning and to pull out their roots from the bottom. Instead, the children took the easy way out by clipping the tops off just below the surface of the water. The lilies bloomed again, stronger than ever.

When the Ackermans moved into the lake house in 1958, they were in the country, not part of any town or city, so they did not have city water or sewage. Water was no problem because they had a good well and acquired a second one when they bought the little stone house.

Sewage was a problem. They had to have a septic tank and the lateral field was between the house and the lake. It was not uncommon to be looking out the window at newly-fallen snow and all of a sudden notice an enlarging wet spot, leaking sewage. A second lateral field to the west was added, and sewage was pumped uphill, a project that alleviated the sewage problem.

Ray and Lou wanted to be annexed by Oklahoma City but most of the 20 lake residents wanted to become part of Warr Acres, where taxes were slightly lower. After two meetings of the Lake Association at the Ackermans home, Ray and Lou won the battle with the help of the late Bill Collins, the attorney who engineered Oklahoma City's massive annexations in the 1950s.

In the 1920s, the lake had been a weekend retreat for the affluent in Heritage Hills. It was a fairly long drive in those days in Model T's on dirt roads, similar to Oklahoma Cityans now driving to eastern Oklahoma lakes on weekends. The last of the summer homes, owned by the Sullivan and Turner families, was directly across the lake from the Ackerman house. The owners had huge parties and made lots of noise on Memorial Day, the Fourth of July and Labor Day. The house was eventually converted to a permanent house about 1970.

Lou and Ray taught patriotism and respect for the flag to their children. They had a flagpole behind the house on the west side and another one in front of the house on which the flag was raised only on Sundays and holidays. Ray would march the children out on the front deck, have them stand at attention, run up the flag, and have them recite the Pledge of Allegiance.

Ray, like his father before him, always searched long and hard for a perfect Christmas tree, preferably one about nine to ten feet tall. One year, he thought he found the perfect tree in a lot on the northeast corner of Northwest 39th Street and Pennsylvania Avenue. As was his custom, he left the tree outside for a few days in water, brought it in on a given night, with plans to trim it the following evening. To his dismay, every time Ray hung an ornament, he was met with a shower of needles on the floor and suddenly realized the tree was dead. He took it down, put it on top of the station wagon, drove back to the lot and asked for another tree. The lot operator said all sales were final and ignored his request. Ray went back home, found a large two foot by three foot piece of cardboard, and with paint and brush, lettered on both sides, "These Trees Are Dead." He attached a stick, went back to the lot, marched around for approximately 30 seconds, after which he was on his way home with a new tree.

Another Christmas, electric-powered racing cars were the rage. On Christmas Eve, Ray and his father had completed assembling doll tables and chairs and beds for the girls and turned their attention to an electric car set for Ray K. The racetrack was on a large plastic mold with ridges on which metal strips had to be presssed to carry the current. Each time Ray and his father tried to press a strip into place, two or three strips they had just installed popped off. After a frustrating hour, with bleeding fingers, Ray placed the pieces of the car set in the trunk of his car.

The day after Christmas, Ray attempted to return the electric car set to Kerr's Department Store. He placed it on a counter and asked for his money back. The clerk said, "Well, maybe you aren't mechanically minded!" Ray called for the manager and said, "I'll bet you $20.00 you can't put this together." Ray got his refund and was exonerated a few weeks later when *Time* Magazine reported that electric racing cars were so popular that some manufacturers, including the company that made the set Ray bought, had rushed into production faulty sets that could not be put together.[6]

The agency became a driving force behind successful bond issues for city improvements and as a pro bono asset for the United Way, the arts, local colleges, churches, hospitals, the Salvation Army, and the Cowboy Hall of Fame.

The advertising business was good, but not great. For the first 10 years after Ray bought the Knox agency, he belonged to an informal group called the Oklahoma City Association of Advertising Agencies (OAAA), consisting of 10 members, all with good reputations. Quarterly the group met to discuss common problems such as how to defeat the oft-introduced state legislation to tax advertising.

The OAAA had an unwritten rule: no soliciting of another member's accounts. Ray, being the youngster of the group, was not in favor of the rule because the older agencies had the big accounts. However, he initially observed the rule. But one day Ray heard that an industrial account headquartered in Oklahoma City, Folding Carrier Corporation, was contemplating switching advertising companies. He called the ad manager, Gene Von Stein, introduced himself and asked if he could make a presentation. Von Stein said, "I have already made a decision on a new agency. Had I known of your firm, I would have given you an opportunity to solicit our business."

Ray wrote to the other members of the Association enclosing a copy of the Ackerman client list, inviting them to call on his clients, because, he wrote, "I'm going to be calling on yours."

A few days later, a media representative told Ray there had been a meeting of four or five of the other nine members who were dividing up the account list to make calls. In any event, the rules of competition were changed dramatically and Ray's company began to prosper from that point on.

In 1965, the Ackerman agency was thrilled to land University Sound as an account. A division of LTV, University Sound was moved to Oklahoma City from White Plains, New York. Ackerman personnel should have known it would be a short-term relationship because when the agency asked for a briefing on products, markets, and competition, University Sound ad manager, Irv Greene, said, "We don't have time for that. We've got a lot of ads to crank out."

Sure enough, Ackerman lost the account in January, 1968. However, Ray wrote a five-page letter, dated February 2, 1968, to president Haskel Blair, pointing out all of his organization's shortcomings. Some excerpts, "If you were to honestly think of your biggest mistake when you moved your company here from

White Plains, N.Y., it was bringing Irv Greene with you—we had to work with him for 2 years before you fired him. Bill Simonite became our primary contact at University Sound and I could go on-and-on about his shortcomings—but it should suffice to say he tees up his ball in the rough. I know he's gone now but I'll bet you're still finding deals he made that you are trying to unravel." There is a sweet ending to the story. On May 12, 1969, Haskel Blair rehired Ackerman as the University Sound ad agency.

In 1962, newspaper publisher J. Leland Gourley hired the agency for a very modest monthly fee to do personal public relations for him. Two years later, Gourley began to give consideration to running for governor. David Hall, the county attorney in Tulsa, was the heavy favorite and had been told by his friends in Oklahoma City and Tulsa to hire the Ackerman agency. Ray told Hall he could not commit unless his present client, Gourley, decided not to run.

Fortunately for the agency, Gourley procrastinated long enough that Hall hired somebody else. Ray was grateful to Gourley for "keeping the agency from handling a Governor who ended up in prison."

Gourley spent $6,000 through a research firm back east to evaluate his image. Results of the survey gave clear direction not to run. Ray remembered, "The bad news was that 9 out of 10 people didn't like Leland; the good news was that only 1 out of 10 knew him!"

Staring that information in the face, Gourley asked Ray how much money it would take to win the race. Ray answered, "If you had $5 million to spend on the campaign, [a huge campaign budget in 1964], I'd put it in the bank and not run." Gourley decided to run anyway, and after the race reported, "I finished 13th in a field of 12."[7]

Another client, Bob Wootten, Republican candidate for Oklahoma lieutenant governor, almost upset the popular George

Nigh in 1966, primarily because of a television commercial. The ad began with a black screen. White circles appeared as eyes with white dots as pupils, moving around in the circles to the sound of a buzzing fly, while the copy spelled out, using the eyes as the o's in the candidate's name, "Look out George, here comes Wootten. " The sound of a flyswatter stopped the buzzing as the eyes looked down.

A large painted outdoor sign at Northwest 50th Street and Classen Boulevard carried the same message, starting with a totally black board, with a tiny bit of the message added in white each day. Nigh won by only 24,000 votes, 328,580 to 306,053. The result was amazing because the unknown Wootten agreed to run as the GOP "sacrificial lamb" just so the party would not be embarrassed by not having a candidate for the major office.

A week before the election, after checking the polling data, Ray called Wootten and said he thought Wootten could win if he had $5,000 more for television. Ray recalled, "He didn't have it, and couldn't get it."[8]

Also in 1966, Ray was elected president of the United Way of Greater Oklahoma City and of the Better Business Bureau in Oklahoma City. He also was selected as Notre Dame Man of the Year by the Oklahoma Alumni Chapter.

In 1967, Ray believed he needed an office in Tulsa if he were to realize his ambition of becoming a truly statewide advertising agency. His Tulsa operation began with one account representative, Chad Steward, one secretary, and no business. Ray figured that if nothing happened within six months, he could simply close the office.

Three months after opening the Tulsa office, John Whitney, owner of one of the two largest Tulsa ad agencies offered to sell his business to Ray. Whitney, who taught part time at the University of Tulsa, was offered a lectureship at Harvard University and needed to be there within 60 days. He and Ray struck a deal.

By 1967, Ackerman in Oklahoma City was billing $2.5 million annually with 30 employees and 60 clients. With the addition of the $1.5 million annual billing of the Whitney Agency in Tulsa, all at once Ray headed up a $4 million agency. However, Whitney had been a one-man agency and the Ackerman agency lost almost $1 million in annual billing the first six months it owned the Tulsa operation. Ray nearly closed the Tulsa office before landing the First National Bank and Trust Company of Tulsa account, putting the office on its way back to profitability.

RODEO MAN

In 1965, the Oklahoma City Chamber of Commerce was successful in attracting the National Finals Rodeo (NFR) to Oklahoma City. Labeled the "World Series of Rodeo," the NFR was launched in 1959 but failed financially in its first six years, three in Los Angeles, California, and three in Dallas, Texas.

Ray accepted the general chairmanship of the NFR with the primary responsibility of selling enough tickets on an all-performance basis to assure a profit. Frankly, the NFR was a tough sell. One prominent civic leader, hearing that cowboys would parade their horses through downtown, said, "We don't want those horse droppings fouling up our streets!" The minimum sale for two box seats for all performances was $96. Ray called Pat Henderson, the chief executive officer of TG&Y Stores, to sell him two tickets. After 30 minutes, and through clenched teeth, Henderson said, "Ray, I'll buy those tickets, but only because it's you doing the asking."[1]

The first NFR in Oklahoma City was an outstanding success, both to fans and to its sponsoring organization, the Professional Rodeo Cowboys Association (PRCA). The event made over $40,000 in profit that first year and averaged $52,000 profit over the next 20 years.[2]

Thousands of rodeo fans converged on Oklahoma City from

The six Ackerman children in 1965. Left to right, front, Ray, Susie, Amy, and Mark. Back, row, left to right, Patsy and Annie.

all 50 states and Canada. It was such an economic boom to the capital city that non-believers began to support the event the following year. Beginning in 1973, the 8,929 seats in the Jim Norick Arena at the State Fairgrounds were sold out for every performance. The rodeo was moved to the Myriad Convention Center, with 11,704 seats, in 1979 and continued to sell out every performance.

The competition was open only to the top 15 money-winners

in each event who competed throughout the year in team roping, bull riding, steer wrestling, saddle bronc riding, bareback riding, and barrel racing. The first year's prize money was $44,500, and grew to $900,000 in 1984.[3]

Ray and Lou, Stanley and Edye Draper, Jr., and Paul and Theo Strasbaugh made an annual pilgrimage to Denver, Colorado, to the PRCA annual meeting to negotiate a new contract for the following December's NFR. As Ray recalled, "It took a long time for the cowboys to warm up to the city slickers from Oklahoma City; but when they did, they were the best of friends."

Ray and the chamber staffers had to earn the trust of the cowboys. On their first visit to Denver in January, 1966, the Oklahoma City delegation was told to report to the PRCA suite at the Brown Palace Hotel at a certain time to make a report on the first NFR in Oklahoma City. They knocked on the door, which opened about one inch, with one eyeball looking out. The door closed, only to reopen a minute later. A quiet voice said, "If you'll wait in the lobby, we'll call you when we want you."[4]

Once Ray made the mistake of having a very small brochure about the NFR printed by his advertising agency. When Ackerman Advertising Agency turned up on the financial statement as an expense, the cowboys looked at Ray suspiciously. From that moment, Ray always hired another agency to handle design and printing.

By 1970, with the NFR well established in Oklahoma City, Ray and Stanley Draper, Jr., decided to lure the Miss Rodeo America pageant away from Las Vegas, Nevada. Only 22 states were represented in the pageant which definitely played second to the Phyllis Diller show at the Desert Inn. Ray and Draper were in the audience in Las Vegas when the comedienne forgot to announce the Miss Rodeo America ceremony as the next item on the program. After a minute of deafening silence, Diller jumped out of the wings and said, "And now, here is Miss Ro-day-o

America!" Ray and Draper knew it would be easy to attract the contest to Oklahoma City. They made a presentation to Miss Rodeo America headquarters officials in Springdale, Arkansas, and convinced the pageant directors to move the event to Oklahoma City.

Tom Poteet, Todd Van Every, and Ray, Claudia, and Lu Anthony bore the burden of producing the Miss Rodeo America pageant in Oklahoma City for years. Together with the Ackermans and the Drapers, they traveled to Springdale each year just before the Fourth of July for meetings and to ride in a special NFR float in that city's rodeo parade. The pageant became a huge success, drawing contestants from as many as 45 states.

The budget for the NFR in Oklahoma City had ballooned from $150,000 in 1965 to over $1 million in 1984. However, the expenditure was worth it. Ray and other Chamber of Commerce officials agreed that the NFR was pumping more than $10 million a year into the Oklahoma City economy in the early 1980s.

The success of the NFR helped Oklahoma City earn the title of "Horse Capital of the World." The reason was that promoters of horse shows saw how strongly the capital city supported the NFR and how the State Fair had expanded its facilities to handle

Ray, left, receives an Expression of Appreciation for his work as general chairman of the 1965 National Finals Rodeo in Oklahoma City, including the fact that he personally sold one-fourth of the box seats. Making the presentation is Glen Farris. Ray did such an outstanding job for the NFR that he kept the job for the 20 years it stayed in Oklahoma

As general chairman of the National Finals Rodeo, Ray was one of the leaders in keeping the event in Oklahoma City after its successful run began in 1965. Courtesy Michael Ives and Ackerman McQueen.

thousands of horses. Within a few years the World Championship Quarter Horse Show, the United States Dressage Championships, the Sunbelt Cutting Horse Futurity, the Grand National Morgan Horse Show, the Arabian Horse Pentathlon, the National Steer Roping Finals, the World Championship Appaloosa Show, and other events called the Oklahoma State Fairgrounds, the Myriad Convention Center, or the Lazy E Arena near Guthrie, their home. In 2001, the horse shows, rodeos, and horse racing combined were estimated to have an annual economic impact of more than $75 million upon Greater Oklahoma City.[5]

The NFR drew peripheral events each year to Oklahoma City. In the days before the Finals actually began, it seemed as if almost every cowboy in America was drawn to Oklahoma City for events such as the World Championship Bull Riding contest, an exhibit and trade show at the Myriad, large rodeo stock sales, major cattle breed shows and sales, and an annual reunion of rodeo oldtimers.

All of the activity translated into a gold mine for merchants.

At a 1980 Oklahoma City Chamber of Commerce National Finals Rodeo appreciation luncheon, Chamber President William "Bill" Swisher, left, introduced Ray; Lou; Oklahoma City Mayor Patience Latting; Miss Rodeo America Kathy Martin; and Don Fedderson, assistant NFR General Manager.

Each year, the Oklahoma City Chamber of Commerce hosted a kickoff party for sponsors of the National Finals Rodeo. In 1980, Stanley Draper, Jr., left, events manager for the chamber, joined Ray, right, and local television personality Jan Stapp at the kickoff. Draper and Ray spent countless hours, days, and months to maintain the NFR in Oklahoma City for 20 years.

As the rodeo purse grew each year, the largest part of the total income came from increasing ticket sales. The American Bus Association selected the NFR in 1982 as one of the Top 100 Events in North America. The NFR certainly became Oklahoma City's best draw.[6]

For three years, 1981 to 1983, Ray chaired an effort to demonstrate "horsepitality" to the directors of the numerous horse shows that helped Oklahoma City earn its place atop the horse world. These were appropriately called "Events I, II, and III," and featured a barbecue, an evening of Western entertainment, cutting horse demonstrations, and a premier presentation by the fledgling Oklahoma City Police Department Mounted Patrol.

In 1983, the NFR celebrated its Silver Anniversary in Oklahoma City. A record $800,000 purse was budgeted for cowboys and another $50,000 for the Women's Professional Rodeo Association. The rodeo was a success despite rumors that a delegation from Las Vegas, Nevada, would make a strong and lucrative bid to win the event for their city in the future.[7]

PRCA officials were soured by an April, 1983, decision by National Cowboy Hall of Fame Director Dean Krakel to stop participating as a major sponsor of the NFR. Krakel said the NFR was "not financially profitable to us anymore." Ray remembered what he perceived to be the real reason, "Krakel looked down his nose at rodeo cowboys, thinking of many of them as second-class citizens, compared to ranchers and working cowboys." Proof of the problem was that, even though the Cowboy Hall of Fame established a special wing to honor rodeo cowboys, it was a minimal effort, resulting in the PRCA establishing its own Rodeo Cowboy Hall of Fame in Colorado.[8]

Ray and Draper helped pacify the PRCA, at least for 1984, by convincing the Oklahoma City Economic Development Foundation to take over the Cowboy Hall of Fame's sponsorship role.

Behind the scenes, Ray worked with local business leaders to do everything possible to keep the NFR in Oklahoma City. A $900,000 purse was approved for 1984, with help from Hesston Corporation's television rights, contestants' entry fees paid by Tener's Western Outfitters, and major contributions from the Oklahoma City Chamber of Commerce, Winston Rodeo Series, Adolph Coors Company, and Resistol Hats. But when Las Vegas came courting, the PRCA decided to listen, and Oklahoma City turned up the heat.

Nearly 900 people attended a steak and potatoes luncheon at the Myriad Convention Center on December 6, 1984. The event, held beneath glass-bead chandeliers in the Great Hall, honored cowboys and cowgirls who were NFR finalists, rodeo officials, and sponsors of the event.

Rodeo general manager Clem McSpadden, Ray, and 1985 Miss Rodeo America Leslie Patton, presented 129 cowboys and cowgirls with gold awards for their past year's achievements.

Oklahoma-born country and western singer Reba McEntire,

whose career had been launched by her singing the National Anthem at the NFR in the mid 1970s for a $35.00 performance fee, entertained the crowd at the rodeo appreciation luncheon as whispers of the NFR moving to Las Vegas dominated conversation among diners who paid $25.00 a ticket.

Local rodeo officials declined to talk about the Las Vegas issue, but McEntire did. The red-headed superstar told the audience, "If we leave Oklahoma City, it's going to be a big mistake." Her remark brought a round of applause and whistles.[9]

Even while the 20th annual NFR was playing to sold-out audiences at the Myriad, Ray and dozens of Chamber of Commerce volunteers were putting the finishing touches on Oklahoma City's presentation that was scheduled for the PRCA board meeting in Colorado Springs, Colorado, the following week on December 12.

Inside information from friends in Nevada revealed that Las Vegas would offer $750,000 more prize money each year than Oklahoma City. Armed with the news, Ray, Strasbaugh, Draper, and others quickly won commitments from Oklahoma City business and civic leaders for $2.25 million, $750,000 a year to add to the $1 million prize money from operations in 1985, 1986, and 1987, to match the Las Vegas prize money pot. Also in the Oklahoma City bid was the promise to build a new arena dedicated to the NFR and to be ready by 1988. The NFR had become so popular in Oklahoma City that no one doubted a special bond issue could be passed to build the stadium.

The Las Vegas challenge was recognized as the most serious one since Oklahoma had lured the NFR away from Dallas 20 years before. Both Oklahoma City and Las Vegas had special friends on the 11-person PRCA board which heard presentations from both cities on the afternoon of December 12, 1984, in Colorado Springs.

A straw vote early in the board meeting which began at 5:00 P.M. showed Oklahoma City winning the bid, 7 to 3. However, when the real vote was taken six hours later, at 11:00 P.M., PRCA directors split 5 to 5. The chairman, Shawn Davis, cast the deciding vote in favor of Las Vegas.[10]

In the end, Oklahoma City simply could not compete with Las Vegas on several fronts. The new Thomas & Mack Arena in Las Vegas seated 16,500 for rodeo events, nearly 5,000 more than Oklahoma City's Myriad Convention Center.

In addition, Las Vegas promised purse increases each year and added free hotel rooms for all NFR contestants, 10,000 first-class rooms available at a $30.00 rate for NFR fans, 200 $20.00 a night hotel rooms for media members, special discounted air fares for contestants and fans, two million square feet of exhibition space for trade exhibitors and sponsors, a milder winter climate, and, of course, nearby gaming tables and spectacular productions.[11]

Ray and Draper went to the first Las Vegas NFR, hoping it would be a failure so they could bring it back to Oklahoma City. The Thomas & Mack Center was built for basketball and roping events were "bastardized," with cowboys chasing calves in a circle instead of a straightaway. After the rodeo, Ray saw one of the ropers in a casino. He smugly asked, "Well how do you like roping in that tea cup?" Ray fully expected the roper to say, "I want to go back to Oklahoma City!" Instead, the roper replied, "For this kind of money, I'd rope in my bathtub."[12]

The NFR was undoubtedly gone for good, or least for as long anyone could envision. The prize money in Las Vegas passed the $5 million mark in 2000. With the NFR gone, Miss Rodeo America followed it to Las Vegas one year later.

It had been a great run for Oklahoma City. However, Chamber of Commerce officials never missed a beat in drumming up support for new horse shows and other horse events utilizing the superb facilities in Oklahoma City to take advantage of the vacuum left by the exit of the NFR.

MAYOR? ADMIRAL? BOTH?

RUNNING FOR PUBLIC OFFICE had never really seriously crossed Ray's mind even though he had served in the public spotlight for years as head of civic and charitable groups. About the closest tie to politics was Ackerman Associates, Inc. serving as the advertising agency for a group known as the Association for Responsible Government (ARG).

ARG was born in 1960 when a majority of city council members in Oklahoma City were under the shadow of a grand jury investigation and charges, made at a public meeting by the city manager, that he had been subjected to pressure from council members to fire certain city employees. The ARG's announced intention was to sweep out the entrenched council and enact numerous changes aimed at ending either real or perceived corruption in city government.

The reform group's mission was simple: elect leaders who would adhere to the city charter and allow a professional city manager to do his job. Anyone could join the ARG by paying $1.00, attending meetings, and supporting candidates.[1]

In 1963, the ARG slate won four council seats and the mayor's office. Two years later, reform slate candidates won three more of the eight council seats.

The entire Ackerman family got into the action of the mayor's race in Oklahoma City in 1967. Handing out brochures outside a local grocery store were left to right, back row, Ray, Lou, Ray K., Patsy, and Annie. Front row, left to right, Amy, Mark, Susie.

In early 1967, ARG had "gotten a little lazy" and, eight weeks before the March election, had not lined up a candidate for mayor. Quail Creek builder and ARG President Jack Johnston approached Ray and suggested he run for mayor.

Ray was shocked. He told Johnston, "Jack, I have six children at home, the first two are about ready for college; I just opened an office in Tulsa; and I've taken on several big civic jobs in Oklahoma City. So I'd like to do it, but this just isn't the right time." Frankly, it was the only political office Ray ever thought he might seek someday.

Johnston, persistent in his belief that Ray could lead Oklahoma City to greater prosperity, had a perfect rebuttal. He said, "Sometimes the bus only comes by once."[2]

Convinced he was the man for the job, Ray tossed his hat into the ring. His closest advisors believed the Oklahoma Publishing Company would not support Ray and would actually look for an opponent. For that reason, Ray's candidacy was kept secret with Ralph Bolen, another ARG member and prominent automobile dealer, agreeing to be a decoy. When probed by reporters, Bolen kept answering, "I'm giving it serious thought but haven't made my mind up yet."

Another man rumored to be interested in the mayor's office was Cain's Coffee Company founder William Morgan Cain.

Six weeks before the election, Ray's candidacy had to be made public so he would have time to campaign. ARG announced its slate; Ray, for mayor; and attorney Ben Franklin; housewife Patience Latting, who later served as Oklahoma City's first woman mayor; Dr. Charles Atkins; and insurance company executive Rowe Cook; for members of the city council.

A campaign brochure in Ray's mayoral race urged voters to "chARGe" to the polls, a symbol of Ray's support from ARG, the Association for Responsible Government.

At a news conference at the Sheraton-Oklahoma Hotel in downtown Oklahoma City, Ray and the other members of the ARG slate were introduced to the media. Ray said, "I believe Oklahoma City, with the proper coordination by its leadership, can become the greatest city in the world."[3]

Ray's platform was straightforward. He believed the mayor was the city's most important ambassador and would play a major role in developing an acceptable water conveyance plan from southeast Oklahoma to Oklahoma City and in the development of Will Rogers Field into a world-class airport to attract new industry.[4]

The Saturday after Ray announced his candidacy, he received a call from KWTV Television owner Edgar T. Bell who had inside information that Ray's friend, Tag Kimberling, was announcing for mayor that afternoon. However, a few hours later, Bell called back, laughing, and reported, "They just found out that Kimberling doesn't live in Oklahoma City and can't run for mayor."[5]

ARG opponents scrambled, looking for a worthy opponent for Ray. They settled on James H. Norick, a former mayor who had been defeated in his bid for re-election four years earlier. Norick, whose 1963 defeat was attributed to opposition from OPUBCO, was hesitant to enter the race. But, at the last minute, he agreed to run for his old office.[6]

As a relative unknown, compared to the former councilman and mayor, Ray accepted every invitation to appear at civic clubs, churches, and any other group that wanted to hear his ideas about the future of Oklahoma City. One night he spoke to a union meeting in Capitol Hill in a flight suit with his tuxedo underneath so he could attend the symphony later in the evening.

Campaign brochures described Ray as "a man in love with a city" and "an Oklahoman by choice," and outlined his plan for the city's future. Among improvements suggested by Ray were pay increases for policemen and firemen, relocation of the sewage

Ray, with only six weeks to campaign for mayor of Oklahoma City, took advantage of every opportunity to speak to groups from 10 to 300, wherever voters would listen to his ideas about the promotion of Oklahoma City.

Ray announced his candidacy at a news conference at the Sheraton-Oklahoma Hotel, Oklahoma City.

disposal plant, establishment of sub-police stations, expansion of city bus service, street and park improvements, redevelopment of downtown Oklahoma City, construction of new technical training and recreational facilities, and construction of a freeway bypass around the Classen Traffic Circle, a perennial bottleneck in northwest Oklahoma City.[7]

Norick anchored his campaign for mayor with the slogan aimed at the ARG, "Vote for straight government, not slate government."

In the March 21 election, Norick led Ray by only 300 votes of more than 38,000 cast, 17,685 to 17,385. Because the other three candidates in the race, H.R. Sidwell, Leo Santifer, and Jack K. Gillespie received 2,621 votes, Ray and Norick were thrown into an April 4 runoff.[8] Ray was confident about his chances in the runoff. He was elated that he ran so close to a former councilman and mayor after only a six-week campaign.

The Daily Oklahoman came out in support of Norick. Ray believed that his candidacy was opposed because of the perception that he was "in bed" with W.P. "Bill" Atkinson, publisher of the *Oklahoma Journal,* a newspaper launched to compete with *The Daily Oklahoman.* The newspaper's inaccurate perception was probably based on the fact that Ray's agency handled Atkinson's successful campaign for the Democratic nomination for governor in 1962. It was a little known fact that Ray actually refused to continue in Atkinson's general election campaign because Atkinson changed planks in his platform with which Ray disagreed. Atkinson was swamped by Republican Henry Bellmon in the November, 1962 general election.[9]

As the old saying goes, "Perception works just like reality." Knowing OPUBCO favored Norick, Ray, in hindsight, thought he should have gone to see publisher Edward L. Gaylord early on in the campaign to try to win his support. Had he known the content of two front-page editorials which would appear in *The Daily Oklahoman* on the Friday and Sunday before the election, he undoubtedly would have asked for a visit with Gaylord.[10]

The first editorial was entitled "Divided Interest," making the point that Ray's agency had numerous contracts with the City of Oklahoma City and had a lucrative $48,000 contract with the Urban Renewal Authority. The fact was that the Ackerman Agency handled two bond issues in the early 1960s, both successfully, but was paid by the business community. The agency never received a penny from the city. Of the $48,000 Urban Renewal Authority contract, Ray's agency received $18,000, *The Sunday Oklahoman* was paid more than $10,000 for a special section, and the other $20,000 was for miscellaneous small media contracts and out-of-pocket expenses. At Ray's request, a retraction appeared in the newspaper, but it was small and buried toward the back.[11]

The second editorial entitled, "Norick Preferred," attacked Ray for saying the city was broke when Norick left office before. What Ray had actually said on several occasions was that the city was "on the verge of bankruptcy" when Norick completed his first term as mayor, which was close to *The Daily Oklahoman*'s own accusation four years earlier that the city was "living from hand to mouth" in an anti-Norick editorial.[12]

In the runoff, with more than 30,000 votes cast, Norick defeated Ray by only 787 votes. After the votes were counted, Ray and Lou went with friends to the Oklahoma City Press Club. Hugh Morgan, a columnist for The *Oklahoma Journal,* wrote that Ray's strength was "ebbed by bewilderment." Morgan described the scene, "His muscles tensed. He rocked back and forth on the balls of his feet. He listened patiently while all of the 'hindsight' journalistic experts, including me, told him what he had done wrong in the campaign for mayor."

Morgan's observation of the election was summed up in one sentence, "Ray Ackerman, a vigorous young man cast in the mold of a John Lindsay [Mayor of New York City], had been defeated by smooth-talking James Norick."[13]

There was an unusual twist to Ray's loss in his political contest. After the election, he received a wire from Captain Davy Crockett, commanding officer of the Dallas Naval Air Station. It said, "We regret Oklahoma City did not recognize head and shoulders talent. Their loss is our gain!"[14] What Crockett meant was that Ray was being considered for promotion to wing staff commander of the 3,000 Naval reservists who trained each month at the Dallas facility. His superiors had struggled over a concern that if Ray had been elected mayor, he might not have sufficient time to be wing staff commander. The command post was an important factor in any future consideration for Ray's promotion to rear admiral.

Years after he lost the mayoral election, Ray reflected, "Obviously, I wanted to be both Mayor and Admiral, but maybe it worked out for the best. Once an Admiral, always an Admiral. But you're only a Mayor for four or eight years!"[15]

FATHER KNOWS BEST

RAY RECEIVED GREAT SATISFACTION from work-
ing his way into leadership positions of civic and charitable organizations. He was driven by the sincere belief that pro bono work
done on behalf of community projects was an "amazing and
meaningful contribution to the fabric of a quality life." Almost
every year he took on a new responsibility. In 1968, Ray was
elected chairman of the Salvation Army Advisory Board in Oklahoma City and president of the Oklahoma City Council of the
Navy League. The following year, he took over as State President
of the Navy League.

Even though community work was satisfying, it was Ray's
family that truly made life the most interesting and worthwhile.
With six children in the family, every day was a new adventure.

Ray and Lou were a good team. She was absolutely dedicated
to creating a wonderful home life for Ray and the children. Had
she not married Ray in 1948, Lou would have attended the
Kansas City Institute of Art to follow her art career. However, as
her marriage produced children early, the art career had to be
postponed.

As soon as their youngest child entered school, Lou took

Ray was Lou's biggest supporter as she displayed her art at the Oklahoma City Festival of the Arts.

lessons and began to paint again; first oils, then watercolors. Her recognized strength was painting faces of girls and women, a strength that Ray said "proves the fact that she is a really good person. Her paintings reflect that goodness in a beautiful way."

Being a natural promoter, Ray often wanted to promote Lou, but she would have none of that. She was comfortable with her station in life as a wife and mother—and artist when she had time. She painted at her own pace, often completing a work for a special birthday or Christmas present for a member of the family.[1]

The nurses were probably right when they said the Ackermans' first child, Patricia Ann, "Patsy," was the prettiest baby they had ever seen. She had a full head of long black hair that the nurses had tied a bow in when they delivered her to Lou. She was born on March 25, 1948, only 87 minutes after Lou woke Ray up and said, "Let's go to the hospital!"

Patsy graduated from St. Charles Borromeo Grade School and McGuinness High School in Oklahoma City; attended St. Mary's College in Leavenworth, Kansas, for two years; and graduated from the University of Oklahoma with a bachelor's degree in Spanish and English literature. She later earned a master's degree in counseling at the University of Northern Colorado. She and her husband lived in Redmond, Washington, in 2002, where Patsy worked in a high-fashion clothing store.

Patsy remembered her father as a "hugger and kisser" but as a tough disciplinarian. Even though her mother "whipped the hardest," with a handy hairbrush, a threat that "Dad will take care of this situation when he gets home" caused ripples of fear through Patsy and her younger brothers and sisters. Ray closely monitored his children's academic progress by meticulously reviewing periodic report cards. If there were Bs on the report, Ray told them, "You can do better."[2]

Admitting that as a little girl she had a crush on her father, Patsy recalled Ray being larger than life. She said, "He would sweep my mom into his arms and give her this romantic kiss that I will always remember."

Ray and Lou enjoyed dressing up in western wear, especially for events each year when Ray was general manager of the National Finals Rodeo in Oklahoma City.

Ray's access to creative people at his agency allowed the Ackerman family to produce an annual Christmas card to send to clients, friends, and family. At right is the front of the 1962 card and below is the inside. . .

Dec the halls

Ann *Pat*

Susie *Ray*

with wreat of holly

Amy *Mark*

and may *your* holidays be jolly!

The Ray Ackermans

. . . posed in the Ackerman living room, far from the snow it depicted. Left to right, Annie, Ray K., Susie, Mark, Amy, and Patsy.

Merry Christmas
. . . come on in!
The Ray Ackermans

The 1965 Ackerman family Christmas card.

Lou and Ray had a thoughtful plan for paying the expenses of a college education for each child. They told the children they had opened a savings account for each at birth, had contributed to it regularly, and taught them to deposit in the account gift money from relatives as they were growing up. Each child was guaranteed sufficient money would be in their account at age 17 to pay for the first year of college. However, the children were required to get a job to pay for miscellaneous expenses. Beginning with their sophomore year. Ray and Lou would pay one-half of the cost of tuition, books, and room and board. They would loan a child the other half, expecting repayment in the years following graduation.

As oldest daughter Patsy neared high school graduation, Ray went over the plan in detail with her. Patsy thoughtfully said, "I don't think I want to go in that much debt." The "Ackerman College Education Plan" immediately was modified.

During her junior year at the University of Oklahoma, Patsy took up skydiving. On Sundays, she went with a group to Stroud, Oklahoma, to make several jumps. She talked to her father one night about dropping out of college to go barnstorming as a skydiver. Fortunately, Ray talked her out of it. After a doctor discovered she had double-jointed shoulders that began popping out when her parachute opened, Patsy gave up the sport.

Lou and Ray certainly did not raise any "dummies." About a month before Patsy's marriage to Phil Conley in March, 1971, Ray overheard her talking with Lou about the combo that was playing at the wedding reception. With six children, one just out of college, several in college, and several on their way, dollars were not exactly flowing freely. Ray asked Patsy, "Who said you could hire a combo for the reception?" Her reply, with a look of wide-eyed innocence, was, "Daddy, you said I could when I asked you last Christmas Eve."

Patsy and Phil had a son, Jason, the first grandchild of Lou and Ray, who graduated from the University of Washington, passed his CPA exam on the first try, and was employed by a

Tempe, Arizona, accounting firm, Deloitte and Touche, in 2001. Patsy and Phil divorced when Jason was young. Later she married Mike Mehring, employed by Microsoft.

One of Patsy's fondest memories of childhood is brushing Ray's hair. She remembered, "He had fine, soft hair, and a lot of it, when he was young. It relaxed him for me to brush his hair while he was driving on long trips in the car." While Patsy brushed Ray's hair, he was prone to break into his rendition of "The Yellow Rose of Texas" or "When Irish Eyes Are Smiling." Patsy said, "My dad was a great singer."[3]

Ray paced the floor during Patsy's first date. When the doorbell rang, he yanked open the door and gave the young man a quick military inspection, head to toe. The next morning Patsy asked her father what she thought of her date. Ray replied, "I didn't like him. He had mud on his shoes. Any guy dating a daughter of mine should be spic 'n span." Patsy went crying to her room but admitted two weeks later that the boy always had mud on his shoes and she was terminating the budding relationship.

One of Patsy's early Valentine's Day cards to her father summarized her feelings. She wrote, "No matter how grown up I get, no matter how far I go, no matter who I meet, I'll never forget my first love, the first man in my life, my very first and always Valentine."[4]

Born on April 18, 1950, second daughter, Ann Carol, "Annie," shared a room for 21 years with Patsy, an accommodation that either brings sisters together as lifelong friends, or causes terrible animosity. Fortunately, for Patsy and Annie, and their parents, the girls' relationship was harmonious.

Ray remembered, "It's amazing that Annie grew up to be such a wonderful lady." Ray, who was always nauseated by dirty diapers, seldom had to change one. However, after Lou had gone to church one Sunday morning, Annie "filled one up." Holding his nose with one hand and unpinning her diaper with the other,

The Ackermans sat for a formal family photograph in 1967. Back row, left to right, Patsy, Annie, Ray K. and Amy. Front row, left to right, Susie, Mark, Ray, and Lou.

Ray washed the baby off under the spray of a warm shower. Annie cried a bit harder, but only for a minute or two.[5]

Annie was very creative and always finished on time whatever she wanted to do. But some activities were cliff-hangers. On the morning of her high school prom, she bought a pattern and material for a formal dress. When her date called for her that evening, she was putting the last stitches in the hem.

Annie graduated from elementary school at St. Charles Borromeo; McGuinness High School, where she was a cheerleader; and the University of Oklahoma where she majored in art history. In 2002, she lived with her husband, Ron Adams, in Dallas where she worked as a freelance graphic designer. Annie and her brothers and sisters worked at least once in their lives for Ray's advertising agency. Annie spent more time at the agency than any of the other children except Mark.

Ray's kindness struck Annie as very special. She explained, "He was nice to everybody. He didn't leave anyone out. When he walked into a room, he paid attention to every one."[6]

Discipline meted out by Ray was swift and often loud. "He did yell at us from time to time," said Annie, "but we laughed later when we relived it." Once Ray got over his immediate anger, he sat down with a child and explained in great detail how they had "messed up."

Ray made his children feel important. Even though he worked impossible hours to build his advertising business, all his children remember special times. When Annie was in the seventh grade, she could not serve a volleyball over the net, a prerequisite for making her school team. Ray taught her to serve and hit the ball well over the net.

The 1967 Christmas card depicted a "posed" photograph of the Ackerman family playing in the surf at St. Petersburg, Florida. Left to right, Annie, Susie, Patsy, Ray K., Amy, Ray, Mark, and Lou.

Ray was not particularly handy around the house, Annie remembered. Once when Lou asked him to paint a wall in the kitchen, the project did not go smoothly. Annie overheard Ray say, "Hells bells!" It was funny to young Annie but not funny to Ray when she repeated the words later at dinner.[7]

The 1970 family Christmas card illustrated six books on a shelf with a picture of one of the children on each spine, together with a book title indicative of each one's personality at the time. The card was labeled "For Your Library of Best Wishes for the Holidays." Patsy's volume was "A March Marriage," Annie's was "You Think Pauline Had Perils?," Ray's was "Long Hair Looks at Sea Cadet Boot Camp," Susie's was "Dancing Through Life," Mark's was "The Art of Goldbricking," and Amy's card was labeled "Life As a Bowl of Cherries."[8]

In her early twenties, Annie was dating a fellow named Chip, whom she knew Ray did not like. Ray's opinion was based upon the fact that Chip had said he wanted to work hard until he was about 40, then retire and fish for the rest of his life like his father. Regardless, Annie decided to marry Chip and the announcements were at the printer when Ray came home one summer afternoon and saw Annie and Chip talking down by the lake. Ray told Lou, "I'm going down there, put my arm around Chip, and lie, when I say, 'Chip, I'm glad you're coming into the family.'" Lou answered, "Don't bother. Annie is down there calling off the wedding." The presses were stopped just in time.[9]

About six or seven years later, Annie was engaged to a young lawyer named Kevin in Dallas. The Ackermans were about to go on their annual vacation to Padre Island, Texas, and Ray told Annie to invite Kevin; that the family would pay for his lodging and meals. Kevin accepted. Ray at first liked the young man but had second thoughts when Kevin made no effort during the vacation to pay his own green fees at the golf course. Some months later, Ray was delighted when Annie called off the marriage just three days before the wedding. Lou and Ray frantically called relatives all over the country with the change of plans and returned wedding gifts. Ray even ended up at the door of the church on the wedding day to break the news to guests who had not been contacted.[10]

In 1986, Annie, at age 36, started seeing Ron Adams. All the family liked him and secretly hoped Annie would marry him. Ray, wanting the best for his daughter, and not mincing words, got Ron off in a corner at Amy's wedding reception two years later and boldly said, "If you're serious about Annie, you need to get married now before it's too late for her to have a baby. If you're not serious about marriage, go away while she still has time to find another guy who will want to marry her and have a baby."

Ray remembered, "I had never seen a guy's eyes bug out like Ron's. And to this day, I can't remember whether he had any response or not." What Lou and Ray did remember was that about three months later on a Sunday morning they were eating breakfast when they received a call from Santa Fe that Annie and Ron and eloped and were on their honeymoon.[11]

Three months after the marriage, everyone was delighted to find out that Annie was pregnant. They were devastated when Annie lost the baby a few weeks later. Fortunately, she was pregnant again in six months and delivered a beautiful little girl, Elizabeth Veronica, whose initials E.V. became her nickname, Evie.

Ray recalled a very special valentine from Annie that read, "Dear Dad, you have always been a romantic to me, sometimes naïve, never jaded. Thinking about you touches my heart. Happy Valentine's Day to my sweet, romantic Daddy. I love you."[12]

The Ackermans' third daughter, Beth, was born April 23, 1953, but died six weeks later because of an enlarging heart.

Ray K. was the first boy in the Ackerman family, born October 5, 1954. Beginning with Patsy, and later with Annie, Lou and Ray had grown accustomed to attending parent-teacher meetings and beaming while the teacher extolled the virtues of their children. When they sat down to hear the first report on their son's progress, they learned that he was not doing very well in school. The teacher tried to soften the blow, explaining why she knew he was smart. However, she said, he tended to show off, trying to entertain other students, and did not pay attention.

The family struggled through counseling sessions, all to no avail. At the end of the third grade, it was as if a light turned on in Ray's head one day when he suggested to Lou that he consult with Father Charles Beckman, their pastor at St. Charles Borromeo. When Ray visited the rectory, Father Beckman was not at home. However, his assistant, Father Paul Gallatin, had great advice. He recognized that Ray K. lived in a female-dominated house with his mother, two older sisters, and a younger sister and a father who was gone from home most of the time.[13]

Ray admitted he was making the common mistake of coming home at night and kissing his wife and daughters but shaking hands with his son. Father Gallatin suggested Ray walk in their door that night, pick up his son first and kiss him soundly on both cheeks. Ray followed the priest's admonition and thought Ray K. was going to faint. However, problems in school stopped immediately, and, as Ray reflected, "He's been nothing but a joy ever since."[14] Ray K. graduated from St. Charles Borromeo and then from the original Putnam City High School.

Ray and Lou paid very little of Ray K.'s college expenses. He earned good money as a waiter, then a cook at local restaurants. Ray did encourage his son to sign up for Navy Reserve Officers Training Corps (NROTC). Ray K. had enjoyed three years as a Sea Cadet with summer cruises from San Diego, California, to Portland, Oregon, at the submarine base at Groton, Connecticut, and at the Great Lakes Naval Training Station. He thoroughly enjoyed the duty so Ray thought he was a natural for NROTC. But, after thinking it over, Ray K. said, "Dad, the Navy's not for me." Although mildly disappointed, Ray understood.

After graduating with a degree in broadcast journalism at the University of Oklahoma, Ray K. traveled as a representative of the Sigma Phi Epsilon fraternity and worked at several radio stations in Oklahoma City. While in high school, Ray K. watched the devotion of his parents as good Catholics. He admired their regular attendance at Mass and their support of the local church.

When he thought that he might want to be a priest, he passed off the idea as "the most ridiculous notion I could ever conceive." Later, in college, when the idea resurfaced, Ray K. said he thought "it was the most cruel joke God could play on the Catholic Church."[15]

Ray K. worked as a standup comedian, in addition to his full-time job as a radio time salesman and disc jockey. Once, his employer tried to convince him to give up his Catholic faith and attend a non-denominational charismatic church. Ray K., possibly being "chased back to my own church," became more active in his Catholic congregation, became a lector, and joined the choir. Soon, he entered St. Meinrad Seminary in Indiana. During his training, he studied in Rome, San Antonio, and Mexico City, and after six years, was ordained a priest in 1991. He was first an assistant pastor at St. Phillip Neri Church in Del City, Oklahoma, then president of Mount Saint Mary's High School in Oklahoma City. In 1999, Ray K. was assigned as pastor of St. Joseph's in Ada, Oklahoma, where he was given the responsibility for the welfare of 230 Catholic families.[16]

Ray and Lou insisted that their children perform household and yard tasks and not expect any remuneration for the work. Work projects for each child were posted weekly on the family refrigerator.

Ray K. remembered the memos. "They taught us not to procrastinate. We knew we would get in trouble if we did not meet dad's expectations. Often, I was mowing the lawn at twilight, hoping that dad's car would not turn into the driveway before I finished," he recalled. Ray taught his children to complete the most difficult job first, making it easier to complete the "things-to-do" list. Every child had a chore; the youngest usually began by picking up sticks from the large yard.[17]

There was a reward if the Ackerman children completed their tasks. Their father and mother hosted parties at Broadlawn Lake. When family, the Karl Ackermans, the Veecks, the Rockwoods, or the Flanagans, arrived for a visit, the Ackerman property became one big party site. Parties consisted of swimming, badminton, volleyball, basketball, horseshoes, and lots of great food. However, family picnics brought a fair share of work for the children. The lawn had to be manicured, tables set up, and food carried from the kitchen to the patio.

Ray did not hesitate to admit when he was wrong in dealing with his children. One day, when Ray K. was 16, a home hot water heater malfunctioned and young Ray obtained advice on replacement of the thermocoupler from a neighbor. Ray K. bought a new part at a hardware store and proudly repaired the water heater. But, his list of chores remained undone.

When Ray arrived and discovered the uncompleted items on the chore list, he accused Ray K. of "dinking" all day. With his lower lip trembling, Ray K. explained he had spent the day repairing the water heater. Instantly, Ray apologized to his son.

Ray K., taking advantage of his father's shocked look, said he also did not like the word "dinking." Ray admitted he was completely unaware the word offended his son. "Dinking" was never used in subsequent conversations.[18]

The most touching moment Ray K. remembered about his father was when he burst into the bedroom one night and found his father, in his nightshirt on his knees, saying his nightly prayers. Even though Ray K. had completed seminary, it was the first time he ever saw his father during the private time of saying prayers. Ray K. recalled, "I went back to my room and sat there and cried. I was so proud of my father for his devotion to his faith."[19]

Ray cherished a Father's Day card from Ray K. It read, "Thanks for all the life lessons I learned from you. I appreciate the gift of your loving care more and more each year. You are a big part of what I have to share in the priesthood and I thank God for you every day, Dad. Love, Ray."[20]

Daughter, Susie, born April 29, 1957, reminded Ray of the lyrics of the old song, "If you knew Susie like I know Susie, oh, oh, oh, what a gal!" While the Ackerman children were away at school, he never recalled getting a telephone call bearing bad news. But he did remember many telephone calls from Susie that brought good news.

Susie also graduated from St. Charles Borromeo and was a cheerleader at Putnam City High School for four years while the Pirates football team went undefeated. However, she decided not to try out for cheerleader at the University of Oklahoma. But new Sooner basketball coach, Dave Bliss, moved to "spice up" home basketball games with a squad of Pom-Pon girls. Bliss recruited Susie, as leader and choreographer, and four other girls to try to improve fan support and morale. Rumor had it that even the cheerleaders often did not show up for OU home basketball games.

Susie dropped one of those bits of good news in her proud parents' lap on the day before the Oklahoma-Ohio State football game in the fall of 1977. On the Friday before the game, a picture of Susie and the other girls was prominently displayed on the front page of the *Oklahoma City Times.* She called with news that the Pom-Pon girls would be part of the game's program in Columbus, Ohio, and, at Coach Barry Switzer's request, would perform at all OU football games from then on. Susie and her squad appeared on national television at least eight times during the Ohio State game. It was the introduction of Pom-Pon girls to college football, in the same manner as they were introduced by the Dallas Cowboys to the National Football League.[21]

Susie's cheerleading led to great summer jobs. In 1977, when the National Association of Cheerleaders and Pom-Pon girls was paying Susie to tour the country by air to put on clinics for young girls, she wrote Ray, "I want to share a little poem with you that reminds me of our relationship: 'You've not only been my father, but also my closest friend. Don't walk in front of me, I might not follow. Don't walk behind me, I might not lead. Just walk beside me and be my friend.' I've always felt so lucky, Dad, and I guess Father's Day is a good time to tell you I love you with all my heart."[22]

In 1981, Susie married Doug Fuller of Ponca City, Oklahoma, a senior vice president of the Bank of Oklahoma. She remembered that her Dad wanted to sing "Daddy's Little Girl" at her wedding. But she cried so hard when he was practicing, they dropped the idea. Susie and Doug had two children, Alexander and Alyssa. In 2002, Susie was an exercise physiologist and adjunct professor at the University of Central Oklahoma.[23]

Susie remembered her family eating on the "European schedule." The children ate dinner around 6:30 P.M., did their homework, and went to bed. Lou waited until Ray came home, often as late as 9:00 or 10:00 P.M. to have dinner.

When Susie drove a National Finals Rodeo official car into a post, her father reacted gingerly, saying, "I don't know what to say to you. I know you already have kicked yourself around the block several times.[24]

Ray refused to succumb to the popular trend of allowing children to have their own telephone lines. He also once purchased an hourglass to force the children to limit their phone calls to one, two, or three minutes, depending on who was being called.

Susie and her brothers and sisters enjoyed riding to school with Ray some mornings. They envied their father going off to the office with a stress-free life.

Mark, born June 15, 1960, was the Ackermans' second boy. Of Mark, Ray wrote, "If you were to be marooned on a desert island for six months with only one male, and you had your choice of who that would be, take Mark. He has the best disposition and best sense of humor in the family, a hair-trigger mind, and a ready wit."[25]

A barbecue to celebrate the groundbreaking for the clubhouse at Quail Creek Golf and Country Club in the spring of 1960 was held on what became the 18th green. As charter members, Lou and Ray attended and 30 days later Mark was born. Ray realized that even as a little boy Mark watched golf on television. Then he noticed Mark dug holes in the back yard, found an old golf ball, and was hitting it with a stick! A set of golf clubs and lessons followed shortly. Mark turned out to be a great natural golfer and Ray always believed the Quail Creek barbecue had something to do with it.

Ray did not coddle his children when competing with them in sports. Mark remembered "knock down, drag out battles," especially in basketball and ping pong. He said, "We'd play horse or shoot free throws and play ping pong for hours." It was tough for Mark to overcome Ray's competitive spirit and finally beat his father in a particular game.

Mark was especially proficient in golf and ping pong. While Mark was still quite young, Ray was often heard saying, "OK, then let's make it five out of nine, or let's go to seven out of twelve." Finally he would give up and admit Mark was the true sports champion of the family, in his father's words, "a super-athlete in all sports."[26]

Mark followed Ray K. and Susie through St. Charles and then Putnam City High School, majored in oral communications at the University of Oklahoma, and worked at a bowling center for several years where he bowled a few 300 games. In 2001, he was employed at the Tulsa office of Ackerman Mc-Queen. He was groomed for the job by Ray and Lou's nephew, Bill Winker, chief financial officer and chief operating officer of Ackerman McQueen. Ray did not encourage his children to make advertising a career because it meant many 60-plus hour, seven-day weeks. But Ray believes Mark is a "natural ad man."

Mark frequently provided drama, humor, or a mix of both, on vacations. Coming back from the west coast on their 1962 vacation, the family accidentally left Mark, who was only two years old, in a service station. About five or ten miles down the road, Ray realized he needed to call the Air Station in Dallas about his upcoming drills and stopped at a roadside phone. He was in the phone booth when a Sinclair gasoline truck drove up, the driver opened the door, and Mark got out with the maddest look on his face Ray had ever seen. Mark stomped to the station wagon and climbed in, not saying a single word to anyone.[27]

The family tried South Padre Island on Texas' Gulf Coast in 1963, spending a night en route at the Sand Dollar, a brand new motel in Rockport, Texas. Mark locked himself in the bathroom. He loved to eat ice and there was a bucketful by the bathroom sink. Talking to him through a big space under the door, Ray promised Mark some of the ice to eat if he would get off the toilet and open the door. Ray recalled, "Hallelujah! I could see Mark walk to the ice bucket, take out a piece, and slide it under the door to me. But he did not unlock the door!" A workman had to take out the bathroom window to let Mark out. Unbelievably, the same thing happened the following day.

It was Mark's first encounter with salt water waves and he did not like it a bit. His father tried to keep him from being scared but was unsuccessful. Even though he was only three, Mark was smart enough to put his shoes on when he got up in the morning, knowing he would not have to get in the water as long as he was wearing them.

Ray always communicated well, and often, with his children. When he did yell at them, he always made up later. Mark remembered, "When he got upset, you knew it if you were in the house. But I don't remember a time when he did not make up at some point, come back to my room, and tell me why he was frustrated at me."28

In 1989, Mark married Deanna Winfrey. In 2002, they lived in Broken Arrow, Oklahoma, with son Raymond Bryan, and daughter, Samantha Riley Ackerman.

Mark wrote Ray one Father's Day, "I love your sense of humor, even making not-so-funny things like yard work into memorable moments with your wit. I'm proud to be your son and pray that I can be the kind of a father to my children that you have been and still are to me." 29

Amy was the final child of the Ray and Lou Ackerman clan, born November 15, 1961. In 2001, Ray said of Amy, "She's a beautiful little waif. Even as she approaches 40, her 'at peace' face could pass for the face of a teenager."

Amy enjoyed growing up on Broadlawn Lake. On summer days she could sit on the dock for hours, dangling her feet in the water, listening to the summer sounds of beetles and grasshoppers. In early 1982, when Lou and Ray decided to sell the lake property and move to a smaller home, Amy was hardest hit by the news. Through gushing tears, she asked her father, "Couldn't you wait to sell the house until one of your children is rich enough to buy it?"[30]

The only less-than-perfect aspect of Amy's life was she genuinely believed that no one liked her at school. Her parents could not imagine why she did not appear to have a host of friends. On the night of Amy's graduation from Putnam City High School, Ray "almost took a header off the top row of the stadium," when Amy was introduced as "the most popular girl in school." After the ceremony, Ray asked her, "Nobody likes you, huh?" Amy gave her Dad a little impish grin and said nothing. She was a good athlete, particularly in volleyball and track. Watching her in action, Ray thought, "grace personified."[31]

In the spring before Amy started college, her sister Annie had decided to sell her Volkswagen Beetle and Ray bought it from her. For the next few months, he had it reupholstered, checked mechanically and structurally, and painted a beautiful University of Oklahoma red. It was presented to Amy as her Christmas present that year, for her transportation to and from school in Norman.

She switched majors a couple of times, and in her fifth or sixth year at OU, told her father she needed a new car. Ray said she would have to get by with the VW until she could graduate, get a job, and buy a new car. However, when Ray overheard Amy telling her mother that she could "see the highway through the floor" of the VW, he bought her a new Honda within 24 hours.

"Dad ran a tight ship at home," she recalled. Amy earned a degree in dietetics from the University of Oklahoma and a degree in physical therapy from Langston University. She married

Dr. Jeffrey Shaver, a third generation opthalmologist. In 2002, Amy lived in Edmond, Oklahoma, with her husband and their five children, Sophie Elizabeth, Lucy Bernadette, Henry Maximillian, and Annie Clare and Lily Therese, twins born January 28, 2002.

Amy described her father as "a real Catholic family man." Ray expected the truth, the whole truth, and nothing but the truth from his children. He insisted the youngsters practice the Golden Rule. [32]

The older children believe that by the time Amy came along, Ray and Lou had loosened their rules slightly. Amy disagreed, citing instance after instance of Ray expressing strong convictions about everything, from boys she dated to what subjects she should take in school.

"My dad was full of love," Amy said. "He picked us up and hugged and kissed us. He sang and danced and sang to me 'Once in Love with Amy.' He entertained us on car trips with jokes and songs like 'Old Man River' and 'She Has Freckles on Her Butt, I Love Her.'" Ray finally got to sing "Daddy's Little Girl" to all four of his daughters at Amy's wedding reception.[33]

The children saw how kind their father treated their mother, how much they were in love. Amy said, "He was in love with her bubbly eyes."

Amy's major responsibility on the family chore list was keeping the street egress to the Ackerman home clean. Amy was embarrassed when she overheard neighbors say, "Oh, there's that little Ackerman girl cleaning up the street again for us. Isn't that sweet!"

As Ray allocated chores for the children, Lou was concerned about their eating habits. Amy cannot recall ever seeing white bread in the house. She remembered taking her lunch to school and not being able to trade with other kids, "Everybody around me had white bread and bologna and cheese and a bag of Cheetos and a Twinkie. No one wanted my egg salad sandwich and apple."[34]

As all the children reached dating age, Ray set down strict curfews. To monitor when the children came home, he installed a "pig bell" on the door. When the door opened, the bell rang out. However, Amy figured a way around the pig bell. She learned to open the door slowly, reach inside, and hold the bell's clanger, while she entered the house.

Ray closely reviewed boyfriends who came calling on his daughters. If he did not like the boys, the girls inevitably moved on to another beaux.

Even though he was known for his tough dealing in business, Ray was a "softie" in his feelings for his children. When each left the nest and went away for college, he sat at his desk and cried. Amy said, "His greatest achievement may have been raising his kids." [35]

Ray most remembered a birthday greeting from Amy. Her note said, "I love you with all my heart. Thank you for teaching me about discipline, commitment, and unconditional love—I thank you and Mom for the gift of life and thanks for being a great daddy! Your baby, Amy."[36]

Being blessed with six living children out of seven, Ray and Lou were always thankful they had never even thought about whether or not they could afford them. However, Patsy and Annie, home for a visit when their younger sisters still lived at home, noted that the smaller family had "eased up on financial matters." They said, "Our parents drove a Pontiac. Susie and Amy's parents drive a Mercedes."

NEW YORK, NEW YORK
AND NATIONAL PREZ

WITH THE THEME, "Madison Avenue Comes to Oklahoma City," Ray began a new era in his advertising agency in 1969. For years Ray dreamed of building his agency to a size that could handle the largest advertising accounts in Oklahoma, such as Phillips Petroleum Company, with a $20 million annual budget that was handled by a New York City agency, and strong enough to survive and grow after his career was over. When Jack Wyatt dropped into Ray's office in August, 1969, with a proposition, it hit Ray that he was not on track to fulfill his dreams and that Wyatt might have the answer.

Ray was proud of having increased the size of the agency 20 times over in just 17 years, from $250,000 in annual billing to just under $5 million. On the other hand, he did not see any clear path for future growth.[1]

At age 47, Ray decided to join forces with Lennen & Newell (L & N), the world's 17th largest advertising agency, heavy in food products clients, headquartered in New York City. The idea came from Wyatt, a partner in the Wyatt and Williams Agency in Dallas that had already merged into L & N. Ray believed

Ray signs the contract formalizing the merger of Ackerman Associates with Lennen and Newell (L & N), a major New York City advertising agency, on December 1, 1969. Watching Ray are, left, Jack Speirs, executive vice president of L & N, and Jack Wyatt, of Wyatt and Williams Agency in Dallas.

merging Ackerman with L & N, which employed 750 people in 17 cities, would result in a bright future for his agency. L & N had major national accounts such as Muriel cigars, the Florida Citrus Commission, McCormack food products, Stokely-Van Camp, and Reynolds Metals Company, and billed $130 million annually, a giant in the industry in those days.

Merger may have been the wrong word for the marriage of Ackerman Inc. and L & N. The New York City agency actually purchased 80 percent of the stock of Ackerman, Inc. Ray took the agency's half ownership of the Ackerman Building on Mosteller Drive as part of his payout. Shareholders of Ackerman, Inc. also were guaranteed annual payments for five years.

The merger was announced at an important Oklahoma City Chamber of Commerce meeting at the Biltmore Hotel. L & N CEO Adolph Toigo was scheduled to come to Oklahoma City for the announcement. However, Toigo canceled at the last minute and sent as his replacement, Jack Speirs. When the L & N official rose to speak, he grabbed hold of the podium with both hands and said nothing. The man's hands were shaking and Ray knew there would be no speech.

The silence was deafening. Ray rescued the man by getting up, putting his arm around the "speaker," and saying, "This announcement is so important to Oklahoma City, so overwhelming, that Mr. Speirs is just choked with emotion." Ray had never been so embarrassed in his life and suspected Speirs needed his martinis before lunch like he always had in New York.

Later Toigo's wife admitted to Ray, in all seriousness, that her husband did not want to come to Oklahoma because he was afraid of being attacked by the Indians. To Toigo, there was "not much out there" west of the Hudson River.[2]

The association with L & N got off to a great start when Ray was able to convince Jim Fuller, vice president of public relations for Bell Helicopter, to move its account to Ackerman from Wyatt & Williams (W & W). This opportunity presented itself because W & W's biggest account, LTV, had acquired the distribution rights in the United States to a French helicopter, the Alouette, and could not handle both accounts. More than half of Bell's business was with the military so Ray wore his Navy uniform during a visit to the Bell plant in Arlington, Texas, to meet with company officials.

Fuller made the decision to move the Bell account to Ackerman with Ray as the account supervisor out of Oklahoma City, provided that Ackerman open a service office in Fort Worth, Texas, manned by both military and commercial account executives from Bell's former agency, and Ackerman's sister agency, W & W. Of course it did not hurt Ray's solicitation of the account that Fuller knew Ray's pretty sister, M' Fran, 25 years earlier when he was a sportswriter in San Diego and she was advance publicist for the Ice Capades. Ray agreed to the terms.

However, one hurdle remained in sealing the deal on the Bell Helicopter account. Ray was assigned the task of selling Bell international sales manager Dwayne Jose on the idea. Jose had been out of the country when Fuller made the decision. Ray, and the former W & W account supervisor on the Bell account, and a good friend of Jose, met with Jose for dinner at an upscale Washington, D.C., restaurant, during a helicopter convention.

The former account man did not have a good night. He was drinking heavily before and during dinner. Later Ray was informed that the man's fiancée had accompanied him to Washington, D.C., for the purpose of getting married. However, she had jilted him.

After Ray told Jose all about the Ackerman agency, he said, "Well, what do you think of being served by us?" At the moment Jose answered, "I don't like it worth a damn!" the former account supervisor, almost on cue, fell asleep with his face in his plate.[3]

Ackerman never overcame that miserable start with Bell. The new office in Fort Worth handled the account for six months, after which the Alouette flew back to France, Bell Helicopter flew back to W & W, and Ackerman closed its office and flew back to Oklahoma City.

Nothing good happened with Lennen & Newell after that. Ackerman had been doing a little business with the *Los Angeles Examiner* when suddenly the newspaper announced, "Cash in Advance". When the words, "A division of Lennen & Newell" were added to Ackerman's contracts and insertion orders, the agency suddenly had bad credit. It was alarming, to say the least.

There was a glimmer of hope when Wilson Foods moved its headquarters from Chicago to Oklahoma City in 1970. Wilson had been a big L & N account in the past but had changed agencies because their account manager left L&N. Because the manager was back with L&N in New York, Ackerman's chances of regaining the Wilson account looked good. It did not take Ray long to make a call on the Vice President of Marketing for Wilson, Harry Barger.

Barger hit Ray with the worst verbal barrage to which he had ever been subjected. Barger accused Ray of spreading a rumor that the reason L & N acquired Ackerman was because of an understanding that L & N would get the Wilson account back.

In reality, the Wilson move and the L & N acquisition were totally unrelated. Ray tried to convince Barger of that fact and that he had not even heard the rumor. He was only half successful at best.

Several follow-up solicitations were made until Ackerman discovered that Wilson was receiving extended credit from its agency in Chicago, Campbell Ewald, and Ray really did not want an account that was using its agency as its bank. Much later, in 1985, the agency did do some work for Wilson.

As national President of the Naval Reserve Association, Ray often traveled to Washington, D.C., for visits with Secretary of Defense Melvin Laird, left. The organization represented 15,000, mostly retired, Navy officers.

A sample of print ads developed by Ackerman, Inc., for the Daisy Manufacturing Company, maker of Daisy air rifles. In the 1950s, the company moved from Chicago, Illinois, to Rogers, Arkansas. Ray solicited the account at that time but was politely informed his agency was too small to consider. At the same time Marvin McQueen solicited the account successfully for D'Arcy out of St. Louis and handled it for many years. So the Ackerman agency was not a stranger when it successfully landed the account in 1977. A national campaign introduced Daisy's new compressed gas pistol, an attempt to expand the company's market from the traditional BB-gun. Football stars Johnny Unitas and Gale Sayers joined hockey great Bobby Hull in promoting Daisy products.

Ray was spending a lot of time in Washington because of his Navy duties, particularly on Capitol Hill. He ran into the CEO of L & N, Adolph Toigo, on several occasions and always saw a peculiar look in Adolph's eyes. He knew Toigo was thinking, "I wonder why the president of that tiny little agency in Oklahoma is up here?" Ray never told him.

One day Ray picked up his phone and it was Adolph Toigo on the line, unloading his problems. Having heard that the name of his psychiatrist was Dr. Ackerman, Ray suddenly realized Toigo thought that was who he was talking to. Ray surmised that Toigo probably said to his secretary, "Get Ackerman on the phone" and she got the wrong guy.

Undoubtedly, the right thing to do was for Ray to tell Toigo about the mistake. He did. Later, as things got worse with L & N, Ray wished he had "hung in there and listened to Adolph talk to his shrink!"[4]

The contract with L & N protected the Ackerman agency for five years during which Ackerman shareholders were to receive their annual payout. The New York office could not interfere with the operation of its Oklahoma shop during those years. However, L & N management tried little things, such as making Ackerman pay into a transportation pool, when very little traveling was needed. Ackerman just refused.

The rumors of the demise of L & N grew stronger when Ray heard in the summer of 1971 that the agency was selling assets. He began to hope L & N would come to him with an offer to sell back the 80 percent ownership.

Ray was with the family on vacation at Padre Island that summer when he received a call from Jack Speirs at L & N, telling him that a man named Marvin McQueen, who headed up D'Arcy's New York office, would like to meet him.

Because of financial problems, L & N had been talking merger to a number of large agencies in New York, including D'Arcy, so Marvin had seen L & N's books and knew they controlled a small agency in Oklahoma "that was making a buck or two." As D'Arcy was talking about a merger with McManus and Adams, an automobile agency headquartered in Detroit, Marvin was concerned about his future. His only daughter was married to a doctor in Tulsa and he thought the timing might be right for him to go back to the middle of the country where he was born, raised, educated, and worked, to join a local advertising agency, in a sort of senior citizen advisory capacity.

Ray met Marvin at a Hilton Hotel in Tulsa late that summer. They laughed later about their initial handshake, when each wondered if the other knew how bad the situation was at L & N. Marvin talked to the owners of several other agencies in Tulsa and Oklahoma City and decided to become associated with the Ackerman agency. A deal was struck for him to go to work in the Tulsa office effective January 1, 1972.[5]

In the meantime, Ray was waiting day by day for L & N to come to him with an offer to sell, rather than vice versa. Finally, they did and 16 key employees of Ackerman bought back all of the stock on December 13, 1971.

In 1969, Ray was elected as national President of the Naval Reserve Association, a 15,000-member group of mostly retired Navy officers between the ages of 40 and 65. Many of the organization's members were exceptionally successful in their civilian careers and influential in state and local politics.

Ray was active in expressing his opinions on Naval readiness to military leaders. He was concerned about the deteriorating condition of the Naval Air Reserve airlift capability. His ideas were valued by Navy Chief of Naval Operations, Admiral Elmo Zumwalt, Jr., who wrote, "We in the Navy acknowledge the deteriorating situation and plan to implement a continuing, if very modest, improvement despite a severe budgetary climate."

Ray, at Admiral Zumwalt's request, completed a tour of temporary duty as chair of a study group to recommend public affairs actions in support of American prisoners of war, men and women missing in action, and their families. Zumwalt wrote Ray of his appreciation, "I am grateful for the good works which you are doing for the Navy. The patriotic donation of your time and acumen is playing a vital role in keeping our Navy strong."[6]

Navy officials did not just file away Ray's recommendations for improving Navy readiness. When Ray made detailed suggestions on increasing effectiveness of Navy training methodology, including the upgrading of pay tables for Navy personnel, Vice Admiral D. H. Guinn, Chief of Naval Personnel, ordered a full review of the subject. Many of Ray's recommendations were ultimately adopted by the Bureau of Naval Personnel.

Ray took his concerns about Navy readiness to Secretary of the Navy John H. Chafee. In private discussions, and by letter, Ray "pulled no punches" in making observations and recommendations on how to improve the ability of the Naval Reserve to assist the active military forces in defense of the country. Chafee wrote, "I have enjoyed our chats and, like you, I do feel that these interchanges are of great importance."[7]

Chafee awarded the Navy Distinguished Public Service Award to Ray in September, 1971. It is the highest award given by the Secretary of the Navy for contributions to the Department of the Navy.

Possibly Ray's most important accomplishment during his two years at the helm of the Naval Reserve Association was to establish a successful Legislative Committee. He insisted that membership on the committee be limited to men and women who had attended school with, worked with, and personally knew members of Congress on a first name basis. Ray wanted only members on the Committee who could "just walk into a senator's or congressman's office."

In 1970, the bill funding the Navy aircraft carrier CVN-70, passed the United States Senate by only two votes. Ray took great pleasure in the fact that six members of the Legislative Committee had spent considerable time in the offices of six key senators in the days before the crucial vote.

THE MCQUEEN CONNECTION

ALTHOUGH JOINING L & N obviously did not work out as planned, Ray would have never met Marvin McQueen if the New York merger had not been made

With his vast experience in management, McQueen quickly became head of the Tulsa operation and president of the agency with Ray as chairman. Key people with him in the Tulsa office in the 1970s were Cecille Bales, Chad Stewart, Charles Hawkins, Claudia Lewis, John Kirk, Sammie Klaassen, Donna O'Rourke, Joan Hagers, Jeff Nauser, Leslie Bullock, Julie Blakemore, Debbie Nauser, Melanie Hill, and Tom Twomey.[1]

Just a few months prior to Marvin McQueen's coming on board, an unusual series of events led to a new client that became a bedrock or baseline account for the beginning of the McQueen era—the Nocona Boot Company.

In the fall of 1971, one of Oklahoma City's oldest advertising agencies, Humphrey/Williamson & Gibson (HW & G), closed its doors. HW & G CEO Mitch Williamson was among staff people Ray persuaded to join the agency and they brought

enough business with them to pay their salaries and overhead. Don Loewen, the dean of advertising art in Oklahoma City, was one of them, and he stayed for 20 years.

Shortly after arriving at Ackerman, Williamson received a call from the Nocona Boot Company in Nocona, Texas, wanting help with the production of the company's annual catalog.

In 1969, looking for new business, Williamson had played a speculative jingle for the company's advertising director who died two years later. The jingle was kept by Mel Chapman, the new advertising director, who tried to call HW & G when he was in Oklahoma City in December, 1971, for the National Finals Rodeo (NFR). When he found the advertising agency was out of business, he called Williamson at home. The next morning, Williamson rushed into Ray's office and told him about the call. The "chance" contact, plus Ray's position as NFR general chairman, resulted in Ackerman winning the Nocona account.

Miss Enid Justin, the only daughter of H.J. Justin, founder of the Justin Boot Company, was the owner of Nocona. Justin established his business in 1879 in Old Spanish Fort, Texas, where the Chisholm Trail crosses the Red River. He measured cowboys' feet, made the boots while they were on the trail going north, and the cowboys picked them up on the return trip to Texas.

Shortly after Justin died, his sons elected to move the boot company to Fort Worth, Texas. Miss Enid said, "Daddy wouldn't have done that," so she borrowed $5,000 and started Nocona Boot Company. A woman running a company, particularly what was considered a man's business, was unheard of in those days. Miss Enid sold firewood, appliances, and meals to oilfield workers to keep her small business going and she and her sister traveled all over Texas in a Model-T Ford selling Nocona boots.[2]

Since Al Fiegel had left Ackerman in 1970, Ray had been less than pleased with the creative work of the agency. Several people turned out credible, but not great, work. That changed when, at Marvin McQueen's recommendation, Ray visited Marvin's son, Angus, who worked at D'Arcy Advertising in New York City.

For the meeting, Ray wore what he called his "West Coast" sport clothes. He never knew until his retirement, 20 years later, just how startled Angus was when Ray showed up wearing lime green pants, white shoes, a green checked sport coat, and a bright green tie. Angus wrote Ray, "I knew immediately you were a man of great courage."

Ray told Angus he was looking to the future, searching for someone to follow in his footsteps, to grow the agency, to have a million-dollar client, and even "someday buy a computer."

Angus joined Ackerman, Inc., on July 1, 1973. Ray was nearly 51 and was looking for someone to succeed him someday as CEO of the agency. None of his current staff, before the arrival of Angus, was interested.

Angus was extremely qualified to immediately add creative excellence and future leadership to Ackerman, Inc. He had been a television director in St. Louis, Missouri, and Houston, Texas, and directed NBC news coverage of the Gemini space flights and the Apollo moon-landing mission. He also had written and produced advertising campaigns for national advertisers such as General Tire, Royal Crown Cola, Gerber Baby Foods, Lufthansa Airlines, and the USO. He was a member of "The November Group" that helped re-elect President Richard Nixon.

In the 1950s and 1960s, the Ackerman agency hit some home runs, particularly the B.C. Clark "Jewelry Is the Gift to Give" jingle and the "Oh Thank Heaven for 7-11" line for 7-11 Food Stores.

But from the day Angus McQueen joined the agency in 1973, the agency really got hot creatively, starting with the Nocona Boot Company.

The famous "Let's Rodeo" campaign introduced their new line to young people and quickly vaulted Nocona into a top position with Justin and Tony Lama. The music for the campaign was created by Mark Keller and the vocals were performed by him and Angus' wife, Jodi.

Creativity kicked into an even higher level with the "manageable controversy" campaign for Nocona Boot Company, voted best in the Southwest, an ad campaign which became legendary in footwear advertising throughout the country.

Beginning with the famous "rattlesnake ad," the campaign grew to a series of 12 ads, many of which also appeared on tee-shirts, posters, greeting cards, and outdoor billboards.

The Nocona story may best exemplify Angus McQueen's dedication to creative excellence. A new campaign for Nocona had been developed. Everyone felt good about it but Angus, at midnight, before he and others were to drive to Texas at 5:30 A.M. to make the presentation, thought of the "rattlesnake ad." He believed it was the idea that finally jelled after months of thinking about how to gain an advertising advantage for Nocona.

Angus called Mark Keller to come to his home, and within hours the new idea was illustrated and presented to Nocona management. It was received with enthusiasm. Ray recalled, "That was a home run with the bases loaded!"[3]

The advertising for Nocona brought in the Resistol account, the leading manufacturer of cowboy hats. The agency promptly created the award-winning line well known to rodeo fans, "Best All-Around."

A television commercial for Vickers Petroleum Company finished second to a Texaco commercial for a Clio Award. A television commercial for the First National Bank of Tulsa was voted one of the 100 best produced in the United States in 1976.

Three kinds of gas for your kind of car.

Unleaded.

Beginning with the 1975 models, all cars manufactured in this country will require unleaded gas, the cleanest of all automobile fuels. Generally, cars that run on regular will perform equally well with unleaded gasoline. Cars requiring premium, however, will not be able to use unleaded.

Regular.

Most of the cars manufactured today are geared to run on regular, the most economical of the three fuels. If regular gasoline is recommended for your car, continue to use it, but keep in mind that in most cases your car will perform equally well using an unleaded fuel.

Premium.

The premium user is pretty well locked in. If your car is designed to run on premium, the high performance fuel, it *requires* premium. The use of a lower octane fuel can cause serious damage to your car's engine.

We're selling all three.

Some oil companies have stopped selling premium. Not Vickers. We're going to continue to offer you whatever kind of gas you need — regular, unleaded or premium — because we know the right kind of gas is the key to your car's performance. So, keep us in mind. We're the little company that's *still* selling all three kinds. Look for the "V" — the Vickers sign.

We're the little company that's selling all three kinds of gas.

Major oil companies were criticized in 1976 for dropping premium gasoline when they had to add unleaded. Vickers Petroleum Company hired Ackerman, Inc., to promote it as "the little company selling all three kinds." This is one of the newspaper ads created by Ackerman. The agency hired actor George Gobel to appear in Vickers television commercials.

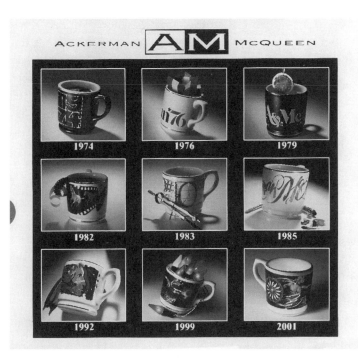

ACKERMAN AM McQUEEN

1974   1976   1979

1982   1983   1985

1992   1999   2001

Nine of the Ackerman Christmas coffee mugs. 1974-the first cup given at Christmas, 1973; 1976-in celebration of America's bicentennial; 1979-the cup announcing the name change from Ackerman to Ackerman McQueen; 1982-celebrating the art of film; 1983-the tenth cup in the series; 1985-An "artsy" Ackerman McQueen; 1992-in celebration of Oklahoma's Native America campaign; 1999-Rudolph leading us to the new millennium; and 2001. Courtesy Ackerman McQueen.

FACING: When Ackerman, Inc., took over the Nocona Boot Company account in 1971, the company's boots were becoming old fashioned. Ackerman assisted Nocona in developing new directions and aggressive campaigns that broadened the customer base enough to require doubling the manufacturing facilities. Ackerman staffers found that the new generation wanted rounder toes, brighter colors, and fancier stitching. The new line was introduced with the famous "Let's Rodeo" campaign, followed by the mini-drama campaign kicked off with this award-winning "rattlesnake" ad.

From the day Angus came aboard, Ray never worried about the agency's creative product. Angus gathered around him an impressive group of creative talent, including Gail Daniels, Mark Keller, Michael Ives, Don Juntunen, Tim Oden, Jeanette Elliott, Dub Brunsteter, Sherry Enrico, Jon Minson, Sherry Duran, Lael Erickson, Don Loewen, and David Lipson. Ray's sister, Kit Winkler, traffic manager for 17 years with the agency, had a great professional relationship with Angus, and was a key player in the rapid growth of the business.

Ray was thankful he brought Marvin and Angus McQueen into the agency, without a doubt the best move he ever made for the advertising agency business in Oklahoma. Ray remembered, "It didn't take long to realize Angus was the man to succeed me. He and Marvin brought to the company a new dimension in the ad business with the experience and expertise normally found only in the biggest cities in the United States."[4]

Ray was actively involved in promoting the placement of a bronze statute of longtime Oklahoma City Chamber of Commerce manager Stanley C. Draper outside the Civic Center in 1974. This photograph shows the plaster mold for the statue in the sculptor's studio. Ray wrote the inscription for the base of the statue, "He dreamed impossible dreams—then inspired and united all who could make them possible. He strengthened our stakes, lengthened our cords—and the dreams soared to reality. His was the spirit of Oklahoma City. Look around you! What you see today, was his tomorrow—yesterday."

By 1977, annual billing at Ackerman, Inc., had topped $8 million and represented clients across the country. The agency was listed as the 200th largest agency in the United States, up 56 places from the year before.

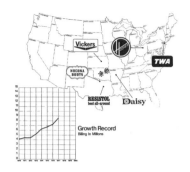

Ray, in his Resistol "Best All Around" cowboy hat, and Marvin McQueen, right, opened an Ackerman office in Dallas, Texas, at the Apparel Mart, in 1978. Although the agency only handled two accounts out of the Dallas office, Nocona and Resistol, the office was vital to Ackerman being selected as the agency to handle Sheraton Hotels in Dallas, Oklahoma City, and Houston as the only one of competing agencies to have offices in two Sheraton cities. Its initial Sheraton business led to Ackerman handling Sheratons in New Orleans, Tulsa, St. Louis, Salt Lake City, Monterrey, and Orlando and being designated as Sheraton's pre-opening agency. Assignments to create weekend promotion packages also went to Ackerman. Patti Weinbrenner was the office manager and account supervisor on all Dallas-based accounts.

East Meets West in Dallas is the apparent story here as agency President Marvin McQueen, in a three-piece suit, and Chairman Ray Ackerman, in western wear, pose together by the marquee in front of Ackerman's new Dallas office, located at the Apparel Mart.

Beginning in 1973, Ray, Marvin, and Angus ran the company. The three met "religiously" every Saturday morning, for up to six hours behind closed doors, as Ray recalled, "with Marvin and me both smoking cigars and Angus smoking at least a pack of cigarettes by noon, and all of us drinking buckets of coffee."

The Ackerman executive committee was not always in unanimous agreement. Sometimes, any one of them thought the other two were ganging up on him. Angus stood firmly with Ray against his father about keeping Oklahoma City as the agency headquarters instead of moving it to Tulsa. On the other hand, Ray reflected, "Marvin was always the first to congratulate me when I brought in a new account. Even though our relationship strayed occasionally for a day or two, the three of us really hung together for the most part and built a helluva advertising agency."[5]

Although they would not have admitted it publicly, Ray and Marvin would say privately to each other that Angus began to run the agency the day he came aboard. The reason was simple, Ray said, "Because Angus is a bit of a genius!"

With the Navy and civic activities taking a lot of Ray's time and his lack of big league experience in advertising frequently being frustrating to Angus, Marvin would always remind his son that Ray was the guy who started the agency 20-plus years before. Marvin said, "It takes a particular type of person to do that and Ray provides unique assets to the agency." Ray enjoyed the compliment but reminded Marvin and Angus that George Knox had actually started the company in 1939 and that Ray had inherited an impeccable reputation for integrity and creativity, a great base upon which to build an advertising agency.

Marvin taught Ray the value of getting quick payment from clients, because you could run the company on cash flow rather than invested cash. Marvin tactfully reminded any slow-pay client that Ackerman was "the little guy," with remarks such as "The Scotch you spill is worth more than the amount of our invoice on your desk." The agency usually received a quick check. The agency had a good record of not incurring bad debts and in 1965 it was the first agency in the Four As to institute a finance charge on past due accounts. However, Marvin's quick collection technique worked better.

Marvin also touted the theory that the agency should be paid for what an idea was worth, not just what agency personnel invested in time and overhead. A five-minute meeting resulted in the brilliant idea of naming a new bowling ball manufactured by Brunswick "Rhino," instead of uninteresting former designations of balls such as "U-22. "Even though the idea took only a few minutes to create, it was worth a lot of money to the client and a substantial fee to the agency," preached Marvin.

On another occasion, a short brainstorming session of agency creatives produced "PennWell" as the new name for the Petroleum Publishing Company of Tulsa, publisher of the famous *Oil and Gas Journal* and other oil industry publications. The name change was necessary because the company was diversifying into the publication of magazines about computers and other products. The company said they wanted a name that would still be indicative of the oil business but also suggest the company was founded in Pennsylvania and was in the printing business. "PennWell" was the perfect and priceless name.

On the other hand, agency staffers could spend two days on a project such as a client wanting a clever idea for his daughter's 13th birthday party invitation. The agency certainly could not afford to bill for the time spent on what was really a request for a "freebie."

Ray worked hard at building the agency's reputation. Warren K. "Doc" Jordan, president of a competing agency, observed, "He tried to elevate the prestige of the industry both locally and as a participant in national trade organizations. He was always a booster of our city and state and sought a professional approach to advertising."[6]

As an annual gift for clients, prospects, the media, and suppliers, Marvin came up with an agency-designed coffee mug for 1974, distributed at Christmas, 1973, with a new design planned for every year. He had no way of knowing that the mugs would become collectors' items, that persons with full sets would be a rarity. Only 500 of the mugs were produced initially, but growth of the agency and popularity of the mugs grew the list to 1,500 in the year 2000.

In the beginning, the mugs cost the agency only about $5 each. Even when the price doubled, it was well worth the impact. In 1976, a Tulsa newscaster had one of the Ackerman mugs on his desk in front of the television cameras for two months.

The morning after Ray received the exciting news of his promotion to Rear Admiral in 1974, he was awakened with an early-morning call from Navy Vice Admiral Emmitt Tidd, from Washington, D.C. Tidd, a Navy ROTC graduate from the University of Oklahoma, headed up the Navy recruiting command to which Ray was attached as a naval reservist. Tidd's first words over the phone were, "Don't try to jump into your trousers; you still need to put them on one leg at a time even if you are a Rear Admiral."[7]

Ray had especially strong fitness reports following his promotion to captain in 1965, but still felt his chances for making Flag Rank were slim because of his two passovers for promotion, one to the rank of lieutenant and one to the rank of commander. So the news that he made it was particularly pleasing, making him

In 1973, Ray chaired the committee that organized a Navy Ball in October. More than 1,000 people attended the event, making it second in size only to the Navy Ball in Washington, D.C. Left to right, Ray, Lou, Mouza Zumwalt, and Admiral Elmo Zumwalt, Jr., Chief of Naval Operations. The Ball was co-sponsored by the Central Oklahoma Chapter of the Navy League and the Naval Reserve Association of Oklahoma.

often wonder how many others in the modern Navy have made it to flag rank, if any, with such a poor record of promotions to lower ranks.

Shortly after he put on his Navy Blues with the "big gold stripe" for the first time, Ray was walking down the street at Naval Air Station Dallas and ran into retired Navy Captain John Lacouter, who was Commanding Officer of Ray's fighter squadron in 1947 when Ray commandeered a Corsair in order to get home according to his orders. John's first remark while shaking Ray's hand was, "How in h_ _ _ did you ever make Flag?" The two had a nice meeting but Ray was just as curious as to why Lacouter never made Flag.

Lacouter was well-known and respected throughout the Navy and was a prolific writer of articles for *Naval Proceedings* and other Navy publications. It was then that Ray realized there is always an element of luck in being selected for Flag rank. Ray said, "I had good luck and John Lacouter had bad luck."[8]

In 1974, Peggy Howard was hired as Media Director of the agency. With considerable experience at much larger agencies in Dallas, Howard brought the same expertise in media that Angus brought to the creative side of the agency. Other important staff members who joined the agency in the 1970s were Bruce Anderson and Patti Weinbrenner.

Also in 1974, at its annual meeting in Lisbon, Portugal, Ray was elected international president of Affiliated Advertising Agencies International (AAAI), an organization of agencies in about 50 cities in the United States and an equal number of cities overseas.

The morning after the election when delegates were scheduled to depart by air or train, a revolution broke out in Portugal, closing all airports and train stations. Fortunately for Ray and Lou, a car they had rented for a post-convention vacation in Spain was delivered to their hotel shortly before revolutionaries began turning over cars in downtown Lisbon. Ray and Lou made their escape down the strip of Portugal on the west side of Spain and crossed the border into Spain only an hour before the border was closed. With Ray holding Portuguese money, worthless in Spain because of the revolution, it took Lou's last six American dollars to buy enough gasoline to reach their destination in Marbella, Spain.[9]

At an AAAI meeting in Stockholm, Sweden, Ray wore his Nocona boots and Resistol hat. He was the hit of the meeting and probably could have sold a thousand hats and pairs of boots in Stockholm that weekend.

Business at Ackerman had been pretty flat from 1969 to 1972, going from just under $5 million in annual billings to just over $5 million. However, the agency rose to $8.5 million in 1977. By the end of the decade, annual billing had grown to $12 million.[10]

In the 1970s, Ackerman creative staff attracted Vickers Petroleum Company; Trans World Airlines; Petroleum Publishing Company, publisher of *Oil and Gas Journal;* Daisy Air Rifles, and Hoover retailers in six states. In the following decade came Food & Wines from France, Droste Chocolates of Holland, Kerr-McGee, Oklahoma Gas and Electric, OPUBCO, the National Rifle Association, Brunswick, Williams Companies, the Oklahoma Department of Tourism and Recreation, the Oklahoma City Chamber of Commerce, Rheem Heating and Air Conditioning, Sheraton Hotels, Pizza Hut, Memorex-Telex, St. Anthony Hospital, Globe Life and Accident Insurance Company, C.R. Anthony Company, Southwestern Bell, Zebco, Remington Park, and the Bank of Oklahoma as major Ackerman clients.[11]

Ray was sleeping soundly early one Friday night in April, 1975, when a phone call advised that his office building was on fire. He jumped in his clothes and sped toward the office on the Northwest Expressway. He silently prayed that when he topped the hill at Portland Avenue, he would see no fire. Unfortunately, he did.

There's no better time to visit New Orleans than during the 1984 Louisiana World Exposition. And there's no better place to stay when you're here than the Sheraton New Orleans Hotel.

The most dazzling entertainment. Elegant restaurants. Intimate cafes and enticing happy hours are all yours in a hotel overlooking the French Quarter – just five blocks from the Fair.

Two specially priced World's Fair Vacation packages are available which include tickets, buffet breakfasts, and children 17 and under stay free when sharing an adult's room using existing bedding. Call now for reservations at **800-325-3535** or contact your travel agent. Spend your World's Fair Vacation at New Orleans' most celebrated hotel.

"Mr. Seymore D. Fair", official and distinguished mascot of the 1984 Louisiana World Exposition.

Sheraton New Orleans Hotel

SHERATON HOTELS, INNS & RESORTS WORLDWIDE
500 CANAL STREET, NEW ORLEANS, LOUISIANA 70130, 504-525-2500

Ackerman McQueen developed a series of colorful print ads for a dozen Sheraton Hotels throughout the country.

JOHNNY RUTHERFORD: Husband, Father, Race Car Driver,
Three-time Indy 500 Winner,
Pilot, Network Commentator, Member of
the National Rifle Association.

"I grew up learning how to handle guns bird hunting
with my dad in Kansas. Now my family
enjoys hunting, too, what few chances we get. If we had
more time, I'm sure it would be a family affair.

"Shooting parallels racing in many ways.
It's a very serious sport, a challenge you can't take lightly.
You have to put your skills and strength of concen-
tration against it. And of course, safety is number one.

"My son and I joined the NRA not only for the
literature and programs it offers, but also because we like
what it stands for. Being an NRA member is important
for everyone who wants to ensure our freedoms to own, enjoy
and compete with guns. I just can't
fathom it any other way." **I'm the NRA.**

The NRA's programs, activities and publications help teach millions
of outdoor enthusiasts about hunting safety, good sportsmanship and the principles
of responsible wildlife management. If you would like to join the NRA
and want more information about our programs and benefits, write Harlon Carter,
Executive Vice President, P.O. Box 37484, Dept. RU-5, Washington, D.C. 20013.
Paid for by the members of the National Rifle Association of America.

The Daisy Manufacturing Company Vice President of Marketing, Jack Powers, was instrumental in Ackerman's successful effort to be the advertising agency for the National Rifle Association (NRA). An NRA official said some of the competing ad agencies in New York City "didn't know which end of the gun the bullet came out of." Ackerman developed this ad to show that the NRA was not made up of "rednecks," but ordinary Americans, such as race car driver Johnny Rutherford. In fact, the NRA was made up of priests, educators, movie stars, nuns, doctors, athletes, people from every walk of life. The theme of the ad campaign was "I'm the NRA."

Giant flames darted through the roof of the two-story building. Before fire fighters could extinguish the blaze, there was considerable damage. Agency personnel worked all night and the next day trying to clean up. Over the weekend, they were able to move salvaged furniture and equipment to unoccupied space in the new Ciudad Building across the street and arrange for telephone service by Monday morning.

The fire caused some loss of business because some materials were destroyed. It took almost a year for the Ackerman Building to be repaired. However, the Tulsa office was operating smoothly and handled many of the accounts while the Oklahoma City office managed in cramped space.

In 1975, Ray and Lou decided to end their 25 years of sending out customized Christmas cards. With a growing list of family and national friends from the Navy and the advertising business, the list had grown to 1,200. It had taken a large production line of all six children each Christmas to sign, stuff, seal, address, and stamp the cards and envelopes. In retrospect, Ray and Lou wished they had written "last one" on the 1974 card because some people were upset in 1975 when they did not receive the annual greeting, believing they had been cut from the Ackerman list. On the other hand, 1975 brought the first card from Patsy with her husband and the Ackermans' first grandchild, Jason.

On July 1, 1977, Ray was transferred to Retired Reserve with a final rank of Rear Admiral, upper half. He had flown over 2,100 hours in 25 of his 35 years of Navy service, most of it in fighters including the Corsair, the Cougar, and the Fury. He missed flying and the camaraderie with the men in his command but enjoyed the extra time with his family. Navy weekends in Dallas had been a hardship at times. One year, Ray missed Easter, Mother's Day, and his wedding anniversary in a three-month period. On three consecutive weekends, at another time, he was in Seattle, Washington; San Diego, California; and Washington, D.C.

The Ackerman clan had "matured" by 1978. Left to right, back row, Patsy, Ray, Lou, and Annie. Left to right, front row, Amy, Ray K. Mark, and Susie. Ray's service to at least a dozen different civic and charitable groups, the agency's growing prominence, and his Navy career earned him an annual listing in Who's Who in America.

One Sunday when Ray was out of town on Navy duty, Lou came out of church with the children. A lady approached her, introduced herself, and said she had been admiring the children and just wanted to meet their mother. Then she said, "Is your husband dead?" Lou, with a surprised look replied, "Well, no." The lady continued, "Well, isn't it too bad he's not a Catholic." Obviously, Ray had missed a lot of Sunday Masses with his family.

In 1978, Ackerman was chosen as the advertising agency for the Oklahoma City Convention and Tourism Commission. The Commission's goal was to promote Oklahoma City to vacationers as a destination point rather than a stopover place and to continue to increase the state capital's convention business.

Ackerman did much more that just create print, radio, outdoor, and television advertisements. Annual reports, brochures, catalogs, audio/visual sales presentations, and employee relations materials were regular projects. In 1978, artist Gail Daniels even designed the cover for country and western singing star Roy Clark's newest album, "Labor of Love."

On January 1, 1979, the name of the Ackerman agency was officially changed to Ackerman & McQueen, Inc. (AM). Ray and Marvin became co-chairmen of the board and Angus McQueen took over as president of the newly-named agency.

Other key employees during the 1970s and 1980s were Tim Oden, Bob Lamons, Steve Young, George Sauter, Marie Holley, T.J. Austin, Walker Randall, Phil Risinger, Ralph Cissne, Linda Webb, Susie Avery, and Sharyn Chesser. Honors piled up as AM annually won more ADDY awards than any other agency in annual competition of the Oklahoma City and Tulsa Advertising Clubs.[12]

Marvin McQueen was truly a master of the English language with a sense of humor to match. He loved to use words slightly off target to force the reader to the dictionary. In 1981, when a young account supervisor, Bruce Anderson, recommended a new system of weekly time reporting on the First National Bank of

Tulsa account, a move that surely would have doubled the time of servicing the account, Marvin wrote to Ray and Angus, the other two members of the executive committee:

> Let me repeat, for the record, at least to the executive committee, that I predict noisy, embarrassing, and agonizing failure for this misbegotten piece of accounting mischief.
>
> This miscegenation occurs when ambitious and enthusiastic client/agency romances flourish and need a law to protect the innocent.
>
> We agency folks are Shelley's Blithe spirits. If we were bookkeepers, we would wear eyeshades and straw sleeves. Our genes are those of Michelangelo, Milton, and Woody Allen. Our antecedents didn't design the Aztec calendar or lay out Stonehenge.
>
> Oh, Lord, deliver me from the shadow of didactic children who indulge their first intoxicating taste of power!

EVOLUTION OF
THE EIGHTIES

Despite the loss of a leader and the scheduled retirement of another, the 1980s was a decade of amazing agency growth from $12 million to $84 million in billings. The final transition of leadership to Angus McQueen, the addition of extraordinary people to the staff, a giant step-up in facilities and technology, and a real merger, resulted in a truly national agency in every respect.

On the creative side, the agency started the 10 years with a new advertising slogan for the Oklahoma City Convention and Tourism Commission in 1982. It was called "Where Success Meets the West." In presenting the new campaign to the commission, Ray said, "People don't come to Oklahoma to fish and ski, they come for the dozen major horse events a year. Only Oklahoma can claim the title as horse capital of the world."

The slogan, "Where Success Meets the West," appeared in national trade magazines and commercials scheduled for the first half of 1983. In an interview about the campaign, Ray told a reporter, "We have an image and it's a damn good one. We are the West. We are the best of the West. We have the romance, the warmth, the hospitality and the friendship of the West and that is what we must promote." Ray strongly believed that Oklahoma City should never forget to promote its Western heritage, including, of course, horses.

In 1983, after 25 years of cherishing the lakefront property where their children were raised, Ray and Lou moved off the lake to a beautiful new home in Val Verde, an exclusive subdivision in northwest Oklahoma City. Ray was not enthusiastic about moving from the lake but remembered, "Lou was smarter that I was. A year later I had to have a hip replacement which began a series of health problems that would have made it impossible for me to maintain the two-plus acres on the lake."

Also in 1983, Ray was named to the Governor's Hall of Fame of the Oklahoma City Advertising Club and received the American Advertising Federation's Silver Medal Award for lifetime achievement in advertising.

William F. Winkler, Jr., Ray's nephew, joined the agency in 1983 as Director of Accounting; later he became Chief Financial Officer and Chief Operating Officer. Winkler came aboard just "in the nick of time," Ray recalled. New business was pouring in faster than the agency could handle it with antiquated accounting machines and procedures. Ray said, "Without Bill's expertise in cash flow management and cutting edge knowledge of escalating computer technology, the agency very easily could have gone under."

Another new key employee was Debby Johnson who joined AM in 1984, coming to Oklahoma City with her Air Force husband. The Johnsons originally intended to stay in Oklahoma City only three years. However, they fell in love with Oklahoma and stayed. Debby later became the agency's Executive Vice President of Marketing, Research, and Strategic Planning.

Almost all of AM's great creative campaigns since the late 1980s have been the work of, or greatly influenced by, the creative genius of Jeanette Elliott who joined the agency as an account executive in 1980. Typical of her genius is the line of copy on a poster designed by the agency's Jon Minson for the Oklahoma City Chamber of Commerce's recognition in 1989 of the 100th anniversary of the city's founding. It reads, "The Eve of the Run, three tall cottonwoods stood on an otherwise barren prairie. Set against a wide blue sky, their huddled silhouette foretold the heights to which this frontier countryside would rise. Overnight, a town surrounded them and in the space of just one century, a wise and mighty city stood where there once were three tall cottonwoods." Elliott's greatest work may have been the role she played in the creation and production of the "Native America" campaign for the Oklahoma Department of Tourism.

Rodney Lipe joined the agency in the mid 1980s as a part-time delivery boy while a student at the University of Central Oklahoma. In 2001, Lipe was executive vice president of account service in the Oklahoma City AM office.

In 1984, Ray lost his friend and AM co-chairman Marvin McQueen, who died from injuries suffered in an automobile accident in Superior, Wisconsin, where he was attending a meeting as a trustee of the University of Wisconsin at Superior. Ray will never forget the funeral service arranged by Angus, particularly the playing of Marvin's favorite hymn, "Amazing Grace," on the bagpipe. Ray remembered, "His burial plot under a shade tree in Memorial Cemetery in Tulsa is perhaps the most serene one I've ever seen. It's too bad Marvin did not live to see the real growth of Ackerman McQueen under his son's leadership."

The agency billed more than $25 million in 1984 and outgrew its building, necessitating a move to 18,500 square feet on the ground and 11th floor of the building located east of Penn Square at 1601 Northwest Expressway in Oklahoma City. The space included a new photography and recording studio complex. The beautiful, perfectly-situated building is now called The Tower, after a succession of names including Penn Square Bank Tower, Northwest Tower, Citizens Tower, and Equity Tower.

Oklahoma's two largest advertising agencies joined forces in 1986. Left to right, Chuck Hood, Angus McQueen, and Ray sign the merger agreement that joined Hood, Hope and Associates of Tulsa and Ackerman & McQueen (AM). The Tulsa agency had billed $28 million the previous year while AM had led state ad agencies with $35 million in billing. At $63 million, the merged agencies formed one of the largest in the Southwest.

Ray's office was on the 11th floor of the new building. Thirty-two years before, he had begun in George Knox's agency on the 11th floor of the historic downtown Colcord Building, and in the interim he was on the second floor of three different buildings.

Ray insisted that his name not appear on his old building once it was sold. Even though the name in metal letters was removed, a yard sign with the "Ackerman" name was painted over by new owners. But the Oklahoma weather faded the paint and brought the name back. Ray was glad when the building was finally sold and converted into a Quality Inn.

The story of AM getting the Food and Wines of France (FWFF) account in 1983 is a particularly fascinating story of how great creative talent in an advertising agency brings in new business and underlines the importance of the baseline Nocona account to the beginning of the McQueen era.

One day the agency received a call from a man in New York "with a heavy French accent." He had seen AM's Nocona boot ads in *Atlanta Magazine* and liked the agency's creativity. He wanted AM to create ads for them to place through a New York agency. AM's Bruce Anderson fielded the call and explained that AM did not sell its creativity for another agency to place in the media but would like to handle the account.

The Food and Wines people came to Oklahoma City and were convinced to make AM their agency of record. The celebration was hardly over when FWFF advised that the photography had to be done in New York. However, Ackerman convinced company officials to set up a competitive test. Ackerman won hands down on a quality/value comparison.

After the second celebration, as the winner of the photography competition, the agency learned it was required to send people to Paris and sell Sopexa, a French corporation that controlled FWFF. Contact was made with Jacques Harland, CEO of AM's French member of Affiliated Advertising Agencies International (AAAI), who agreed to assist with the presentation as translator. However, the FWFF staff in New York said it would be smarter for Ackerman to just ship the presentation to Jacques, have him make it alone, and avoid the negatives of translation. Ray remembered, "That was done and Jacques carried the day!" It was undoubtedly the most important benefit the agency ever received from its membership in AAAI. Two months later, Droste Chocolates of Holland followed FWFF into the agency.

In 1986, the wine and spirits division of Food and Wines of France was added as a client because of the great work on cheese. However, every two years, Sopexa sent a new manager to New York. One of the first questions always was, "With hundreds of agencies in New York, why do they have an agency in—where is Oklahoma City?" The new manager would be brought to Oklahoma City for a presentation and AM would retain the account.

Ray shakes hands with future President George Bush at a July, 1986, rally in Oklahoma City for Republican gubernatorial hopeful Henry Bellmon.

Ray and Lou at a 1985 national advertising agency convention. As Angus McQueen took over daily control of the agency, Ray and Lou had more time to travel and spend time with their children and grandchildren. Ray's role was even further reduced when AM merged with a Tulsa advertising agency in 1986.

That ploy worked for three manager changes, but not the fourth.

Ray's heavy civic involvement continued. In 1984, he served as president of the St. Anthony Hospital Foundation and chaired the Foundation's initial gifts division, helping to raise nearly $4 million in the hospital's first public fund drive in more than 20 years. He continued to serve as president of the governing board of the Omniplex Science Museum. Ray also served on the boards of the Last Frontier Council of the Boy Scouts of America and the Oklahoma City Youth Park Trust.

He was a director of Let's Race/OK County, a group of Oklahoma City leaders supporting pari-mutuel betting in Oklahoma County. Ray believed voters in the August, 1984, election were smart to approve the question which paved the way for the construction of Remington Park in northeast Oklahoma City.

In 1985, Ray and Lou were selected as Ambassadors to the People's Republic of China, a people-to-people program established during the President Dwight D. Eisenhower administration. The program encouraged experts in certain fields to teach seminars in China; this year, the Chinese requested advertising professionals. As a representative of small advertising agencies, Ray gathered samples of different kinds of retail advertising campaigns, including a very humorous ad campaign for a Chinese restaurant in New York City. After making a presentation to Chinese advertising personnel, Ray wondered why they were so quiet and reserved. Quickly, he learned that the Chinese man in the funny hat in the ad was none other than the revered Mao, the former leader of Red China. Ray had not recognized Mao and thought sure he and Lou would be murdered in their beds that night. Thankfully, Deng was at the peak of his power and Mao's legacy had been diluted by the new regime.

Ray became known as the "balloon man" on the China trip. He gave away thousands of balloons provided by Founders Bank in Oklahoma City. He was convinced that many of the Chinese children had never seen a balloon.

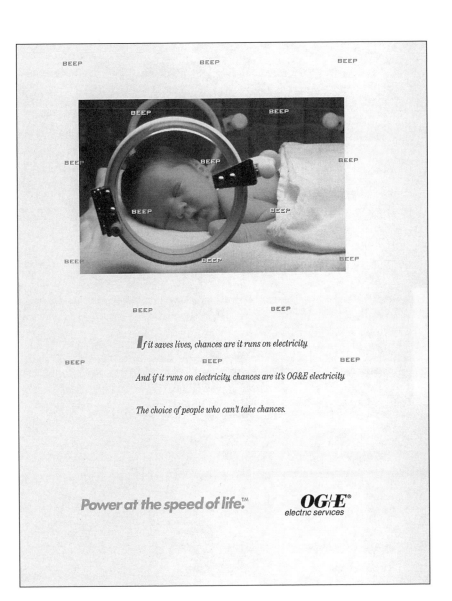

If it saves lives, chances are it runs on electricity.

And if it runs on electricity, chances are it's OG&E electricity.

The choice of people who can't take chances.

Power at the speed of life.™

OG·E®
electric services

OG+E has been an Ackerman McQueen client since 1989.

Trans World Airlines (TWA) called upon Ackerman McQueen to develop an advertising program to unveil TWA's increased emphasis on carrying small air freight.

KERR-McGEE & THE SEA.

Ever since 1947 – when we launched the offshore industry with the **world's** first successful well beyond the sight of land – Kerr-McGee has ventured beneath the sea for oil and gas.

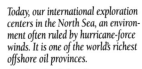

Today, our international exploration centers in the North Sea, an environment often ruled by hurricane-force winds. It is one of the world's richest offshore oil provinces.

Our first North Sea discovery was off Scotland in 1976 – and our commitment since has steadily grown.

Exploration in the Gulf of Mexico has also continued to expand. On shore, we're active in Wyoming, Texas and Canada.

It's proof that the same pioneer vision that **started** this nation is alive at Kerr-McGee. That spirit – that vision – is what this company's made of. It's What America's Made Of.

OIL & GAS
REFINING & MARKETING
COAL
CHEMICALS

Kerr-McGee Corporation, one of Oklahoma's largest companies, appointed Ackerman McQueen as its agency-of-record in 1989.

HAS YOUR BANK BROUGHT YOU TO THE BRINK?

Doing a slow burn over sorry bank service?
Errors, missing information, runarounds and delays are
bringing customer frustrations to a boil. But remember
– you don't *have* to sit there and simmer.

Burns Hargis
Vice Chairman
Bank of Oklahoma

Mark Funke
President and COO
Bank of Oklahoma

Count To Ten And Call BOk.

We're ready to listen,
advise, right the wrongs
and get your banking
back on track.
We call it Building On
Common Ground.℠

405-272-2000

BANK OF OKLAHOMA N.A.
Building On Common Ground.℠

Bank of Oklahoma became an Ackerman McQueen client in 1982.

The Daily Oklahoman *became an Ackerman McQueen client in 1987.*

In 1989, Ray and Oklahoma Press Association director Ben Blackstock led a brief but successful fight against a proposed tax on advertising. Ray predicted that imposition of such a tax would have disastrous consequences on the advertising business in Oklahoma. Moments after this photograph was taken, Ray stuck a pin into the balloon, "taking the air out of the ad tax proposal." Courtesy Jim Argo and Oklahoma Publishing Company.

In 1986 Ray continued his service to the annual Allied Arts Fund Drive. He chaired the campaign that raised more than $1.2 million for support of Ballet Oklahoma; the Oklahoma Symphony Orchestra, now the Oklahoma City Philharmonic; Omniplex; Lyric Theater; the Oklahoma Art Center, now the Oklahoma City Museum of Art; and the Arts Council of Oklahoma City.

Longtime Oklahoma City civic leader Mex Frates remembered Ray's never-give-up attitude toward raising money for Allied Arts. She said, "He was determined to find new money because we were really short and it seemed impossible to raise the

From time to time, the issue of assessing sales tax on advertising arose in the Oklahoma legislature. In August, 1989, Oklahoma Governor Henry Bellmon called a surprise special session of the legislature to deal with a budget shortfall. Over the next few months, a proposal to levy a four percent tax on about 30 services, including advertising, was put forth by some members of the legislature searching for additional state revenue.

Ray went on the attack. Armed with information from the American Association of Advertising Agencies and the State Advertising Coalition in Washington, D.C., he drafted a memo to state senators and representatives. Oklahoma Press Association director Ben Blackstock made certain the memo was hand-delivered to each solon. Ray warned that imposition of a tax on advertising would cause Oklahoma advertising firms to transfer employees to other states because otherwise large accounts headquartered out-of-state would leave AHM rather than pay a tax on advertising. He also said that if agencies tried to absorb the tax, the slim profit margin that existed would be obliterated, forcing many agencies out of business.

The Daily Oklahoman, under a headline "New Taxes Would Hurt," emphatically supported the opposition to the advertising tax.

Legislative action was swift. By Thanksgiving, legislative leaders announced that the tax on advertising was no longer a part of the revenue-raising legislation.

In 1990, Ray was named to head the Kirkpatrick Center museum complex in Oklahoma City. He succeeded Oklahoma Gas and Electric Company CEO James G. Harlow, Jr., as chairman of the board of governors and chairman of the Kirkpatrick executive committee. By 1990, the Kirkpatrick Center complex had developed into one of the most attended facilities in the state with many attractions, including Omniplex, a "hands on" science museum, the Air Space museum, the Red Earth Center; and the International Photography Hall of Fame and Museum.

Ray's work at the Kirkpatrick Center was special because of

his long-standing relationship with the Center's benefactor, John E. Kirkpatrick. Both were Navy Rear Admirals who loved Oklahoma City. Kirkpatrick said of Ray's civic work, "He had so much energy, he wore me out. He was always full of ideas."

Ray and Lou went back to Bellevue, Pennsylvania, in 1990 for his 50th high school class reunion. When one of his classmates said he talked funny, Ray recognized that his Pennsylvania twang was gone and he had finally arrived as an Oklahoman! It dawned on him that only a few years earlier, new Oklahomans he met had stopped asking him where he was from. The same year, Ray was selected for membership in the Fortune Club.

Early in 1990, under the chairmanship of Bill Durrett at the Oklahoma City Chamber of Commerce, Ray was very active in the massive effort to lure United Airlines to build a maintenance facility in Oklahoma City. Ray spoke to a rally of several hundred people in front of the Myriad Convention Center. "I have never seen our people so united in 50 years," Ray told the crowd that had gathered to kick off the campaign to convince voters to approve a penny sales tax increase to help pay for construction of a United maintenance center at Will Rogers World Airport.

Political advertising veteran Don Hoover, with funds provided by "Let's Get United," a group made up of civic leaders, labor union officials, and major corporations, produced a series of ads that promoted the benefits of a 33-month tax as being essential to Oklahoma City winning over 800 cities competing for the United facility. A billboard was placed outside United headquarters in Chicago. It read, "United: Your Sure Bet! Oklahoma City." Hundreds of United workers, some of them, hopefully decision makers, passed by the billboard location each day. Voters responded positively to the effort and overwhelmingly approved a temporary one-cent sales tax by a two-to-one margin. Community support for the United Airlines project was overwhelming. Edward L. Gaylord, publisher of *The Daily Oklahoman*, wrote Ray, "This will get us moving again." *Journal Record* Publishing

Company Chairman Dan Hogan said, "It is amazing what can happen when people properly organize to work within the framework of a serious action plan."

For a year, United tantalized Oklahoma City with the potential construction. The issue took so much of Ray's time he began to believe that when he walked down the street, his head was shaped like the big red and blue "U" of United Airlines.

Unfortunately, United did not choose Oklahoma City for the site of the new facility. However, Ray considered the teamwork that went into passing the temporary sales tax as laying vital groundwork for future citywide promotions.

Also in 1990, Durrett, Frank McPherson, and Ray chaired the effort to raise $1.8 million to assure that the Oklahoma School of Science and Mathematics would be located in Oklahoma City. Spurring the campaign was the alarming annual decrease in college students in the United States graduating in science and math following World War II. The alarm had resulted in North Carolina's establishment of a special school for juniors and seniors in high school who had high IQ's and aptitude in science and math. Because North Carolina had done well with the idea, and because the need existed, Oklahoma passed legislation to authorize the school.

Oklahoma City submitted a bid for the school. In the late 1980s, it was announced that Oklahoma City, Stillwater, and Tulsa were finalists. Oklahoma City offered a no-longer-used elementary school building in the Oklahoma Health Center area and $1.5 in financial incentives to refurbish the building. Actually, $1.8 million in private money needed to be raised to include the cost of financing $1.5 million in pledges over a three-year period.

The state legislature had been leaning toward Stillwater for the school's location but Oklahoma City's proposal, culminating in successful fund raising from the business community, became "an offer they could not refuse." The old school building to house the Oklahoma School of Science and Mathematics was renovated by HTB, an Oklahoma City architectural firm that won national design awards for the facility.

Later that year, John E. Kirkpatrick and Ray flew to Washington, D.C., with General Revere Young, commanding officer of the Oklahoma Air National Guard, to seek artifacts from the Navy Yard Museum for the Kirkpatrick Center. Construction workers had been digging a foundation for an expansion of the Navy Yard Museum and had unearthed a number of old cannons.

In answer to their question, Kirkpatrick and Ray were told they could select two cannons to transport back to Oklahoma City. They asked museum officials about the vintage and whether the two specimens they selected were from a fort or ship. The cannons were from the Civil War era and were used both in forts and on ships. When Ray asked which ship or fort did their selection come from, the reply was, "Which ship or fort would you like them to be from?" Ray has been suspicious ever since of the authenticity of military hardware in museums.

In 1992, Ray rejoined the Rotary Club of Oklahoma City after a 20 year hiatus.

THE RIVER

F ROM CHILDHOOD, RIVERS MESMERIZED R AY.
He grew up in Pittsburgh, the American city best known for its
rivers. His mother was born along the Monongahela which, to-
gether with the Allegheny River, forms Pittsburgh's downtown
Golden Triangle, the tip marking the beginning of the mighty
Ohio River. His grandparents lived on the banks of the Ohio in
West Virginia.

Ray swam in the river, played along its banks, traveled on the
river in a paddle-wheel steamboat, and saw it swollen by spring
floods. He saw the 12-feet high-water mark on a building in
downtown Pittsburgh which the flooding rivers had reached in
1936 and, in 1941, spent a night in Pittsburgh because the Allegheny River had closed the bridge on which he traveled home
from work.

So, it was no great surprise that interest in its river would be
the hallmark of Ray's imprint upon the development and history
of Oklahoma City, his adopted home.

When Ray arrived in Oklahoma City after World War II, he
thought people were joking when they pointed out the North
Canadian River. There was no water! Ray listened with

amazement to stories of great floods of the river. He soon learned that the river played a key role in Oklahoma City history, dividing the north and south halves of the capital city, both geographically and, often, politically and socially.

The North Canadian, in Ray's opinion, was never a positive asset to Oklahoma City's first century of growth. It was either dry or out of its banks until the 1920s; then it was just dry. The joke, "The North Canadian is the only river in the world that is mowed three times a year," was based on fact.

The river really is not its own river; it was officially named the North Fork of the Canadian River, thanks to 18th century French explorers. It originates in the northeast corner of New Mexico and enters the Oklahoma Panhandle southwest of Guymon where it is known as the Beaver River. The Beaver flows across Texas, Beaver, and Harper Counties until, according to the official state map, the river is given its common name of North Canadian in Woodward County.

The river's first recorded white visitor was Indian trader Thomas James, who led an 11-man exploration party from St. Louis, Missouri, up the Cimarron River and crossed the North Canadian near Woodward in 1821.

Historians W. David Baird and Danney Goble wrote of the James party, "They often resorted to the use of dried buffalo chips, or manure as fuel for fire on the treeless plains." The James party ate buffalo meat, described in journals as "more savory than the steaks dressed by the most delicate cooks in civilized life."

James traveled on the North Canadian in 1822 as part of a trading expedition to the Comanches who, along with other bands of Native Americans, had made their home along the river for centuries. James loaded more than $5,000 worth of merchandise into keelboats for the trip to a settlement called Spring Valley, most likely a site northeast of Banner, in present Canadian County. When the water in the river was too shallow for navigation, the 20-man party loaded its cargo into dugout canoes and tied them onto tired horses. From Spring Valley and a campsite in present Blaine County, James and his men "had a very successful trading season, taking in 400 horses and mules and more buffalo hides and beaver pelts than they could carry to market."

During Oklahoma City's earliest days, the North Canadian was a popular gathering spot lined with trees, the Delmar Gardens amusement park, baseball fields, a zoo, and walking and hiking trails.

Delmar Gardens was Oklahoma City's version of Coney Island from 1902 to 1910. A Greek immigrant, John Sinopoulo, transformed 140 acres of worthless, sandy soil along the North Canadian into a wonderland for children and adults alike. The park featured a 1,200-seat theater where actor Lon Chaney appeared in plays and Indian chief Geronimo signed autographs. There was a scenic railway, a beer garden, race track, restaurant, and hotel. The city's new streetcar system brought many of the 600,000 visitors to the Gardens in its glory year of 1905.

It was the largest amusement park west of St. Louis, decades before Disneyland in California could lay claim to that distinction. However, annual flooding brought hordes of mosquitoes and destruction, causing Delmar Gardens to close in 1910. Floods also forced the zoo and ballpark to move to drier locations.

The North Canadian was a river of fantasies and nightmares. One historian said, "It was either feast or famine for the water level in the river." The North Canadian was dry, or ran at a trickle, for most of the year. However, when spring rains soaked the surrounding countryside, the river became wild. It often flooded adjacent lands and even towns.

In 1923, the river escaped its banks and devastated much of downtown Oklahoma City. Civic leaders, led by Chamber of Commerce manager Stanley C. Draper, convinced the United States Army Corps of Engineers to straighten the river, remove most of the trees and shrubs that once lined the waterway, and dredge rock and sand from river bottom to pile along the sides, creating tall berms that still line the banks.

This Corps of Engineers flood control project, completed in the 1950s, stopped the flooding nightmares, but it also killed a scenic, recreational waterway. Ray was so naïve about river development at the time that when he saw the rip-rap built by the Corps along the banks, he thought surely the river would be full of water in no time.

The North Canadian River was on Ray's mind for decades. On his Navy duty, when he flew over Texas cities such as San Antonio, Austin, and Waco, he saw rivers running through sections of town where there had been no rivers before. On the ground, he marveled at the success of the River Walk area of San Antonio.

In 1967, Ray was on a small yacht in the Tennessee River, went through a lock, and "stared with amazement as the water level was lowered hundreds of feet below the dam." He recognized that the North Canadian was not in the league with the Tennessee River for electric power development but it reminded him of the question, "Why can't we dam up the North Canadian in Oklahoma City for the kind of economic development it could create and sustain?"

In Wichita, Kansas, watching on television the landing of the first space shuttle while he ate lunch, Ray looked out the window of the Petroleum Club and realized Wichita had magically added a river running down the middle of town. He learned that Wichita had accomplished the feat with a series of rubber, inflatable dams. Ray began dreaming, thinking, "Why couldn't Oklahoma City have a true river of fresh, running water flowing close to its downtown area?"

Frankly, the idea for developing the river through downtown Oklahoma City was not new. Shortly after the city was founded in 1889, two of its founding fathers, Henry Overholser and Charles G. "Gristmill" Jones, wanted to build a gristmill to grind flour, but needed a source of power. Overholser and other city leaders looked for a way to generate electricity and turned to "water power."

Because the flow of the North Canadian was so erratic, Overholser and Jones convinced townspeople of the tent city to invest in the Oklahoma City Ditch and Water Power Company. The plan was to build a six-mile diversion channel, with solid banks and a constant flow of water to power a gristmill and electric-generating turbines.

The project was a disaster. Historian Bob Blackburn wrote, "When the canal was completed, they opened the gates and water flowed down the channel. The first day, there were celebrations. The second day, the water level dropped and, finally, within a few days, the water disappeared." Leaks in the sandy bottom could not be stopped, even though much of the canal was timbered. The project was abandoned in January, 1892.

Ray read about the early canal failure but continued to envision water in the North Canadian all the time and a canal to the Myriad Gardens through Bricktown. When he read the story of the Hoover Dam and what it meant to economic development in the entire West, Ray was again reminded that harnessing a river like the North Canadian through dams could be as rewarding for Oklahoma City as damming the mighty Colorado River was to 25 percent of the country.

Ray was not interested in putting water into the North Canadian River just for the sake of having a prettier river, important as that was. He once told a Rotary Club audience, "One of our major assets in attracting new industry is that we have plenty of fresh water. But when companies interested in us as a possible relocation site or for a new plant come to see us, they travel over a river from the airport and see people cutting weeds on one side and toasting marshmallows on the other side, all in the middle of the river bed." Ray believed the "dry and dusty image" hurt Oklahoma City in its competition for new and expanding industry.

Cruising the North Canadian River remained a dream. When architect I.M. Pei was hired in the 1960s to plot a course for future Oklahoma City, he did not even recognize the North Canadian as a river. Instead, the North Canadian was simply referred to as the "Oklahoma City Floodway."

Close to home, Tulsa had success with re-working river channels. Tulsa developed widely used recreational trails, a park system, and a center for an array of outdoor activity ranging from classical music concerts to raft races. Ray, in his frequent travels, was well aware of the success of other cities in harnessing naturally flowing rivers for economic and scenic benefit.

Although he never liked the name given the project, Ray fully supported a 1980 effort, called the "String of Pearls," that planned to use massive federal dollars to develop parks and dams from Lake Overholser eastward through downtown Oklahoma City. Ray said, "The name didn't fit the river." Included in the master plan was a series of dams that would create a 22-mile scenic waterway between Northeast 63rd Street and Air Depot Boulevard and Lake Overholser. Planned were picnic areas, bicycle paths, an equestrian park, sports center, and theme parks. Water was to be impounded by dams at the cost of more than $100 million.

However, because of the energy crunch and staggering federal budget deficits, including a change of attitude in the nation's capital about such projects, the String of Pearls never became a reality. But Ray and other interested citizens including Pat Downes, Bert Cooper, Dusty Martin, Don Kaspereit, and Jack Cornett never gave up hope of someday being able to develop the North Canadian.

Ray looked for solutions. Some people were afraid the North Canadian might not hold water and cause a repeat of the 1890 gristmill fiasco. Still others believed it might flow too much water and flood basements of downtown buildings. Ray's solution was to find a way to prove its feasibility, then go to the public for a vote on funding.

The Oklahoma City Riverfront Redevelopment Authority (OCRRA) was created to plan a development of the North Canadian from the Oklahoma-Canadian County line to Midwest Boulevard in eastern Oklahoma County. The OCRRA was patterned after similar organizations in other cities that cleaned up streams and embankments, transforming entire cities, from Detroit to Denver to San Antonio, into oases, drawing millions of tourists and hundreds of conventions each year.

Ray discovered that the OCRRA trust owned operating oil and gas properties along the North Canadian and had enough in the bank to finance a feasibility study to determine if the riverbed would hold water and not flood. Ray sat in on a selection committee meeting of the OCRRA trust when RGDC, an Oklahoma City engineering firm, was selected over a Tulsa firm to do the study.

When the RGDC study was concluded in 1990, proving that it was feasible to build dams and impound water along the North Canadian, Ray was ready to move ahead. The timing was perfect because members of the Greater Oklahoma City Chamber of Commerce had chosen him as Chairman of the Chamber for 1991.

He believed the right time to win support for such long range ideas might be the 1990 annual fall retreat of the Chamber of Commerce Board of Directors.

CHAMBER CHAIRMAN, ST. CRISPIN'S, AND MAPS

TWENTY-FIVE YEARS FROM NOW, historians may well look back on a meeting of the Greater Oklahoma City Chamber of Commerce Board of Directors as a turning point in the city's history. The two-day retreat at St. Crispin's Conference Center in Seminole, Oklahoma, October 29-30, 1990, was well-attended by a Who's Who in Oklahoma City list of industry leaders.

As incoming Chairman of the Chamber, Ray chaired the sessions with a goal of convincing Chamber leaders to formulate a great visionary plan to be completed over a number of years to make Oklahoma City a truly great city.

The time was ripe for designing an ambitious plan of exciting projects for Oklahoma City. Many of the conferees still were agonizing from disappointment at not being able to take advantage of the centennial of the Run of '89 with a World's Fair. The oil bust, collapses of banks led by Penn Square, and a World's Fair in New Orleans that lost $150 million, halted plans for an international celebration to commemorate Oklahoma City's centennial.[1]

Also, a survey of Oklahoma City residents showed that only 17 percent of those responding had a positive image of their community. Worse, 61 percent said they had a negative image. Ray drew only one conclusion from the survey; "No one liked what they saw and there was no plan for anything better in the future."[2]

A quorum of these 1990-1991 Chamber directors were present at Seminole: Bill Durrett; James Harlow, Jr.; Bill Pirtle; Stan Hupfeld; Dean Werries; Ken Townsend; Dean Schirf; Bob Anthony; Clay Bennett; G.T. Blankenship; Bill Cameron; former Mayor Andy Coats; Ed Cook, Sr.; Jim Everest; E.K. Gaylord II; Edward L. Gaylord; J. Leland Gourley; Jean Gumerson; Dan Hogan; Ed Joullian III; John Kilpatrick; John E. Kirkpatrick; Ed Martin; former Governor George Nigh; John Parsons; Oklahoma City Mayor Ron Norick; Lee Allan Smith; Bill Swisher; Ed Townsend; Dr. G. Rainey Williams; and Stanton L. Young. Others present included John C. Andrews and Wayne VonFeldt.[3]

Individual Chamber directors spoke to different interests; sports facilities, both indoor and outdoor, a learning center, hotels, state fairgrounds improvements, renovation of the Myriad and Civic Center Music Hall for the performing arts, and light rail transportation.

Ray spoke about his particular interest of damming up the North Canadian River, now that a study had proven the river would hold water and would not flood downtown basements. He also pushed for a canal from the river to Myriad Gardens, through Bricktown, and a canal or channel from the river into the entrance of Stockyards City. Ray pointed to the amazing success of the San Antonio River Walk. Although Oklahoma City's plans would be different, Ray said, "It offers more potential." He predicted a downtown canal and development of the river would have a revolutionary impact upon the future of Oklahoma City.

An article in *The Daily Oklahoman* on December, 2, 1990, provided an excellent summary of Ray's feelings about the river and canal development:

Shall we gather at the river, the beautiful, beautiful river? For Oklahoma City's 101 years of official existence, the North Canadian River has divided the municipality populations—north and south—and sometimes its politics and vision.

But in 1991, the Oklahoma City Chamber of Commerce and its incoming chairman, Ray Ackerman, want residents to come together at the river and help the city take a giant step in the leap to major league status.

"I have been here 43 years, and the city has not truly been one," Ackerman said last week. "If we put water in that river, put development on both sides, that would draw us together."

The North Canadian is not a rolling river—it just sort of limps along. But the intent of Ackerman and the Chamber is not just for revival meeting of residents on the shore. It's to make converts of companies and their executives looking at Oklahoma City as a place to bring their plants and jobs.

It's image—the big and tangible in the tough economic development plan.

"The city's image to the nation, from a survey of residents in 42 cities nationwide, is of a dry and dusty cow town in an oil and gas setting," Ackerman said.

"In this business of economic development, people slip into town to look you over," Ackerman said. "We look dry and dusty when you drive in from the airport. But engineers say you can put water in the river."

"Everything started (in the leap of cities to major league status) with one significant thing," Ackerman said. "St. Louis built an arch. Indianapolis built a dome stadium. Oklahoma City needs a channel to downtown," Ackerman said.

"Water is natural and an attraction for vacations, hotels and restaurants downtown," Ackerman said.

Ray and Lou, far right, spent a lot of time with friends Lee Allan Smith, left, and his wife, DeAnn. Smith headed up an Ackerman McQueen division called OK Events which promoted special events. His first success for Ackerman McQueen was coordinating the Olympic Festival in Oklahoma City in 1989.

Ackerman went on to say that water in the river alone was not going to change the city's image in the minds of local residents. "They need to be reminded of the positive. For some reason or another, our people think the grass is greener on the other side of the fence and it isn't."

"So I see my job as Chamber Chairman as not only pushing for the river development and the entire Vision package adopted by our board, but also coming up with a campaign to sell Oklahoma Citians on what a great place they live in."[4]

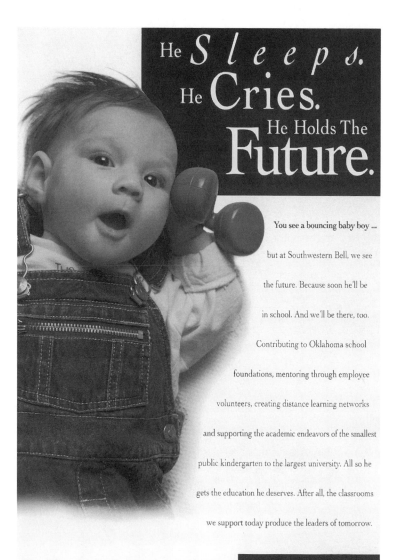

He *Sleeps.*
He Cries.
He Holds The
Future.

You see a bouncing baby boy ...

but at Southwestern Bell, we see

the future. Because soon he'll be

in school. And we'll be there, too.

Contributing to Oklahoma school

foundations, mentoring through employee

volunteers, creating distance learning networks

and supporting the academic endeavors of the smallest

public kindergarten to the largest university. All so he

gets the education he deserves. After all, the classrooms

we support today produce the leaders of tomorrow.

For more information, call
1 - 8 0 0 - 2 4 6 - 3 4 5 6

Ackerman McQueen developed a series of print advertisements to publicize the fact that Southwestern Bell Telephone Company contributed money to Oklahoma school foundations and supported an innovative program in which Bell employees voluntarily tutored high school students.

The Chamber Board of Directors unanimously adopted a plan called "Visions of a New Frontier." The vision included new hotels, a new baseball park, an indoor sports facility designed to accommodate major league sports teams from the National Basketball Association and/or the National Hockey League, an arts and cultural center, a library/learning center, renovation of the Civic Center Music Hall and Myriad Convention Center, expansion of the Bricktown area near downtown, streetcars running from downtown to Bricktown, state fairgrounds improvements with light rail transportation to downtown, a Native American Cultural Center, and development of the North Canadian River with a canal to Myriad Gardens through Bricktown.[5]

The directors also voted unanimously to recommend to the mayor and city council of Oklahoma City that they adopt the

The Bricktown Canal opened in Oklahoma City in 1999. One newspaper publisher suggested it be called the "Ackerman Bricktown Canal," in honor of Ray's idea for, and promotion of, the project. Courtesy Oklahoma Publishing Company.

Visions, determine a way to fund them, and allow the public to vote on all issues with one ballot, rather than voting on each venue or project individually.

In later announcing the plan, Ray said, "This vision will take 15, maybe 20 years to complete, but when it is complete, our city will be competitive with any city in the nation."[6]

The focus of the Visions of a New Frontier was the damming of the North Canadian River by filling it with water from Eastern Avenue west to Lake Overholser and developing biking and jogging trails, equestrian facilities and riding trails, boating facilities, restaurants, hotels, parks, and a golf course along the 16 miles of riverfront and the canal.

The *Capitol Hill Beacon,* a south Oklahoma City newspaper, applauded Ray's vision, writing in a January 10, 1991 editorial, "Three cheers for Ray Ackerman. We're surprised, but pleased to see him tackle this project which has been so difficult to accomplish in past efforts. One reason we can see for Ackerman tackling this is the new attitude toward river development. They're not talking parks. They're talking San Antonio—They're talking jobs, construction, tourism, new people, new life, opportunity—We encourage Ray Ackerman in his plans to develop the river and we pledge our support—Ray Ackerman might be the one with enough vision to get this job done."[7]

The Chamber and the City began quietly working together in 1991 to assemble cost figures on Visions venues and to determine how best to get the support of the public. The Chamber also worked on its other mandate from the public of changing the city's image to a positive one among its own people, so they would become a front line sales force as they traveled around the state and country.

Ray knew in his heart that Oklahoma City had much to offer businesses looking for a place to build new plants and facilities. In 1990, *Fortune* Magazine ranked Oklahoma City as 10th best among the country's top 50 cities in which to locate a business.

The survey cited the Oklahoma City labor pool as having some of the most skilled and loyal workers of any city. Also, the survey found the housing and commercial real estate market in Oklahoma City "a buyer's paradise."

Ray believed the city's shortcoming was not selling itself properly. He said, "First we have to turn our people on to what a good place this is to live, then do a better job of telling the nation."

At every opportunity, Ray asked Oklahoma Citians to "get off the dime" and start talking positively about the city and its assets.

The Chamber, as always, was active on all fronts in 1991. Ray appointed Jean Gumerson, president of the Presbyterian Health Foundation, to chair the committee to oversee a special, federally-funded program to combat drug and alcohol abuse in Oklahoma City.

The Chamber attempted to patch its image problem with members of the state legislature. Ray had seen an "anti-Oklahoma City" sentiment among some rural legislators during debate over additional funding for the Oklahoma School of Science and Mathematics. He and other Chamber leaders sought to establish good working relationships with leaders in both houses of the legislature.

Stan Hupfeld, chief executive officer of the Baptist Healthcare Corporation, put together a key-person network. Members of the Chamber were asked to get to know a specific legislator on a personal basis, through a social function, lunch, or dinner. The Chamber entertained legislators on a special day at Remington Park and on a bus en route to an OU-OSU basketball game in Stillwater.[8]

The Chamber used its influence to work for the defeat of several bills that would have driven up health costs, increased taxes for aviation facilities, and gutted the workers' compensation system.

Ackerman McQueen developed an advertising campaign to promote the revitalization of Oklahoma City and the "Oklahoma, Native America" 1990s campaign for the Oklahoma Department of Tourism.

An advertisement designed after the voters passed MAPS.

America's most ambitious downtown revitalization. A sweeping **$580 million** program now under way ranges from a new ballpark and canal to updated performing arts and convention centers — and many more projects to grow on.

The Economic Development Committee of the Chamber had a successful year, luring the corporate headquarters of Dayton Tire Company from Akron, Ohio, and convincing other businesses such as Oryx Energy Company, SIPCO, Applied Intelligence Group, Phillips Petroleum Company, JAKO, United Engines, and Hormel to expand their operations in Oklahoma City. Hundreds of new jobs were added.

Funded equally by the Oklahoma City Chamber of Commerce, WKY Radio, and Ackerman McQueen, the agency created and produced the "It's a Wonderful Life" campaign, which was centered around a jingle whose lyrics and music were written by Angus McQueen and Mark Keller, a talented musician with the agency who later moved to the West coast doing work for some of the biggest advertisers in the country.[9]

The Oklahoma City Chamber of Commerce had a pro bono committee to promote "It's a Wonderful Life," which was reasonably effective for a few years, but like most pro bono committees charged with doing work on a regular basis, it faded away. Still, the campaign made a memorable impact. Ray said, "So it was not just stopped, but set aside for reintroduction at another time."[10]

Chairman Ray and other Chamber officers and staff had several meetings with Mayor Ron Norick and other city officials, requesting financial assistance to promote economic development in Oklahoma City. In June of 1991, $400,000 was approved by the City Council to help in the effort, the first such assistance from the City of Oklahoma City for the work of the Chamber of Commerce.

Also in 1991, the Chamber supported Oklahoma City Superintendent of Schools, Dr. Marvin Crawford, in forming an Education Round Table. The purpose was to help develop a strategic plan for improving the level of education in the Oklahoma City Public School District, recognizing that the condition of the public schools was a negative in selling Oklahoma City as providing "A Wonderful Life."

The Round Table was chaired in consecutive years by James G. Harlow, Jr., CEO of OG&E, and Frank McPherson, CEO of Kerr-McGee Corporation. The Round Table evolved into the Oklahoma City Public Schools Foundation which has earned the support of many businesses in Oklahoma City, both financially and in key executives' time. In 2001, with the passage of "Maps for Kids," a $710 million program funded by a sales tax and revenue bonds, most Chamber leaders believed that, in the not too distant future, the Oklahoma City Public School District will become the standard by which other districts in the country will be judged.[11] Mayor Kirk Humphreys and Sonic Industries CEO Cliff Hudson led the campaign.

One of Ray's biggest supporters as Chamber Chairman was Paul Strasbaugh, for many years the manager of the Chamber. Strasbaugh, who like Ray hailed from Pennsylvania, called Ray "the consummate civic leader."

In November, 1991, the Chamber's annual Board of Directors Retreat was held at Lake Murray Lodge. Ray, incoming Chairman Frank McPherson, and Mayor Norick pledged a stronger union of the city and the Chamber than ever before. Shortly thereafter, the mayor named the Chambers Vision Statement, "MAPS," an excellent acronym for Metropolitan Area Projects. Before going to Lake Murray, Ray knew he was going to have to have his aortic heart valve replaced. He left Lake Murray with great peace of mind knowing that exciting things were planned for Oklahoma City and with confidence the people would approve paying for the projects.[12]

The Chamber provided funding and staff support to keep the MAPS task force privately funded and out of the public arena long enough to accomplish major brainstorming and organization of ideas.

In October, 1993, the Oklahoma City Council adopted the MAPS comprehensive plan that included the construction of a 15,000-seat stadium meeting Triple-A baseball standards, and an indoor 20,000-seat arena; renovation of the Civic Center Music

Hall and the Myriad Convention Center; improvement of facilities at the State Fairgrounds; restoring light rail transportation; and construction of a new downtown library/learning center complex.

Also included in the package was proposed funding for dams on the North Canadian River that would pool water from Martin Luther King Avenue to Meridian Avenue and for a scenic, shop-lined canal to run north from the river, parallel to Byers Avenue. The canal would turn west at Reno and stop near E.K. Gaylord Boulevard and Reno. Plans to connect the canal to the river, an extension of it into Myriad Botanical Gardens, and a dredged channel from the riverbank to Stockyards City were not included in the MAPS package. The city's leaders envisioned those ideas for the future in a plan that might be called MAPS II. The total price tag for MAPS was estimated at $238 million.[13]

The Chamber of Commerce launched a major promotion campaign to persuade Oklahoma City voters to approve a five-year, penny sales tax increase to fund MAPS. Ray framed the vote as a referendum for the city to "compete or retreat" on jobs, national image, and conventions.

The Daily Oklahoman wholeheartedly endorsed the plan, editorializing, "Voters should approve MAPS, securing a brighter future for Oklahoma City. The MAPS plan is both practical and visionary." Ray served on the steering committee which planned and executed the campaign that led to the December, 1993, MAPS election.[14]

Voters agreed with MAPS visionaries and, with 54 percent voting yes, approved the imposition of the five-year sales tax. At a victory party crowded with MAPS supporters, Mayor Norick said, "Oklahoma City, welcome to the big leagues."[15]

For the next five years, MAPS took shape, literally transforming the Bricktown area of Oklahoma City into a riverfront jewel, on a smaller scale of the successful River Walk in San Antonio. The Southwestern Bell Bricktown Ballpark was opened in 1998 and was immediately recognized as one of the finest minor league parks in America.

Because of the difficulty in 1992 to accurately estimate costs of the MAPS venues without detailed plans and specifications, costs of the different projects exceeded original estimates. With labor and material costs also rising, city and Chamber officials went back to the voters in late 1998 to "Finish MAPS Right." A substantial majority of voters approved a six-month extension of the sale sax to fund the increased costs.

The canal opened in the summer of 1999. Tens of thousands of "home folk and visitors" converged to ride water taxis along a beautiful canal filled with artificially blue-green water. Ray had been watching the construction with excitement. The day he knew the coloring was being added, he was walking east on Sheridan Avenue under the railroad tracks when he ran into Steve Collier and Sandy Price, members of the Oklahoma City Tourism Commission. Collier shook Ray's hand and said, "Congratulations, it's beautiful! I remember when you talked about it at St. Crispin's in 1990 and I thought, 'He's out of his mind!'"[16]

Friday newspaper publisher J. Leland Gourley, one of those present at the St. Crispin's retreat eight years before, suggested that Ray was the father of the idea for the canal, and in an editorial on December 4, 1998, proposed calling it the "Ackerman Aqueduct." Later, he changed his recommendation to the "Ackerman Bricktown Canal." Gourley wrote in a July 16, 1999 editorial, "Everybody in town is raving about how wonderful the new canal is, and well they should be. The naysayers about MAPS in general and certainly the beautiful canal in particular have vanished. Indeed it is the crown jewel of MAPS. It has brought a new spirit of pride and optimism to Our Town, the likes of which we have not seen for years."[17]

Gourley's editorial continued, "It will be a shamefully serious mark of community ingratitude if we allow the 'Father' of the downtown Oklahoma City canal to go unrecognized. For it was

Ray Ackerman, alone and initially, who dreamed and promoted the idea—to start a revival of a decaying city core with a canal running through it—Our town can do no less than name it the Ackerman Bricktown Canal, easy as ABC!"[18]

Gourley urged readers to call their councilmen and write to the mayor and city manager. However, in humility, Ray spurned attempts to name the canal for him. He was just happy to see the project completed, believing strongly that it was a launching pad for a remarkable new era of prosperous economic development for Oklahoma City. Besides, Ray agreed with one man who wrote *The Daily Oklahoman* suggesting the name be the "OK Canal."

Coordinating the North Canadian River redevelopment project was the Oklahoma City Riverfront Redevelopment Authority. The authority's executive director, Pat Downes, was "giddy" as construction began, in the summer of 1999, on the first of three dams that would impound water in the once dry and dusty riverbed. Federal funds made possible the construction of locks on the dams at May and Western avenues, allowing boats to traverse the full seven-mile length of the newly impounded water.

On April 27, 1999, Ray attended the groundbreaking of the Eastern Avenue dam of the river. For 48 hours before, several inches of rain had put enough water in the river that Mike Knopp, president of the Oklahoma City Association of Rowing, had two teams of rowers going back and forth in shells. Ray remembered, "They looked fantastic on that beautiful, sunlit, and cloudless day!" Ray was so excited, he called Jack Barner, Vice President of Development at Oklahoma City University, and suggested OCU make rowing a varsity sport and initiate competitive rowing with the University of Tulsa and Oklahoma State University which already had teams. Tulsa was so enthusiastic about the idea, it donated a shell to OCU to help get started. OCU established a rowing club for both male and female teams. The club's establishment was the first step toward making it a varsity sport. OCU actually successfully competed with universities all over the country in 2001, with its pro bono coach, Mike Knopp.[19]

A boathouse was designed by Smith & Pickel to be built just south of Bricktown. At a cost of $500,000, to be raised from private donors, the boathouse was slated to become the first development on Oklahoma City's new riverfront. Chesapeake Energy Corporation made a major contribution to the cost of the boathouse, which will bear its name.

In 2001, the river project was within two years of completion. Nearly 1,000 trees were planted along the eight-mile corridor, including hackberry, Kentucky coffee, cottonless cottonwood, sycamore, willow, and pecan trees. A two-acre "Grand Lawn" promenade was being developed on the river's north shore between Wiley Post and Wheeler Parks. Future plans included a Native American Cultural Center to be built at the intersection of I-35 and I-40. The impetus of MAPS has private money flowing into downtown and Bricktown, including a $40 million Oklahoma City Museum of Art.

One evening at dusk in late 1999, Ray stood looking at the glimmering water of the Bricktown Canal. His gaze arose above the water toward the dry North Canadian River. He could clearly see the day, soon to come, that Oklahoma City's canal would connect with a vibrant body of water, which probably should be called the Oklahoma River.[20]

Ray Ackerman's dream of bringing potential investors to Oklahoma City and traveling from the airport to downtown, crossing a river teeming with sparkling water, had come true. No longer would Oklahoma City be thought of as "dry and dusty."[21]

RETIREMENT

ALTHOUGH NOT PUBLICLY ANNOUNCED in 1987 on the occasion of merging the Hood, Hope Agency into Ackerman McQueen, Ray had made the decision to retire on his 70th birthday which was still five years away. Ray had given careful thought to the decision. He had handily achieved the two goals he set when he entered the advertising agency world in 1952; increase its size and strength to handle the largest Oklahoma advertising budgets and assure the agency's future, long after he was gone. Ray also wanted to spend more time doing civic work, with family, and traveling. Although in relatively good health, Ray said, "I'm not going to break Methuselah's record!"[1]

Several surgeries had taken their toll. In December, 1991, doctors replaced Ray's aortic heart valve. The following spring, he had his left knee replaced. That surgery, along with a 1985 hip replacement and a 1989 back surgery that left him in a body cast for three months, were necessary because of his inverted ejection in 1960 from his Navy jet when his wingman crashed into Ray and cut his plane in half, adversely affected his entire skeletal system because he could not get his backbone and neck straight. Surgeons said running two miles daily on concrete in hard-rubber soled shoes in the 1960s and 1970s certainly did not help either.[2]

Ray officially retired from the advertising agency, as promised, on his 70th birthday, August 7, 1992. His hip-replacement had to be replaced in 1998, a pacemaker was implanted in 2000, and his right knee was replaced in 2001.

In 1952, when Ray joined the agency, it billed $250,000. By 1970, it had grown to just under $5 million, and, in Marvin McQueen's first year with the agency in 1972, billing surpassed $5 million for the first time. From the time Angus McQueen joined the firm in 1973 until Marvin's untimely death in 1984, the three men ran the agency and annual billing mushroomed to over $26 million. Upon Ray's retirement in 1992 annual billing was $92 million. The growth accelerated to over $250 million in 2000, putting it in the top 130 of 8,000 advertising agencies in the United States, by far the largest agency headquartered in Oklahoma.[3] In 2001, the home office of AM in Oklahoma City occupied 40,000 square feet on five floors in The Tower. More than 250 employees worked in offices in Tulsa; Dallas; Washington, D.C.; Colorado Springs; and Oklahoma City. Ray was given the honorary title of Chairman Emeritus upon his retirement.

In retiring, Ray reflected on the good fortune he had in persuading Marvin and Angus McQueen to join him. He totally endorsed their theory that "You never quit thinking about or working on an ad or campaign until the minute you present it to a client."[4]

Ray's friends responded to his retirement. Express Personnel Services founder Robert Funk wrote, "Congratulations on your move to a more progressive position in life. . . . I hope you enjoy every minute of every day and continue to be Ray Ackerman— The Man."[5]

John O'Toole, president of the American Association of Advertising Agencies (Four A), said, "You built a fine agency that has never sacrificed its principles, and you yourself have been an important and valuable member of the industry."

But the letter that meant the most to Ray came from the young man he attracted to the agency decades before. Angus McQueen wrote:

Dear Ray:

I remember the day we met. You were standing in front of the University Club in New York wearing lime green pants, white shoes, a green checked sport coat and a bright green tie. I knew immediately you were a man of great courage.

On that first evening, over our first Scotch together, you told me you were looking for a guy who would some day want your job. That conversation led to others and then to dozens and hundreds more in which we talked of many "some days." "Some day we'll have a million-dollar client," "Someday we'll open a Dallas office," "Someday we'll buy a computer," and "Someday we'll make some money." And so on, with "someday" after "someday."

Remember, in the glum times, in those tough years, in the face of bad news, how you and my dad would say, "Someday we can stop worrying through the middle of every night."

Well, Ray, I guess that "someday" is this day and I'm sorry it got here so fast. What a grand adventure we had together. What a great company our two names share. For me, whatever pain we endured along the way is long forgotten. I only remember the victories, the good people and good times. And, of course, I wish our partner, my dad, could have been here with us tonight.

Marvin taught us both a lot about advertising, a lot about business and more than we needed to know about Scotch whiskey and good cigars. But, most importantly, he taught us how to stick together. He greatly admired your family, your military career, your devotion to Oklahoma. And, he always reminded me that you were the "real" entrepreneur. You were here first.

Throughout these past few years I've watched you struggle with one frightful challenge to your well being after another. I've seen some of the pain you tried to escape at times, but never stopped you. I've seen the commitments you undertook and kept

In the early 1990s, Ray served on the Founders Bank board. Left to right, standing, are Dr. G. Rainey Williams; Greg Edwards; Mickey Clegg; and E. Carey Joullian, IV. Sitting are Dr. O. Alton Watson, bank president Wayne Stone, and Ray.

on behalf of your city in spite of great risk to your health, maybe even to your life. And, well, yes, I've come to realize that you are indeed a man of great courage. And I'm proud of you.

For the company, there are still many "somedays" still out there to reach for. And you know we'll get our share. But there will always be plenty left for the next guy. The guy or girl who wants "my" job. And that is what you wanted, what you felt on that first night we met, isn't it?

Well here we are and congratulations are sure in order. So here's to you, Ray, with the heartfelt hope that God will bless you with many, many years of good health and joy with your family, your friends, and yes, with us. Because the warmest words I can find to close this letter are simply, "See you on Monday."

Godspeed,

Angus[7]

Left to right, Ray, Lou, Lou's sister Patsy, and her husband, Dr. Charles Rockwood, a world famous orthopedic surgeon.

Ray and Lou at a reception at the Lazy E Arena near Guthrie, Oklahoma.

Charles Van Rysselberge, left, president of the Oklahoma City Chamber of Commerce, and Ray. In 2002, Ray continued to spend countless hours each year promoting Oklahoma City, an assignment he has loved ever since arriving in Oklahoma City in 1947. Van Rysselberge called Ray "a tireless worker." The chamber official said, "If you had 10 or 20 Ray Ackermans, it would be unbelievable what you could get accomplished in a community."

Awards continued for Ray. He was named a distinguished alumnus at Oklahoma City University in 1991, was given the Humanitarian Award by the Oklahoma City chapter of the Arthritis Foundation, and received the Pathmaker Award from the Oklahoma County Historical Society in 1992. In 1993, he chaired Junior Achievement's annual fund-raising drive for the second time. In 1995, he was Director Emeritus of the St. Anthony Hospital Foundation.

He received a special award from the United Way of Metro Oklahoma City in 1996 for 50 consecutive years of service. When Tom Brown, president of the United Way for nine years, retired in 2001, he wrote Ray, "When I think of heroes of this community, I think of you."

In 2001, Ray continued to serve on the governing boards of the Oklahoma City Chamber of Commerce, the United Way of Central Oklahoma, Allied Arts, Omniplex Kirkpatrick Center museum complex, Oklahoma City University, Red Earth Indian Center, the Community Council, the Oklahoma City Public Schools Foundation, and the Oklahoma Heritage Association.[8]

Left to right, Ray, Lou, and Oklahoma Governor Frank Keating at a 1996 Republican rally.

The entire Ackerman clan gathered in June, 1998, to celebrate Lou and Ray's 50th wedding anniversary. Front row, left to right, Alyssa Fuller, Sophie Shaver, Evie Adams, Raymond Ackerman, and Alex Fuller. Second row, left to right, Deanna Ackerman, Samantha Ackerman, Susie Fuller, Patsy Conley-Mehring, Lou Ackerman, Ray Ackerman, Annie Adams, Amy Shaver, Lucy Shaver. Back row, left to right, Mark Ackerman, Jason Conley, Mike Mehring, Doug Fuller, the Reverend Ray K. Ackerman, Ron Adams, and Jeff Shaver.

Ray, always in love with rivers, surveys the Danube River in Hungary during a 1998 European vacation.

Ray with his arm around his bride of 50 years, Lou, on a trip to Melch, Austria, in 1998.

On Sunday, June 14, 1998, Lou and Ray celebrated their 50th wedding anniversary. They renewed their vows and celebrated a special Golden Jubilee Mass at The Catholic Church of St. Eugene in Oklahoma City.

Left to right, Father Ray, Deanna Ackerman, Mark's wife, and Mark Ackerman.

The Ackerman girls. Left to right, Annie, Patsy, Susie, and Amy.

Ray and Lou received a proclamation from Pope John Paul II, in celebration of their 50th wedding anniversary in 1998.

Ray and Lou Ackerman in 1999, still in love after 51 years, seven children, nine grandchildren, and a million miles traveled around the earth.

The Fortune Club
Christmas 1999

The highest award an Oklahoman can receive was bestowed upon Ray in November, 1993. He was inducted into the Oklahoma Hall of Fame, sponsored by the Oklahoma Heritage Association. Ray was nominated by Oklahoma City civic leader Jane Harlow, who wrote, "Boundless enthusiasm. Energy. Tenacity. Extraordinary loyalty. And always, a twinkle in his eye. Oklahoma City has been deeply and lastingly enriched by the contributions of Ray Ackerman." At the ceremony in Oklahoma City's Civic Center Music Hall, Ray was introduced by his longtime friend, Four A president John O'Toole.[9]

Ray considered his induction into the Hall of Fame his most prestigious honor. He said, "Being an immigrant from Pittsburgh makes it even more incredible to receive an Oklahoma statewide honor."[10]

Oklahoma City banker H.E. "Gene" Rainbolt congratulated Ray, "It is a signal honor for one whose life has been dedicated to the public well-being while at the same time building a significant business enterprise. We need more Oklahomans with your vision, commitment, and ability."[11]

Brad Davis, head of a large West Coast advertising firm, acknowledged Ray's entry into the Oklahoma Hall of Fame, writing, "It's outstanding to know that you joined the ranks of Will Rogers, Gene Autry, and Warren Spahn. Does this mean you'll own a baseball team or go on the road doing the Ackerman Follies?"[12]

Appreciation for Ray Ackeman's life of public service was shown often by presentation of awards. Ray believed that heading the list of organizations every businessman in Oklahoma City should support financially were the Greater Oklahoma City Chamber of Commerce, the United Way of Metro Oklahoma City, and Allied Arts. He received the Lifetime Achievement Award from the United Way in 1991. In 2000, Ray received the Governor's Art Award, primarily for 20 years service to Allied Arts and Omniplex Science Musueum, and as co-visionary with

Stanley Draper, Jr., in 1982 of the World's Largest Sculpture, "The Run of '89," which will be placed across the Bricktown Canal and dedicated in 2007, the Centennial of Oklahoma's statehood.

At the end of 1993, Jimmy Lyles unexpectedly resigned as president of the Oklahoma City Chamber of Commerce. Outgoing Chamber Chairman Frank McPherson, and new Chairman Ken Townsend, asked Ray to serve as interim president while a search committee looked for Lyles' replacement.

The request came while Ray and Lou were visiting family in San Antonio on New Year's Eve. Ray could not say no. He played hard to get but secretly relished getting back into the saddle of Chamber work.

Ray took on the temporary job during a time when the city was, in his opinion, "exploding at the seams" with enthusiasm and excitement with increased efforts to land new companies, for working out the details of the MAPS projects, and for fighting any possible closure of Tinker Air Force Base.[13]

Ray was in the temporary job for six months. He operated from the top of his desk, vowing not to get too entrenched by putting anything in the drawers or file cabinets. On the personal recommendation of then United States Senator David L. Boren, Ray asked University of Central Oklahoma President George Nigh to loan university vice president, retired Lieutenant General Richard Burpee, to the Chamber to head a unified effort to save Tinker from closing. The Base Re-alignment and Closure Committee (BRAC) had suggested that two of the five United States Air Force supply depots would be closed. Because of the leadership of Burpee and Major General Ken Eichmann, the commanding officer of Tinker, the BRAC never strongly considered closing Tinker. In fact, jobs from some of the other supply depots eventually ended up at Tinker.

After Ray had served as interim president, duty Ray described as "returning to active duty," the Chamber of Commerce voted

Lou Ackerman at her easel. Even though Lou painted wonderful landscapes, it was "the faces" of her subjects that Ray thought Lou painted with a special gift.

to create the Ray Ackerman Award, given annually to the member of the Chairman's Club who is voted by the Club's members as the volunteer who did the most that year to achieve the Chamber's objectives.[14]

In 1993, at the request of his pastor, the Reverend Bill H. Pruett, Ray accepted the post of chairman of the Communications Board of the Catholic Church of St. Eugene. The first action of the board was to launch a quarterly newsletter. Ray named it "The Gospel Truth" and labeled the pastor's column, "The Word According to Father Bill."

From 1994 to 1996, Ray served as chairman of the Visitors Board of the University of Oklahoma Health Center, following Admiral William J. Crowe, who served as the first chairman.

On April 12, 1995, Ray asked members of the Oklahoma City Advertising Club to act as a pro bono advertising agency for the City of Oklahoma City and develop a campaign to convince its citizens that "It's a Wonderful Life in OKC." This was to re-launch what he began in 1991.

Ray proposed putting all 150 members of the Ad Club to work in committees of announcers, copywriters, and producers for timely radio and television spots. He also outlined single-person assignments such as selling the piano player at the music bar in Bricktown on playing "It's a Wonderful Life" (having fun in Bricktown) about once an hour, getting all the patrons to sing along. Other single-person assignments would use the same approach at half time of high school football and basketball games.

Club members gave Ray a standing ovation after the speech and unanimously accepted the challenge. After the meeting, Chamber of Commerce president Charles Van Rysselberge said, "Ray hit a home run!"[15] Local media covered the idea in detail. E.K. Gaylord II wrote to Ray, "Great idea!" All calls and letters were positive.

Unfortunately, just a week later, a bomb ripped through the Alfred P. Murrah Federal Building in downtown Oklahoma City and the Ad Club members wisely decided to put the campaign on hold. Ray agreed, saying, "In six months or so, the campaign can be started and built from a higher level of pride in its people from the way they handled themselves during and after this tragedy." Unfortunately, a year later, the Ad Club reversed its earlier decision to accept the challenge.

In 1996, Ray was awarded an honorary doctor of commercial science degree from Oklahoma City University, his alma mater.

From 1997 to 1999, he served on a 15-person committee to develop a Cultural Arts Plan for Oklahoma City. An early result was that Allied Arts, historically raising money for only seven organizations, expanded to raise funds to help operate more than 20 arts-related groups.

Ray was inducted in the Oklahoma Commerce and Industry Hall of Fame in October, 1998. The Hall of Fame was established by Oklahoma City University to honor men and women who have made significant contributions to the growth of Oklahoma and the Southwest. Oklahoma Governor Frank Keating, in a congratulatory letter, called Ray "one of our state's finest and most productive business leaders."[16]

More honors came for Ray in 2000, including the Archbishop Eusebius J. Beltran Community Service Award. His selection for a Governor's Arts Award, prompted T.J. d'Andriole to say, "Few people in the state have done as much as, and none more than, Ray to improve the quality of life here." Ray also was chosen for induction into the Academy of Achievement Hall of Fame of the Sales & Marketing Executives Association and was given a Lifetime Achievement Award by the Oklahoma Chapter of the National Society of Fund Raising Executives.

Downtown Now, Inc., honored Ray with the annual Dean A. McGee Award, named for the late co-founder of Kerr-McGee Corporation. Upon reading about Ray's latest awards, Father Bill Pruett, pastor of the Catholic Church of St. Eugene in Oklahoma City, wrote, "I am amazed at your stamina, your creativity and intelligence, but even more—your faith in God and God's people—Like the Lord, you do all things well!"

In 2001, Ray received the Lifetime Achievement Award from Leadership Oklahoma.

IDEAS AT WORK

THE WORLD'S LONGEST SCULPTURE

IN 2000, one of Ray's longtime dreams came true. Two decades before, he and Stanley C. Draper, Jr., had pushed for the commissioning of the world's longest bronze sculpture to commemorate the Land Run of 1889.

The idea for the sculpture came when Ray and Draper sought an idea for a permanent landmark for a World's Fair tentatively planned to be held in Oklahoma City in 1989. Oklahoma City needed something that would be what the Arch is to St. Louis, Missouri, and the Space Needle is to Seattle, Washington. One day in 1982, standing in the old Chamber of Commerce offices in the Santa Fe Parking Garage Building, Draper pointed to a small bas-relief of the Run of '89 hanging on a wall and said, "We ought to cast a giant sized version of that and place it at some prominent highway intersection. Ray added to the dream, saying, "Yes, but the relief should just be the background. There should be 30 or 40 heroic-sized, three-dimensional figures in front of it; people on horseback, covered wagons, people running." Both Ray and Draper agreed that the perfect place for the gargantuan sculpture would be at the intersection of I-35 and I-40 in Oklahoma City.[1]

Sculptor Leonard McMurry created a wax model of the idea and Oklahoma City employee Pat Downes secured tentative approval to build up an area of land at the major intersection for placement of the sculpture.

But the Penn Square Bank failure, the bust in the oil business, and New Orleans' loss of $150 million on its World's Fair caused Oklahoma City to stop its planning for a World's Fair.

Down through the years Ray and Draper unsuccessfully tried to convince several wealthy Oklahomans to memorialize their families or their businesses by sponsoring the sculpture. Unknown to Ray and Draper, Lee Allan Smith saw the McMurry model in the Chamber of Commerce offices and also tried to sell the idea, without success.

In the spring 1999, Ray read where his friend, J. Blake Wade, the former executive director of the Oklahoma Historical Society, had been named chairman of the Oklahoma Centennial Commission by Governor Frank Keating to plan a year-long celebration of the 100th anniversary of statehood in 2007.

Knowing the idea of the sculpture would excite Wade, Ray called Draper and asked him to have McMurry dust off the wax model and replace the arms and legs that had fallen off during the past 17 years. Wade "fell in love with the idea" and said with confidence he believed that state money could be obtained to match private and city government donations.

Smith recommended that other sculptors be invited to produce a competitive design. Ultimately, the design of Norman sculptor Paul Moore, judged to be more exciting than McMurry's, and at a much lower cost to sculpt and cast, was approved by the Oklahoma Centennial Commission. It was Lee Allan Smith's and Paul Moore's idea to place the football-field long sculpture across the Bricktown Canal as a simulated stream. Half of the heroic-sized figures appear to be going into the stream and half coming out of the stream.[2]

Lee Allan Smith raised private money to finance the sculpting until the permanent funding could be arranged because Moore needed to begin work in January, 2000, so it could be completed

by 2007. In 2000, the City of Oklahoma City voted to give $1.7 million to the project. Congressman Ernest Istoook secured a federal grant.

As Ray said, in handing out plaudits to Smith, Wade, and Moore, "Let's face it. Dreams are wonderful, and I am proud to have been one of two dreamers of this sculpture. But it takes a special talent to make dreams happen. The efforts of Lee Allan, Blake, and Paul will give the city an incredible symbol that will give us a distinctive identity, unmatched by any other city in the world."[3]

THE OKLAHOMA RIVER

THE NORTH CANADIAN RIVER lies entirely within the state of Oklahoma except for its headwaters in the extreme northeast corner of New Mexico. It is called the Beaver River in the first four counties of Oklahoma and becomes the North Canadian as it crosses into Woodward County.

In 1993, Ray convinced several area state legislators to promote a name change for the river. State Senator Keith Leftwich, with the personal backing of Ray and the Chamber of Commerce Board of Directors, introduced a bill that would change the name of the river to the "Oklahoma River." Leftwich asked, "Why promote Canada, rather than Oklahoma?" Other sponsors of the bill were Senator Howard Hendrick of Bethany; State Representative Mary Fallin, who later became Oklahoma's lieutenant governor; and Representative Charles Gray of Oklahoma City.

The Executive Committee of the Greater Oklahoma City Chamber of Commerce voted to support the name change as did Mayor Ron Norick and the MAPS oversight committee.[4]

Opposition to the name change came quickly and loudly from Oklahoma City's neighbors to the west, in Canadian County. City councils in Yukon and El Reno passed resolutions to keep the river's name the North Canadian. State legislators from Canadian County rallied behind their constituents and the name-change bill died.

In 2000, Midwest City State Senator Dave Herbert met with Ray and agreed to recommend the name-change to the legislature. Senator Herbert and Ray believe that if the idea is presented properly to the citizens of Canadian County, to introduce the change as their contribution to the tourism industry for the entire state, the North Canadian River might someday soon become the Oklahoma River.[5]

INLAND WATER PORT

ONE OF THE REASONS Oklahoma City has an almost unlimited supply of fresh water for the future is due to the work of the Water Development Foundation, at one time a subdivision of the Greater Oklahoma City Chamber of Commerce. Ray served on the board of directors for years, a board chaired by Robert S. Kerr, Jr. The Foundation's thrust was to continue the work of Kerr's father, the legendary Oklahoma United States Senator Robert S. Kerr, to assure Oklahoma City's fresh water supply for the future and to provide barge transportation to the sea.

Kerr and Arkansas Senator John McClellan were the architects of the waterway which bears their name and which brings saltwater barge traffic into the Port of Catoosa near Tulsa. Kerr was poised in 1962 to lead the Senate to approve additional funding that would have brought the waterway as far as Luther in northeast Oklahoma County. With Kerr's powerful influence in the Senate, barge traffic from Oklahoma City to the sea was all but a "done deal." However, Kerr died on January 1, 1963, and the project has never moved forward. Ray hopes that in the 21st century, Oklahoma will get the project moving again.[6]

WHEN THE LONE STAR STATE came up with the anti-litter slogan, "Don't Mess With Texas," most people agreed it was a classic among such slogans.

Some years later, when Jordan Associates, an Oklahoma City advertising agency, created the line, "Don't Lay That Trash on Oklahoma," Ray wrote Doc Jordan a letter and congratulated him on the idea. Ray thought it was in a class with the Texas line, even if it was a couple of words longer.[7]

At the time Jordan developed the anti-litter campaign for Oklahoma, the word "trash" was strictly a noun. Sometime in the 1990s, it began to also be used as a verb. Ray immediately wrote to the appropriate officials at the State Capitol and suggested Oklahoma's slogan be changed to "Don't Trash Oklahoma!" Ray thought the proposed slogan was equally as good, if not better, than "Don't Mess With Texas." He also suggested "grandfathering" current materials so that tax dollars would not be wasted. The new slogan would simply appear on newly produced items.

As far as Ray knows, no change has been made or is being considered. But, he said, "It should be!"[8]

ADVERTISING OKLAHOMA IS EVERYONE'S JOB

RAY SUGGESTED, in an appearance before the legislature, that it require a front tag for automobiles that could convey a positive message about the state to passing motorists. Research showed time and time again that the biggest negative for tourism in Oklahoma is the image of being dry and dusty, even though the state has more land-locked water than any of the other 17 western states. He said, "Why not have a license plate that reads, "OKLAHOMA! America's Frontier Lake State." As Ray saw it, "We would have four million little billboards driving around the country, advertising our state in another positive way, with the

Native America message on the rear plate." If it is necessary to make it legal to add the second plate to the annual license fee at a cost of about $2.00, Ray proposed that the front license plate could include back-up stickers to those on the rear plate.

Ray also wants Oklahoma to change its official abbreviation from OK to *OK!*, with an exclamation mark. Ray asked, "Which looks better and more exciting?"

Antlers, OK	Antlers, *OK!*
Enid, OK	Enid, *OK!*
Tulsa, OK	Tulsa, *OK!*
Oklahoma City, OK	Oklahoma City, *OK!*

NEW FLAG FOR OKLAHOMA CITY

A NEW FLAG FOR OKLAHOMA CITY is one of Ray's dreams. The current flag, said Ray, "is seldom seen because the city seal is so small it has no meaning and with a white background, it looks dirty all the time." Ray suggested replacing the white background with a Kelly green background with the diameter of the city seal almost the same dimension as the height of the flag so it could be read.

TIE STATE FLAG TO STATE SONG

RAY RECALLED the true story of the playwrights kicking around a name for the new Broadway play that had been initially entitled *Green Grow the Lilacs,* then *Away We Go.* They thought the name "Oklahoma" might be good, but it seemed to lack punch and excitement. That is, until the wife of Oscar Hammerstein, II, said, "What about putting it in italics with an exclamation mark after it and calling the play, *Oklahoma!* As Oklahoman Paul Harvey would say, "Now you know the rest of the story.'

The comparison is shown in this artist's conception. Such a display would complement the name of the famous stage play and song. Present flags could be grandfathered. Courtesy Jon Minson.

In 2000, a state legislator suggested taking Oklahoma's name off the state flag. Fortunately, Lieutenant Governor Mary Fallin led the effort to squash the idea. After taking an objective look at the state flag, Ray recommended the style of lettering be changed from the present stolid, uninteresting block letter form, to an exciting, italic type, ending in an exclamation mark.

EPILOGUE

Over the years, Ray traveled extensively, promoting Oklahoma City, the National Finals Rodeo, the Navy, and his advertising agency. Often, his message and his dress were geared for the occasion.

One week he made three out-of-town speeches; one for the Navy, in his Rear Admiral uniform; another for the NFR, in cowboy hat and boots; and a third trip, in a business suit, to make a presentation to a prospective client. The variety of dress prompted a porter at Will Rogers World Airport in Oklahoma City to remark, "Gee, Mr. Ackerman, you sure have a lot of fancy costumes!"[1]

In August, 2000, Ray wrote of Oklahoma City's future in the OKC Rotary News:

> After we've solved all the problems with the Oklahoma City Public School District, I propose the next priority be MAPS II, the main part of which would be the further development of our recreational water resources.
>
> The Vision for this was approved at the Chamber of Commerce Board of Directors Retreat in 1999 and includes extending the Bricktown Canal into the Myriad Botanical Gardens and dredging two channels from the river, one into Stockyards City and one under the new I-40 and the railroad tracks to terminate below the end of the present Bricktown Canal, which is approximately 18 feet lower than the river's edge, making for beautiful, terraced banks

GREATER OKLAHOMA CITY CHAMBER OF COMMERCE

RESOLUTION OF APPRECIATION
RAY ACKERMAN
CHAIRMAN EMERITUS, ACKERMAN MCQUEEN, INC.

WHEREAS, the Oklahoma City Chamber of Commerce Board of Directors did meet October 29th and 30th in 1990 for the Annual Board of Directors Retreat at Crispin's Conference Center in Seminole; and

WHEREAS, the 1990 Annual Chamber Retreat was chaired by Ray Ackerman, the incoming Chamber Chairman for 1991; and

WHEREAS, the Chamber's Board of Directors determined that Oklahoma City needed formulate a great visionary plan to be completed over a number of years Oklahoma City was to become a truly great city; and

WHEREAS, during the 1990 Retreat, the Board evolved the **"Visions of a New Frontier** as the centerpiece of its **Program of Work** to commence in 1991; and

WHEREAS, this vision included new hotels, a sports facility designed to accommodate maj league sports such as NBA Basketball or NFL Hockey, an Arts and Cultu Center, renovation of the Civic Center and Myriad Convention Cent expansion of Bricktown, street cars running from downtown to Bricktown, Native American Center; and

WHEREAS, the focus of this Vision was the damming of the North Canadian River by filling with water from Eastern Avenue west to Lake Overholser and developing bik and jogging trails, equestrian facility and riding trails plus a golf course along t river; and

WHEREAS, the river development was to include a **"Canal"** to Myriad Gardens throu **Bricktown** and a dredged channel of the river into Stockyards City; and

WHEREAS, Ray Ackerman was the primary spokesman and promoter in pushing for the riv and canal projects that became the focus of the Chamber's 1991 "Visions of New Frontier," later called **Metropolitan Area Projects (MAPS);** and

WHEREAS, most of the Vision projects mentioned herein have now been completed or a in the process of being completed as a result of the citizens of Oklahoma C voting in favor of a Five Year One-cent City Sales Tax in December of 1993, pl a six-month extension in December 1998, to ensure the successful completi of the MAPS Program; and

WHEREAS, Ray Ackerman and others are now envisioning further development of the riv with a transfer plan from the Canal to boats on the river and locks betwe connecting lakes, a river channel into Stockyards City, and an extension of t Canal into the Myriad Gardens.

NOW, THEREFORE, LET IT BE RESOLVED that on this fifth day of Novemb nineteen hundred and ninety-nine, the Board of Directors of the Greater Oklahoma C Chamber of Commerce wishes to extend to Ray Ackerman its most sincere appreciatic gratitude and heartfelt thanks for his leadership and untiring dedication to civic duty in having vision that led to the Chamber advancing its **1991 "Visions of a New Frontier,"** and that v further wish to bestow on Ray Ackerman the honorary title of Oklahoma City's **"Old Ma River"** as we feel he has earned it.

Steven E. Moore
Chairman

Charles H. Van Rysselberge, CCE
President

ATTEST: Dean Schirf, CCM
Corporate Secretary

along the channel's route. People could transfer from the small canal boats to larger riverboats, or vice versa, by steps or ramps.

The best way to extend the present canal into Myriad Gardens is along what is now Reno Avenue. The old I-40 route would replace Reno as the necessary east-west commuter route.

I'm not sure anyone has the vision to foresee how fast the shoreline of over 20 miles of river, canal, and channel will develop, but with the city owning most of the land, it should happen fast! You can be sure that all entities will move rapidly to help private enterprise build hotels, restaurants, golf courses, riding trails, and other 'fun and games' venues along the riverbank, particularly because a large part of it is in a newly-authorized tax improvement district. The establishment of a Downtown Business Improvement District will also be an asset to accelerate development along the river.[2]

Ray is looking forward to hosting a party, beginning by boarding a canal boat at Myriad Gardens for hors d'oeuvres, transferring to a riverboat, and taking his party to Cattlemen's Restaurant in Stockyards City for dinner. Thanks to federal funds that made possible the construction of locks on the dams at May and Western, boats can traverse the full eight-mile length of the river.

At the Chamber of Commerce's Board of Directors retreat on November 5, 1999, a resolution was approved calling Ray "The Primary Spokesman and Promoter in Publicizing the River and Canal Projects."

The resolution bestowed upon Ray the honorary title of "Old Man River," although publisher Edward L. Gaylord was the first to "hang" the title on Ray.[3]

FACING: The Oklahoma City Chamber of Commerce resolution that officially gave Ray Ackerman the title of "Old Man River."

"It was Ray who kept pushing the river project all these years," said Oklahoma City Public Works Director Paul Brum. "And he was right, the river will be the meeting place between north and south Oklahoma City. No longer will the river be the Mason-Dixon Line of our city," Brum said.[4]

As the late Oscar Hammerstein II wrote in lyrics for the stage play Oklahoma!, "You've got to have a dream; if you don't have a dream, how you gonna' have a dream come true?"

Fortunately for Oklahoma City, Ray Ackerman had many dreams, and most of them are coming true.

Newspapers

Capitol Hill Beacon
Oklahoma City, Oklahoma

Friday
Oklahoma City, Oklahoma

Dallas Morning News
Dallas, Texas

Denver Post
Denver, Colorado

New York Times
New York, New York

Norman Transcript
Norman, Oklahoma

Oklahoma Gazette
Oklahoma City, Oklahoma

Oklahoma Journal
Midwest City, Oklahoma

Oklahoma City Times
Oklahoma City, Oklahoma

Stillwater News Press
Stillwater, Oklahoma

The Daily Oklahoman
Oklahoma City, Oklahoma

Tulsa Daily World
Tulsa, Oklahoma

Tulsa Tribune
Tulsa, Oklahoma

Magazines and Periodicals

Oklahoma Today
Oklahoma City, Oklahoma

Sturm's Oklahoma Magazine
Oklahoma City, Oklahoma

Books

Ackerman, Ray. *Tomorrow Belongs to Oklahoma!* Oklahoma City: privately printed, 1964.

Baird, W. David and Danney Goble. *The Story of Oklahoma.* Norman: University of Oklahoma Press, 1994.

Blackburn, Bob L. *Heart of the Promised Land.* Woodland Hills, California: Windsor Publications, Inc., 1982.

Burke, Bob, Kenny Franks, and Royse Parr. *Glory Days of Summer: The History of Baseball in Oklahoma.* Oklahoma City: Oklahoma Heritage Association, 1999.

Burke, Bob. *Good Guys Wear White Hats: The Life of George Nigh.* Oklahoma City: Oklahoma Heritage Association, 2000.

Creel, Von Russell and Bob Burke. *Mike Monroney: Oklahoma Liberal.* Edmond: University of Central Oklahoma Press, 1997.

Debo, Angie. *Oklahoma, foot loose and fancy free.* Norman: University of Oklahoma Press, 1949.

Franks, Kenny A. *You're Doin' Fine Oklahoma!* Oklahoma City: Oklahoma Historical Society, 1983.

Jones, Stephen. *Oklahoma Politics in State and Nation.* Enid: The Haymaker Press, Inc., 1974.

Stewart, Roy P. *Country Boy Hornbook.* Oklahoma City: Oklahoma Publishing Company, 1968.

Stewart, Roy P. with Pendleton Woods. *Born Grown.* Oklahoma City: Fidelity Bank, 1974.

NOTES

PENNSYLVANIA ROOTS

1 Interview with Raymond Basil "Ray" Ackerman, January 10, Feburary 17, March 3, April 2, 2001, hereinafter referred to as Ray Ackerman interview. Heritage Archives, Oklahoma Heritage Association, Oklahoma City, Oklahoma.

2. Ibid.

3 Ibid.

4 Ibid.

5 Bob Burke, Kenny Franks, and Royse Parr. *Glory Days of Summer: The History of Baseball in Oklahoma.* (Oklahoma City: Oklahoma Heritage Association, 1999), p. 54.

6 Ray Ackerman interview.

BIG ACK

1 Ray Ackerman interview.

2 Ibid.

YOU'RE IN THE ARMY NOW

1 Ray Ackerman interview.

2 Ibid.

ANCHORS AWEIGH

1 Ray Ackerman interview.

2 Ibid.

3 Ibid.

4 Ibid.

5 www.ixpres.com/ ag1caf/usplanes

6 Ray Ackerman interview.

7 www.ixpres.com/ ag1caf/usplanes

8 Ray Ackerman interview.

9 www.ixpres.com/ ag1caf/usplanes

10 Ibid.

11 Ray Ackerman interview.

12 Ibid.

13 Ibid.

14 ww.ixpres.com/ ag1caf/usplanes, Enzo Angelucci, *The Rand McNally Encyclopedia of Military Aircraft* (Chicago: Rand McNally & Company, 1981), p. 279.

ON LAND AND SEA

1 www.multied. com/NAVY/ Ranger.html

2 Bob Burke. *Good Guys Wear White Hats: The Life of George Nigh* (Oklahoma City: Oklahoma Heritage Association, 2000), p.67.

3 *Dictionary of American Naval Fighting Ships* (Washington, D.C.: Naval Historical Center).

4 Ray Ackerman interview.

5 Ibid.

6 *Dictionary of American Naval Fighting Ships* (Washington, D.C.: Naval Historical Center).

7 Ibid.

GO WEST YOUNG MAN

1 Ray Ackerman interview.

2 Ibid.

3 Ibid.

AD SALESMAN AND STUDENT

1 Von Russell Creel and Bob Burke. *Mike Monroney: Oklahoma Liberal* (Edmond: University of Central Oklahoma Press, 1997), p. 21.

2 Ray Ackerman interview.

CARPETBAGGER WITHOUT PORTFOLIO

1 Ray Ackerman interview

2 Ibid.

3 Ibid.

THE CRADLE WILL ROCK

1 Ray Ackerman interview.

2 Ibid.

3 Ibid.

4 Ibid.

BUILDING AN AD BUSINESS

1 Ray Ackerman interview.

2 Ibid.

3 Ibid.

4 Ibid.

5 Ibid.

6 Ibid.

SHARED
OWNERSHIP

1 Ray Ackerman
interview.

2 Ibid.

3 Ibid.

4 Ibid.

5 Ibid.

6 Ibid.

7 Ibid.

8 Ibid.

9 Ibid.

A NEAR MISS

1 www.ixpres.com/
ag1caf/usplanes

2 Ray Ackerman
interview.

3 Ibid.

4 Ibid.

5 Ibid.

6 Ibid.

7 Ibid.

TOMORROW
BELONGS TO
OKLAHOMA

1 Ray Ackerman.
*Tomorrow Belongs
to Oklahoma* (Ok-
lahoma City: pri-
vately printed,
1964), p. 3.

2 Ibid.

3 Ibid., p. 21

4 Ray Ackerman
interview.

5 Ibid.

6 Ibid.

7 Ibid.

8 Ibid.

RODEO MAN

1 Ray Ackerman
interview.

2 *The Daily Okla-
homan* (Oklahoma
City, Oklahoma),
November 15,
1985.

3 Ibid.

4 Ray Ackerman
interview.

5 Ibid.

6 *The Daily Okla-
homan*, November
18, 1983.

7 Ibid., December
5, 1983.

8 Ray Ackerman
interview.

9 *The Daily Okla-
homan,* December
7, 1984.

10 Ray Ackerman
interview.

11 *The Daily Ok-
lahoman,* January
15, 1986.

12 Ray Ackerman
interview.

MAYOR?
ADMIRAL? BOTH?

1 *The Daily Okla-
homan,* January 15,
1967.

2 Ray Ackerman
interview.

3 Ibid.

4 Ray Ackerman
campaign
brochure. Heritage
Archives.

5 Ray Ackerman
interview.

6 Ibid.

7 Ray Ackerman
campaign
brochure. Heritage
Archives.

8 *The Daily Okla-
homan,* March 22,
1967.

9 Ibid., March 31,
1967.

10 Ray Ackerman
interview.

11 *The Daily Ok-
lahoman,* April 10,
1967.

12 Ibid., April 15,
1967.

13 *Oklahoma
Journal* (Midwest
City, Oklahoma),
May 1, 1967.

14 Telegram from
Davy Crockett to
Ray Ackerman,
Heritage Archives.

15 Ray Ackerman
interview.

FATHER KNOWS
BEST

1 Ray Ackerman
interview.

2 Interview with
Patricia Ann "Pat-
sy" Ackerman
Mehring, January
12, 2001, here-
inafter referred to
as Patsy Mehring
interview, Heritage
Archives.

3 Ibid.

4 Ibid.

5 Ray Ackerman
interview.

6 Interview with
Ann Carol "Annie"
Ackerman Adams,
January 17, 2001,
hereinafter referred
to as Annie Adams
interview, Heritage
Archives.

7 Ibid.

8 Christmas card
from Ackerman
Family Collection,
Heritage Archives.

9 Ray Ackerman
interview.

10 Ibid.

11 Ibid.

12 Ibid.

13 Ibid.

14 Ibid.

15 Interview with Ray Karl "Ray K" Ackerman, January 31, 2001, hereinafter referred to as Ray K. Ackerman interview, Heritage Archives.

16 Ibid.

17 Ibid.

18 Ray Ackerman interview.

19 Ray K. Ackerman interview.

20 Ackerman Family Collection, Heritage Archives.

21 Ray Ackerman interview.

22 Ackerman Family Collection, Heritage Archives.

23 Interview with Susie Ackerman Fuller, February 15, 2001, hereinafter referred to as Susie Fuller interview, Heritage Archives.

24 Ibid.

25 Ray Ackerman interview.

26 Ibid.

27 Ibid.

28 Interview with Mark Ackerman, February 17, 2001, hereinafter referred to as Mark Ackerman interview,

Heritage Archives.

29 Ibid.

30 Ray Ackerman interview.

31 Ibid.

32 Interview with Amy Ackerman Shaver, February 1, 2001, hereinafter referred to as Amy Shaver interview, Heritage Archives.

33 Ibid.

34 Ibid.

35 Ibid.

36 Ackerman Family Collection, Heritage Archives.

NEW YORK, NEW YORK AND NATIONAL PREZ

1 Ray Ackerman interview.

2 Ibid.

3 Ibid.

4 Ibid.

5 Ibid.

6 Undated letter from Admiral Elmo Zumwalt, Jr., to Ray Ackerman, Heritage Archives.

7 Letter from John H. Chafee to Ray Ackerman, September 15, 1970, Heritage Archives.

THE MCQUEEN CONNECTION

1 Ray Ackerman interview.

2 Ibid.

3 Ibid.

4 Ibid.

5 Ibid.

6 Undated letter from Warren K. Jordan to Oklahoma Heritage Association, Heritage Archives.

7 Ray Ackerman interview.

8 Ibid.

9 Ibid.

10 Ibid.

11 Internal Ackerman Agency memorandum, Heritage Archives.

12 Ray Ackerman interview.

13 June, 1981, memorandum, Heritage Archives.

EVOLUTION OF THE EIGHTIES

1 Ray Ackerman interview.

2 The Daily Oklahoman, June 7, 1983.

3 Promotional brochure, Heritage Archives.

4 Ray Ackerman interview.

5 Ibid.

6 Letter from Mex Frates to Oklahoma Heritage Association, February 15, 1986, Heritage Archives.

7 Ray Ackerman interview.

8 The Daily Oklahoman, November 15, 1989.

9 Ray Ackerman interview.

10 The Daily Oklahoman, October 15, 1989.

11 Ray Ackerman interview.

12 Undated letter from Edward L. Gaylord to Ray Ackerman, Heritage Archives.

13 Undated letter from Dan Hogan to Ray Ackerman, Heritage Archives.

14 Ray Ackerman interview.

15 Ibid.

16 Ibid.

THE RIVER

1 Ray Ackerman interview.

2 Ibid.

3 Bob L. Blackburn, *Heart of the Promised Land* (Woodland Hills, California: Windsor Publications, Inc., 1982), p. 12.

4 W. David Baird and Danney Goble, *The Story of Oklahoma* (Norman: University of Oklahoma Press, 1994), p. 57.

5 Ibid.

6 Roy P. Stewart, *Born Grown* (Oklahoma City: Fidelity Bank, 1974), p. 89-90.

7 Ibid.

8 Ray Ackerman interview.

9 Ibid.

10 Blackburn, *Heart of the Promised Land,* p. 12.

11 Ray Ackerman interview.

12 Ibid.

13 Ibid.

14 Ibid.

CHAMBER CHAIRMAN, ST. CRISPIN'S, AND MAPS

1 Ray Ackerman interview.

2 Ibid.

3 Ibid.

4 *The Daily Oklahoman,* December 2, 1990.

5 *Visions of a New Frontier,* the 1990 Annual Report and 1991 Program of Work of the Oklahoma City Chamber of Commerce, Archives and Manuscript Division, Oklahoma Historical Society, Oklahoma City, Oklahoma.

6 Ray Ackerman interview.

7 *Capitol Hill Beacon* (Oklahoma City, Oklahoma), January 10, 1991.

8 Ray Ackerman interview.

9 Ibid.

10 Ibid.

11 Ibid.

12 Ibid.

13 Ibid.

14 *The Daily Oklahoman,* December 1, 1993.

15 Ibid., December 15, 1993.

16 Ibid., June 22, 1999.

17 *Friday* (Oklahoma City, Oklahoma), December 4, 1998.

18 Ibid.

19 Ray Ackerman interview.

20 Ibid.

21 Ibid.

RETIREMENT

1 Ray Ackerman interview.

2 Ibid.

3 Ibid.

4 Ibid.

5 Letter from Robert Funk to Ray Ackerman, August 9, 1992, Heritage Archives.

6 Letter from John O'Toole to Ray Ackerman, August 15, 1992, Heritage Archives.

7 Letter from Angus McQueen to Ray Ackerman, August 7, 1992, Heritage Archives.

8 Ray Ackerman interview.

9 Oklahoma Hall of Fame file, Oklahoma Heritage Association, Heritage Archives.

10 Ibid.

11 Ibid.

12 Ibid.

13 Ray Ackerman interview.

14 Ibid.

15 Ibid.

16 Letter from Frank Keating to Ray Ackerman, October 15, 1998, Heritage Archives.

IDEAS AT WORK

1 Ray Ackerman interview.

2 Ibid.

3 Ibid.

4 Ibid.

5 Ibid.

6 Ibid.

7 Ibid.

8 Ibid.

EPILOGUE

1 OKC Rotary News (Oklahoma City, Oklahoma), August, 2000.

2 Ray Ackerman interview.

3 Interview with Paul Brum, May 15, 2001, Heritage Archives.